THE IMPORTANCE OF ACKNOWLEDGING
Childhood Trauma
in the Clinical Field

(Surviving Isn't Living)
A Person-Centred Account

Rita Ballantyne

Grosvenor House
Publishing Limited

This book is published by
Grosvenor House Publishing Ltd
Link House
140 The Broadway, Tolworth, Surrey, KT6 7HT.
www.grosvenorhousepublishing.co.uk

A CIP record for this book
is available from the British Library

ISBN 978-1-80381-878-8
eBook ISBN 978-1-80381-917-4

Dedicated to my three children.

*You are the most wonderful gifts
I've received in this life.*

Motto:

'Did you survive?'

I didn't.
I shattered,
I am still silently picking up pieces,
Some forever lost.

(An *Unfinished Mosaic* - random, old screenshot.
If this poem is from you, please raise your hand.)

This book is for every soul
who has ever been discriminated against,
put down and suffered low self-esteem as a
result, everyone who has ever promised themselves
they would never hurt another person
like they've been hurt.

There are many of us. You're not alone,
we feel you, we are you.

Remember what you've come through. Put together,
our kindness can make a difference in the world!

Table of Contents

Part 3: The Road to Recovery

Acknowledgements

It started off with seeing @aurahoffman's videos on TikTok. The quotes rang true and made my experience feel real and worthwhile to share and explore as I realised I was far from alone in how I was feeling.

A special backhanded thank you goes to my old workplace, which will remain nameless, not just for legal reasons, but also for not causing any adverse consequences for some of the people there who don't deserve it. That place, though – it truly reignited a multitude of negative feelings in me that made me relive my childhood, raise all those issues I had tried hard for decades to bury and avoid, never quite having to face them head on in adulthood. Eliciting, experiencing these feelings propelled me back right into my past, to those moments when I had felt exactly the same, crushed, hopeless, misunderstood, humiliated, disappointed in humanity and consumed with overwhelming pain with nowhere to run, feelings so deep that the experience negated all else.

Without the people who mistreated me there, I would have never been brave enough to unearth these memories that engulfed me without warning and against my will. I would have never wanted to see them back, but there they were, urging me, forcing me to work through my sorrows and find sense in all this suffering.

Moreover, interacting with people in that place, individuals who seemed to have very little understanding of how childhood trauma affects an adult, made me want to try to make a dent in that shortcoming in the general awareness of the public.

Most importantly, I'd like to thank my husband, Thomas Ballantyne, for his encouragement at every step of the way, for always being ready to share his thoughts on the subject and, above all, for teaching me about what real love looks like. Thank you for your support and all the times you've listened to my ramblings while I was trying to make sense of the chaotic mind of my narcissistic mother.

Another heart-felt thank you to my publishing team, Melanie Bartle and Tessa Thompson for the detailed feedback, encouragement, enthusiasm and proofreading. Any remaining mistakes are still mine though!

Foreword

There has been a lot of consideration given to childhood abuse in recent times that has resulted in a multitude of policies, guidelines and extensive training materials aimed at providing the childcare professional with an understanding of how to identify the signs of abuse, deal with its repercussions and address the resulting conditions. Day by day, I see wondrous and crucial consequences of such awareness in my professional life, saving and bettering children's lives in ways never seen before.

And yet, a lot of people, some professionals included, sadly, don't quite get it. Not what it's really like to be abused by a narcissist parent, and most importantly, not how devastating a sentence it can remain for the rest of our lives. This book is trying to bridge that gap.

How This Book Came About

(A Sort of Introduction)

How many times have you been told not to dwell on your childhood? That no good comes out of rehashing the past? That it's just a way of blaming others? That you should move on? That it can't have been that bad and others had it worse? Been instructed to grow up and get over it? That you're not a child anymore and therefore it shouldn't concern you? That you don't remember it right? That it was a long time ago, too long ago and therefore it shouldn't affect you now? Just let it go? Forget it? That it had never happened? That it was only family, how could it be that bad? That you must have imagined it? To stop concentrating on the past? Not to mention that our emotionally repressed society is still based on some old, traditional ideals and thus communicating our real feelings is often seen as a sign of weakness, rude, even.

There's this whole padded stratum of forgotten abuse where, in the absence of hard physical evidence, we are simply asked to shove all that's happened under the rug as water under the bridge. Or, if there's some minimal acknowledgement from the listener that the parents' behaviour was wrong, then we are supposed to forgive the abusers because 'they didn't know any better in those days'. Well, you see, the parents acted differently in front of outsiders so that must mean they knew that what they were doing was wrong.

But even if they didn't know and I could forgive, that could not heal all the damage childhood experiences caused. Would it matter if it was forty years ago that you lost the use of your legs, your sight? Should you be over it by now and be able to see clearly? No, because the damage is still there, you fight with it every day, every moment of your life. There's no running away from it, it sticks with you like ongoing punishment for some offence you didn't commit.

Truly listening ears are few and far between, truly understanding ones even less so. Some only try to ignore you and some of these people have no idea what they're talking about. Forcing a muzzle on childhood pain seems to be part of this culture of conventional social wisdom that doesn't just refer to childhood trauma. Society, in general, silences the abused.

Diminishing, dismissing, denying and discarding the importance of our experiences hurts in itself. I'm sure you have felt the effects yourself under various circumstances. It still shocks me to this day how people respond to hearing someone has depression as well. A family member sent me stretching exercises to combat it, for example. Now those might work against sadness, mild depression, I don't doubt it, but expecting it to work against severe, deep-rooted depression with well-established, otherwise oriented causes the sufferer can pinpoint?

To demonstrate this phenomenon, let me give you an example, an exact quote from another well-meaning, but clueless, patronising and invalidating message I received from another family member in support:

'Sweetie, I don't think you really have a reason to experience depression. You are not lonely, you have a beautiful family, skilful and precious children. I know how hard it is to work so much, and that it's November – dark, unfriendly, cold. Try to get over this.

As funny and abstract as it may seem, Munchausen had it right when he held on to his hair and pulled himself out of the swamp. One only has to gather his strength and enjoy what he has.

Depression only robs you of time that could be spent with someone else. Cut a window into the rainy darkness and let in the light. You will have a wonderful experience!'

Nice, right? Really nice. At first glance. I don't doubt the positive sentiment, but just get over it? Again, typically the words of someone who doesn't know how to handle mental illnesses. Let it go and move on. It isn't just completely unhelpful, it is harmful and insensitive as well. They are asking you to lie to yourself. It can only lead to lower on the spiral of being misunderstood, neglected, crushed, till you literally cry so much you're fighting for the next breath. A perfect example of how well-meaning ignorance crushes the world.

These kinds of instructions are communicated way too often in a variety of ways to people looking to be understood, heard, their pain justified. Because it's not enough that we feel these negative emotions, on top of it we are told that we shouldn't; we are criticised further, eliciting, perpetuating more negativity.

When it concerns childhood trauma, this negative sentiment becomes even more reinforced and prevalent within, because often our abusive past has never been properly acknowledged and is negated with this behaviour, as if it were our fault that we feel bad as result of what we have endured. It's infuriating,

saddening,

offensive,

insensitive,

ignorant,

dismissive,

it feels like being accused of lying. It's everything we're trying to fight, inwardly and outwardly. Our feelings are real. They are a result of what we have lived through and nobody has the right to judge them, and render them invalid.

Not to mention that recovery and healing doesn't work like that. We can't simply do as the 'advice' suggests. A great portion of the books on the topic out there are self-help books, promising some magical transformation in just a few steps, not very far off the above described way of society's attitude to mental health. Fix it and fix it quick.

In contrast, while it contains some insight from my own background, tips and guidance, this is not a self-help book. I don't claim to know all the answers like some do. I'd like more psychologists and therapists to admit that they don't know the answer, they just pretend or believe they do. Let's also admit that a lot of psychologists became engaged in the field because of personal experiences, or those of a family member or close friend, maybe in some instances derived from disasters or war experience. So while they know more about the general subject than the average person, they don't know everything. I'd like to start from this facet of the truth foremost, and from this standpoint we can move on to dare and explore for more knowledge.

Thus, I think first we need to understand why our destructive feelings and urges are there and acknowledge them, otherwise we can't make sense of our own behaviours. We cannot bury our pain and expect it to never come back to haunt us. The same way, the aftereffects of trauma hardly ever work themselves out on their own. As I have mentioned, this book is mainly based on my own personal insight in the wider context of familiarity with similar experiences bleeding into societal consciousness and this awareness tells me that overcoming the effects of childhood trauma does not solely rely on trying hard enough, and it certainly does not get solved within the confines of a self-help book.

Which is why I think it is especially important to talk about our past, to stand up and say hey, inflicting this kind of trauma is wrong and in doing so, perhaps I will be able to help not just a similar sufferer, but also prevent some trauma occurring in the first place by raising awareness of its long-lasting, detrimental effects on a person's life. Maybe some parents will think twice. This is not hanging on to the past, it is working out how we've been damaged and how to overcome it.

Parental love shouldn't be conditional, it should not depend on whether or not the child is a certain way, looks a certain way, behaves in a given manner. A child's voice, their choices, should be heard, no matter the age, and not just on some official paper. You see, toxic people, toxic parents, condition you to think that the abuse isn't the problem, that your reaction is the problem. That perhaps you're too sensitive, you're too reactive, you're weak and that you're somehow less because of it. It's called toxic conditioning. Don't fall for it. If you're hurt, it isn't your fault.

If you're hurt, you have a right to ask for a better chance.

Many of us who have experienced forcibly pressed down childhood trauma, finding that part of themselves were never allowed to blossom, search not for just an answer, but for a sign that our feelings and resentments are valid. We want to know with certainty that what is broken, different in us to others, is a result of what we have experienced as children.

I hear you. You're not alone, you're not delusional, there are many of us still out of sight because it is not the commonly accepted societal custom to open feelings up, to 'bring shame on our parents', especially in British middle-class circles who simply choose to change the subject as if it were taboo. They did not do their best so enough of the silence!

I'm hoping that by standing up and sharing my experience, others will do the same and hidden, complex trauma will become more understood and taken notice of in all areas of care and education, because as you will see from the details in this book that I have collected with the help of my degree in psychology and my own experience, consequences of such hidden abuse are way too far-reaching in every area of life to let go of, from fear of intimacy and avoidance to low self-esteem and difficulties trusting, clearly detrimental to relationships and a successful work life. In fact, nobody would 'have to lay a hand on you to destroy you. Regularly said cruel words and actions are enough to shatter a person's sense of self and even affect their future. It is murder with clean hands.' – Shahida Arabi, author of *Power: Surviving and Thriving After Narcissistic Abuse* and the poetry book *She Who Destroys the Light.*

Decades later, in adulthood, people still suffer from conditions such as depression, migraines, addictions as a result of childhood trauma. But these conditions and illnesses are just the tip of the iceberg. We don't get over it, we don't move on, no matter how other people would like to smooth everything over and never hear about our experiences ever again. We're only human. This is why I became a psychologist, first of all, to help myself through these feelings, to learn how to address these issues. And then it gets more interesting, every time I dig into it further.

I have been grappling with the idea of writing about my experiences for years. Sure, a subjective book, but what better person to write about childhood trauma effects than someone who had experienced it firsthand? However, I had always been put off by two factors. First of all, I did not want to think back on my childhood, I wanted to keep it there at the back of my mind, buried, for my own comfort. After all, who would want to wallow in their own pain, shake it all up, accept that they were unloved by their primary caregiver as a child? This self-imposed ignorance, however, didn't save me from suffering its effects every day in the form of returning panic attacks and sleepless nights.

Secondly, I did not at first deem my childhood abusive enough to write a book about. I read many books on the subject and they were certainly about something more outright shocking, such as severe neglect or sexual abuse. So I thought that while I had been hit often enough, my experiences were not as outstanding, it was just the normal, everyday, systematic, devaluating abuse. Yet the aftereffects didn't end and I yearned to find someone to talk to, someone who would acknowledge and understand my loss as the injustice it was. Through this I came to realise how the detrimental influence emotional abuse is undervalued. It is not acknowledged often enough by far, and people suffer the consequences as a result, some sadly not even realising how their self-deprecating, self-sabotaging behaviour is a result of the childhood they suffered.

Then came the dehumanizing déjà-poo* experience with one of my old workplaces. Let it be an example for you of what not to follow: little by little, I became mentally, emotionally and physically exhausted when memories, feelings from my childhood, were triggered by that toxic environment. I am pretty damn diligent and habitually burn myself out by working too hard, be that with housework or something as relatively unimportant as making fan-art. If I have promised something, I will do my best to deliver because, quite frankly, I can't cope with people having negative emotions towards me. Even now. More on the reason for that unhealthy coping mechanism further on in the book, but there I was, an over-pleaser as a result of childhood trauma, giving my everything to that job, from my health to my mental well-being, going the extra mile, hardly ever finishing on time, always offering to do extra tasks for my overly critical bosses. Of course, taking my health from me was not enough, nothing, no belittling was ever enough. How it doesn't occur to more people that frequent criticism has adverse effects on performance is beyond me. Would I have taken this level of negativity from them without revolting if I wasn't crushed into having little self-esteem as a child? I doubt it.

What was fairly normal, mild, baseline depression at the start became worse and worse to the point I often cried uncontrollably for hours after work, tears running down my face while driving, my nights spent thinking about and having nightmares about my situation at work as opposed to enjoying a proper rest. I couldn't think about how to perform the most mundane of tasks because of the stress, not even the ones what would have otherwise been rewarding ones, such as interacting with children. It also reignited my PTSD and my social anxiety went through the roof, with physical symptoms such as chest pains and dizziness, the classical, trauma-induced mental health problems being exacerbated by more trauma and stress. Let me explain how.

Whenever something bad had happened in the past, I always knew from experience that I would only have to wait something like twenty-four hours, or deep dive into a hobby and it would all start to feel better. Timescales might vary for other people, but that's how my nervous system operated. Then the recovery period after the stress experienced at this workplace became two days, a whole weekend. Then it didn't happen anymore, I was just miserable all the time to the extent of seriously contemplating suicide, but of course I wouldn't do that in any circumstances, not really, because of the harm it would inflict on my own children.

Again, as a result of my childhood, I never had much self-esteem, but this also became worse the longer my situation at work lasted. I had no confidence, barely any self-worth left, I turned myself inside out to be the person I was told to be by my superiors, I tried to have characteristics I did not value, such as being too forceful with children and fake in social situations.

After all the effort I had to put into my job, I rarely had any energy left, not even enough to have a conversation with my own children, which I obviously regret. Anybody else would have probably gone off sick a long time before it got to this stage, but I felt like I couldn't do that because I was already thought of as not doing my job properly since I approached things differently. I had been told that often enough and I didn't want to add one more reason for them to undervalue me. I was being pulled up for trivial matters, usually several times a day, things that shouldn't matter, details that weren't directly related to performance, they were just the bosses' personal preferences. With absolutely no praise given, ever, I could do no right, apparently. And there, I found myself in the exact same position I felt as a child, I was nothing but a plaything of a narcissistic woman, who would only feel better when I was down. There was no point in giving any opinions, no matter whether the issue was big or small because there could be only one way to go about it and it wasn't mine. I simply lived in a heightened survival mode, terrified, on edge, scared of when the next 'mistake' would be bounced back to me and just how big of a deal it would be made out to be and based on that, when my life would be ruined for good. How miserable do we have to be before a narcissist is happy?

As a consequence, as you can imagine with this perturbed mental and psychological state, I became forgetful and my muddled thoughts weren't exactly conducive to performance. They left me bleeding on the floor and then complained about the mess. I'm talking about some deep-rooted systemic issues here that I obviously couldn't battle. Micromanagement, which is a form of bullying, and the lack of worker autonomy does not allow for professional development and healthy discourse. That, along with the poor communication, resistance to change, accusing staff members, the lack of genuine interest in friendship and the badmouthing of clients behind their backs made it a toxic environment, conducive to burnout and the development of complex workplace PTSD, manifesting in anxiety, memory problems, hyper-reactivity, self-blame and so on. Clearly, I could never prove the value I know I have to my line manager.

But why did I let this happen to me when I do mind the floor being wiped with me? Why did I linger in a space somewhere between giving up and seeing how much more I can take? Because it was learnt behaviour, it was the only way I could survive as a child, no matter how bad circumstances got. But it's all wrong, from the start. Therefore, it is vital to unearth the reasons behind our behaviours and start to relearn happiness, consciously and purposefully rewire our brains after we come to understand what went wrong.

Understanding where our worries, difficulties, triggers and plights come from is the first step to taking control and becoming the person we were always meant to be.

Let me underline this from the findings of an article from the Journal of General Internal Medicine that are presented here courtesy of the Society of General Internal Medicine: childhood 'abuse has been associated with a plethora of psychological and somatic symptoms, as well as psychiatric and medical diagnoses including depression, anxiety disorders, eating disorders, post-traumatic stress disorder (PTSD), chronic pain syndromes, fibromyalgia, chronic fatigue syndrome, and irritable bowel. Compared with non-abused adults, those who experienced childhood abuse are more likely to engage in high-risk health behaviours including smoking, alcohol and drug use, and unsafe sex; to report an overall lower health status; and to use more health services'[1].

And hey, if you feel like I have done a huge injustice to parents by writing this book, like I hear many say – that no one should accuse people like this who did everything for you growing up – then no, you didn't have that unfair childhood we had and this book isn't for you, because a chunk wasn't ripped out of your soul before it could ever fully form. Your perspective will forever be different to ours. Possibly, for the so-called normal people, it is difficult to comprehend that such evil exists within our midst, that some parents would choose to inflict such pain on their children. It is for this reason that a lot of people who come face-to-face with the actions of a narcissist parent have to spend some time thinking about it as they don't understand the behaviour and its meaning. At some level, they understand that it isn't standard, at another, they can't make sense of it. So don't judge and condemn what you don't understand. It is disappointing how lots of professionals, and, in particular, physicians and counsellors minimise the pain and the hurt of those who have lived through lasting emotional trauma.

So perhaps it would be beneficial to consider that if someone says that they are being abused, and it is hard to believe because the accused appears so agreeable and good-natured and the relationship looks outwardly perfect, then you also need to understand that apparent charm is one of the main criteria for diagnosing a narcissist or sociopathic toxic parent and that the individual claiming they are being targeted with contempt, abuse, scorn, maltreatment, rejection and disdain is in most cases telling the truth about their circumstances and they are trying to put their trust in you in the hope of help. Denying them this, not believing them, or not verifying their narrative could be the difference between life and death.

Ignorance should not be an excuse. One of the saddest things is that most children or grown-up survivors never get help. They are categorised by society as having 'only suffered emotional abuse' at best.

By taking you through my journey, I aim to present how detrimental emotional abuse can be, especially as many still suffer in silence when we shouldn't have to. Please hear our voices!

'I'm not delusional, I lived a nightmare.
I'm not weak, I was
Trusting.
I'm not giving up,
I'm healing
I'm not incapable of love, I'm giving.
I'm not alone. I see you all here.
I'm fighting this.' – Rene Smith

Disclaimer: Unless otherwise stated, this book reflects my personal opinion and is not to be taken as irrefutable facts.

Part 1: The Abusive Environment

What is Childhood Trauma?

Before jumping in at the deep end, we should make sure everyone is on the same page about what we see as trauma, and briefly cover the basics. By my definition, going through very stressful, frightening or distressing events is called trauma. It is some 'very difficult or unpleasant experience that causes someone to have mental or emotional problems, usually for a long time'[2]. So events leading to emotional or psychological trauma can happen at any stage of development and can cause long-lasting damage.

Childhood trauma comes in all shapes and sizes, from the typically referred to violence, physical, financial and sexual abuse, to being degraded and shamed, criticised, screamed at, lied to, treated with contempt or disrespect, cheated or even just being controlled to the detriment of the self.

Doctors Vincent J. Felitti, Robert F. Anda et al. talk about the importance of knowing your adverse childhood experiences (ACE) score by adding one each time one of the following happened:

- loss of a parent
- parent with mental illness
- physical abuse
- sexual abuse

- emotional abuse
- physical neglect
- emotional neglect
- household domestic violence
- household member in jail
- parent with substance abuse.

These adverse childhood experiences can then contribute not only to mental illness but also chronic pain and migraines, autoimmune diseases, liver and lung disease, unhealthy thyroid levels, diabetes, chronic fatigue, obesity and gastrointestinal diseases.

Everyone has a different reaction to trauma, so different disorders can emerge following similar experiences. They are, however, all a result of internal coping and survival mechanisms, which are normal ways for any psyche to try to process trauma.

Talking to everyday people, I often run into the misconception that trauma manifests itself in unpleasant flashbacks and resulting fearful states while thinking of the incident. While there are instances when painful moments replay over and over in our heads, whether we are awake or asleep, this commonplace assumption is nevertheless, in most cases, incorrect, especially in the case of complex trauma, such as a long-standing, botched-up childhood, where the main harm manifests itself in a variety of other mental and other health problems. The effect 'comes back as a reaction, not a memory' (Bessel Van Der Kolk, MD)[3]. It is also a cumulative affliction as additional stress and later traumatic experiences can worsen these primal reaction-based conditions, such as, for example, digestive issues, adrenal malfunction, obsessive-compulsive disorder, chronic headaches, the inability to function and execute everyday chores, eating and sleeping problems, hypervigilance or startled responses, sex and other addictions, anxiety, alcoholism, depression, post-traumatic stress disorder (PTSD), complex post-traumatic stress disorder (cPTSD), memory problems or suicidal tendencies. These are mentioned here purely as examples as I will go back to these resulting conditions one by one, and more extensively, in the course of this book. Also used as examples as opposed to an all-inclusive list, trauma can also manifest itself a result of occurrences where we feel discriminated against, humiliated, undermined, rejected, shamed, harassed, neglected, helpless, unsupported, bullied, threatened, trapped, unsafe or scared, regardless of the cause. Commonly, there is also inconsistency, making it hard for the abused to anticipate the abuser's actions, and/or a forced competition between siblings for the sake of alienating them from each other, manipulation, unpredictable emotional outbursts, scorn, ridicule and other forms of enforcing control.

As seen from the above, it is oftentimes the individual's very existence or parts of their identity that is or feels at risk, so no wonder that we resort to survival mechanisms! What's more, the abused is not allowed to display their well-justified anger, not within the family nor out in society, as the abuser will frequently make sure these children are afraid enough not to mention the abuse. Using institutions such as the church, police, courts, relatives or hospitals to threaten them with is a form of abuse as well, as are other threats, like threatening suicide in case of noncompliance, or harming other loved ones. Other kinds of threats we see involve promising restrictions to the personal freedoms of the child, confinement, rejection, neglect or physical harm. These don't have to be verbal, some abusers manage ingraining intimidation reactions in the child well enough with simple looks, actions, gestures or withholding or destroying the child's belongings. Economic abuse includes misusing the family's money or refusing child support. So is withholding the satisfaction of basic needs to control the child's behaviour or using them as bargaining chips in their other relationships, bossing them around as servants.

Neglect or inconsistent care is abusive too. Disregarding a child, not caring about who they are or want to become, what they need, is like telling them that they are not important enough to be considered over and over again. Toxic people use neglect deliberately to make the victim feel worthless or undeserving.

Of course, not all of these experiences result in trauma, it will depend on the intensity of the harmful behaviours, the resilience of the person on the receiving end and their possibly non-existent interpersonal support network.

When it comes to early childhood trauma, it is rarely a singular event's effect, rather it consists of ongoing events, such as living in a traumatic or drug-dependent environment, or the child going through on and off cycles of harm or witnesses harm to someone else. Also, as examples, childhood trauma can consist of being often shouted at, gang violence, being blamed and degraded, with or without it being accompanied by the obvious physical abuse, having to care for a parent or sibling at an early age, being called bad names and lied to or being forced to do things against their will, akin to the absence or purposeful withdrawal of safety, love and trust, and the chance of a happy childhood.

On top of it all, being completely dependent on our families at these early ages, we cannot escape the abuse and therefore children will start to feel trapped and horrified by it and their prospects. In some cases, entire childhoods are characterised by such environments and it being the norm for the individual leads to complex trauma.

Childhood trauma can also look like being in or witnessing traumatic accidents and fires, the death of a close family member, abandonment, having an emotionally unavailable or dishonest parent, having a parent who consistently does not deliver on promises, divorce, being given age-inappropriate responsibilities, the destruction of personal belongings, bullying and humiliation.

There are certain decisions in the older child's life that should never be taken by another person, such as the basic autonomies of what to do with their bodies, from haircuts to their right for an abortion and being told how to feel.

While mentioning all these examples, it is important to stress once more that childhood trauma isn't limited to the above. What is traumatic for one person, might not be seen or felt as such by another. So, by limiting our position on what can be traumatising and what isn't, what we're really doing is imposing limits on our own potential for figuring out what is happening within us, deducing what our reactions are based on accordingly and as such, we may be subverting our own recovery.

What everyone needs to understand is that invisible, psychological, verbal abuse can be severe enough to affect the person's health and well-being for a long time to come. In fact, it doesn't even need to be severe mistreatment for it to significantly affect the person's future relationships and ability to function. What most people don't realise is that any kind of trauma can literally cause physical and neurological changes in the brain akin to brain injury. It is the effect of an overload on top of our ability to cope and it affects early brain development. Childhood sexual abuse victims regularly struggle with misconduct, sexual difficulties, eating disorders, self-harming behaviours, flashbacks to the traumatic events, phobias, anger[63], a sense of helplessness, being paralysed with shame, despair or powerlessness, emotional numbness, low self-esteem, lack of self-confidence, suicidal ideation and suicide attempts[62]. Some abuse victims simply don't care about their lives anymore, a mental state that can manifest in other kinds of destructive behaviours, for example, habitually driving too fast and perhaps a little dangerously because they don't feel or want to feel anything at that moment or because they don't deem the consequences, such as dying, important enough when they live unhappily day by day.

Nearly every sufferer complained of impaired memory. This is partially due to conscious avoidance of unwanted memories, as well as from the damage to the hippocampus, a part of the brain linked to learning and memory, which will be explained in more detail later. Severe childhood abuse can lead to post-traumatic stress[64], dissociative identity disorder, or could leave the victim perceiving the outside world in an unrealistic manner and moving through life as if in a dream state, or as if their environment was surreal. The addictions[66] childhood abuse victims take on to relieve their discomfort unfortunately can only provide temporary relief from symptoms and involve the use of alcohol, sex, drugs, smoking, food, betting, shopping and other obsessive-compulsive behaviours, amongst other maladaptive attempts to kill the pain[65]. According to the US Center for Disease Control, childhood trauma also contributes to having a low life potential, achieving less in life. To top it all off, those traumatised as children tend to die sooner than those with happy childhoods. The higher the score on the adverse childhood experiences scale, the higher the probability of poor psychological and physical health in adult life.

Trauma can also generate deep-rooted feelings of hurt, uncontrollable bouts of crying, problems with concentration and make people always worry what might happen next. Sufferers might resist change, become codependent in fear of being rejected and crave external validation, or become so used to abuse that they turn a blind eye to it or tolerate it when they are subsequently abused by another person. They might have problems standing up for themselves or ignore their own needs in order to avoid conflict. These are, of course, again only examples of the vast array of consequences.

As my mother is a narcissist, I can provide a targeted outlook on this personality's effect on the child, especially relevant in today's self-obsessed society, currently experiencing an epidemic in the rise of narcissism traits. It is all about the self, evident from phenomena such as the selfie and celebrity culture, attention-seeking social media posts, a boom in the cosmetic industry. Just about everyone is pretending to be something they aren't, using inflation* to conceal and deny their own identity, whether consciously or unconsciously. They present an image that is more likely to be valued and appear grandiose. And it is this very image that stops them from being able to form real connections. So that this presented image can remain untouched, they cannot show their real self and nor can they grasp that other people might have needs too. It is a deep shortcoming that psychologists have long given up trying to fix as it is almost impossible without the narcissist's say-so, who typically, will never admit to vulnerability.

That such persons are idolised, have devout followers and are considered role models for some, is beyond me. Donald Trump is the perfect example. He has no interest in others' needs and overestimates his own worth to the extent of delusion. Numbers tell the same story: the epidemiological evidence described in the book *The Narcissism Epidemic* by Jean Twenge and Keith Campbell, who found that narcissistic personality traits rose as quickly as obesity from the 1980s on, with a change in women especially noticeable. Scores have risen more swiftly in this millennium to the extent of narcissistic traits afflicting almost 10% of people in their twenties, compared with 3% of people in their sixties. These people believe themselves to be unrealistically special and they are keen on voicing this opinion of theirs. They are well-pleased with their own behaviour too, proud of having barrelled through a horde of people, crushing them or the very planet itself under their own steam just to achieve some goal without guilt. They don't even think that not having empathy is a negative trait – just look at Katie Hopkins, who amongst others is unfortunately normalising the trait of being unsympathetic and ignorant. They also tend to be assertive exhibitionists and they only see a person in terms of what benefits their existence or closeness gives them.

This contemporary narcissism epidemic is stoked by materialism and capitalist values, as demonstrated by Vater Moritz and Roepke[70] in their study comparing Western and Eastern German attitudes on the narcissism scale.

In terms of childrearing, the problem is that parents with this type of personality tend to be unsympathetic, overcritical and censorious with their children as well, repeating generational trauma over and over again, damaging entire families, using people, including their children, to advance their own interests. Their self-image is the most important to them, so the child has to be very careful how they behave and present themselves as the narcissist considers them their extension, and as such the child always needs to be presenting themselves in the particular manner that the narcissist parent would like them to be.

Unwanted (Memories) –
It's Some Kind of a Start

As a base of understanding where I come from and how it came about that I possess firsthand insight into these matters, I should share a few personal facts and memories with you. A warning here – many of these might be triggering for some.

The basal problem occurred even before I was born: I was unwanted. You see, my mother, an opportunistic know-it-all with no empathy, as I would describe her now, did not want children to chain her down, inconvenience her. This goal was, however, somewhat hard to accomplish in the Socialist Romania of the 70s, with abortion being illegal and contraception hard to come by. This one fact in itself didn't bother my mother too much, because while officially working as a secretary at the National Theatre, she also had a little underground business going where she took women, actresses at first, for illegal abortions to a doctor she knew. Having been in such a privileged position, she had had abortions performed on herself as well, any time she wanted, both before and after giving birth to me. But when she became pregnant with me she made the mistake of thinking she could have a legal abortion for once because the kinds of sedatives she took for the first few months of her pregnancy were soundly contraindicated and could cause serious damage to the foetus. Knowing this, she was certain that a legal abortion would be granted, but as it happens, one of the three doctors who had to sign the approval, refused. With the pregnancy's existence being out in the open, she could no longer have an illegal abortion without chancing prison. Therefore, here I am.

Now, most of the time, I don't mind existing, not in the least. I am thankful for this opportunity and try to enjoy my time here on this planet, to offer my children and others I work with the happy childhood I never got. But back then, during my early life, my day-to-day experience wasn't so rose-tinted, and our poverty level had nothing to do with it.

I think my first memory is of sitting on the bare linoleum floor of the living room, staring at some remains of my favourite toy, a doll. I remember the name of it too: Helga. Her head was detached and her face was bashed in after my mother, obsessed with her looks, punctured it with her perfect high heels before she left in rage. I remember this as being the first time I can recall the bodily feeling that accompanied the aftermath of such stomps and rages from my mother. I felt physical pain in my chest and arms like being stabbed through from the inside, the resulting thrumming and pulsing and pulling me down with its heaviness, building up stronger and stronger as I did not cry. I wasn't allowed to cry and I certainly did not dare to have a favourite toy after that, not openly at least. I did have a favourite book though, arriving at the same end, ripped to pieces in some rage over something I was blamed for, no idea what. It must have been a particularly savage tantrum by my two-year-old mother because a few days later she arrived home with the same book to give to me, a newer, shinier, unread and coloured version, but to me it was always just a reminder of the attack. She usually destroyed items, including my glasses that flew off my face many times when she landed a good slap if I didn't duck quickly enough. I didn't mind items that much, but I was about twelve years old when I caught the handle of the broom she raised at me, never let go and pulled it out of her hand. It was an empowering moment; it felt the best in my life for many years to come. I never let her beat me properly after that. Still, all the other forms of abuse continued.

But I'm getting ahead of myself. My next memory, I think, is walking home from school with a friend from Primary One. We would usually make our way home alone, without parents, it wasn't at all uncommon at the time, that wasn't a problem. On the way home we played catch, as children do and I somehow tripped and fell and bruised my chin. It wasn't a bad injury at all, I was just terrified of what my mother would do to me when she saw me ruining my white school shirt with blood. I begged my friend to come with me, hoping the abuse wouldn't be as severe if we had company, and it took me a while to convince her, as she didn't understand what the big deal was. I was wrong though. Despite having a witness, my mother welcomed me with a great big slap to my cheek. From that moment on, my friends knew my mother was an abuser, they never talked about her in any other way. When I saw some people at school reunions, I was surprised when the first thing they asked me was whether my mother is still a monster. As a result of that initial encounter, I was no longer allowed to have friends over, not just friends over who might judge her, I wasn't allowed to go out or to play with them other than at school times.

This resulted in isolation, my escape into fantasy, a serious lack of social skills and problems with facial recognition and facial expressions. I learnt not to express my feelings unless I wanted to get some more abuse shouted at me. If I ever did, I came to regret saying anything at all.

The best place was in my head, till it wasn't. She made sure I was bullied for my appearance too. She chose the clothes and she always chose the most outlandish ones that had my classmates roaring with laughter. I had nowhere to turn to, no one to talk to. I wasn't allowed extracurricular activities, anything to gain some self-esteem, anything to learn some skill that could get me out or above my situation. I still find myself saying to myself the same deprecating words she said to me, putting myself down or discrediting myself, dispirited and struggling with ventures and emotions.

The situation was worse than walking on eggshells because that's predictable, here you never knew what else you were going to be criticised about and should concentrate on to avoid. There was an atmosphere of heightened tension at all times because you never knew when your mother would burst into your room to accuse you of something you didn't know was a problem.

People often comment on my lack of sufficient eye contact as well, even ignorantly deeming the behaviour dishonest. They have no idea I spent my childhood in a house where I was regularly told 'don't you dare come in front of my eyes'! Do you think I would dare to make eye contact? That would be as far from daring to come into the room as Antarctica from Greenland! I struggle each day, forcing myself to look into people's eyes, a part of me still terrified because for a long time, it was only being alone that equalled safety. My attention, my hearing, was fine-tuned for every moment, every change. I knew well when the elevator moved outside our apartment, I knew who came up by the way they let the door go and by the time my mother would have the key in the lock, I would have fled into my room, as far away from harm as I could get, so I didn't have to hear how worthless I was. Of course, being able to identify every family member by the sound of their footsteps is another trauma response, a way to protect oneself, vital even – a survival mechanism.

Typical daily interactions would sound like this: 'I'm talking, you shut up,' 'We are past that. Look what you made me do.' Usually, she was being angry at what I 'made her do' – she blamed me for lashing out and breaking things.

She would say, 'you owe me, you need to respect me,' or 'what do you want from me? Am I not good enough for you? You are nothing, I'm the one who shitted you out, not the other way round.' That one was one of my single mother's favourite phrases, along with calling me *szemetlada*, which meant 'trash can' in the ethnic Hungarian language we spoke. That's what I was, a trash can, no better than a trash can. 'You deserved it, didn't you? You didn't do what I told you.' There were other ways she insulted me, such as 'pig' or 'big pile of shit', or she ridiculed something I've done, that was the default. She not only made me feel like nothing, she regularly told me I was nothing for good measure, so even though she didn't physically leave me, I still felt unwanted and my needs were neglected, as I wouldn't dare to voice them.

Any different point of view from hers had to be invalidated and ridiculed, the person neutralised. I am talking mainly about my father and me here, but occasionally she would launch an attack on someone else too. Then she would progress to pointing out 'faults'. Being stupid was another favourite. And so I learnt to feel stupid and dead, fittingly, like a trash can.

My energy was taken with having to scramble every time, to do her bidding, listen out to noise in the house, figure out what she was doing, judge the pitch of her voice, look for clues as to when it was particularly dangerous to be around, and defend myself against unfounded accusations. Punishments varied, ranging from a low number of spanks to not talking to me for days, refusing to give me food, hiding my clothes away so I could not go to school and, in my late teens, when she had less power over me and could not sabotage as many of my plans, hiding my passport so I could not go over the border to visit friends (we lived just a few miles from the border between Hungary and Romania). But do you know what it is called when the child is given the message that they have to try harder to earn love? It is called being groomed, conditioned, accustomed to abuse.

My estranged, alcoholic father was the better parent, as it goes. I was allowed to see him, to stay with him for a few weeks during the holidays, which was a relief. I could never quite blame my father for escaping that narcissistic hag when I was around three years old. Unfortunately, it was around the same time that my brother (fifteen years old when I was born) left for university in a different town, leaving the space open for my mother to do unspeakable things she could never have done with them around. Just picture Dr Jekyll and Mr Hyde.

According to my mother, the blame for everything bad in our lives lay with my father. For our financial situation, for how people viewed us in the community, why we didn't have a car, why the house wasn't repainted, why the vacuum cleaner didn't work. I listened to her complain and playing the victim for hours at a time, slagging him off to her friends on the phone, waiting for someone else to fix her problems. She could play the victim so well, her perceived slights were endless! It was never her fault, whatever it was. It was always someone else's. I could see and experienced the smear campaign in full swing, the master manipulation of controlling how others saw him, including my brother. On these phone calls she also depicted herself as the martyr, listing her suffering, someone who would sacrifice herself for her children. It was rather bewildering to see the mastermind at work. I knew the routine as soon as I knew who was on the phone. In a pre-emptive strike, she labelled others toxic because anyone could be a potential threat to how her friends saw her. She also often rambled about topics she knew very little about, but she pretended she did, giving advice right, left and centre. Of course, that was her outward persona that she put on. I don't know if she ever considered me, but she certainly didn't care about the collateral damage I suffered as a result, as long as it made her look good.

When we had a DIY issue, she always went on and on about my father not being there until eventually, in my teens, I learnt how to assemble a wardrobe, fix a radio, paint the walls. She wouldn't do it, it wasn't her 'job'.

School was a relief, in some ways, apart from homework. You see, my mother demanded perfection.

I had to be a model student, and was beaten up if any of my marks were not straight As. Worse, though, was having to do homework, because that, too, had to be pristine, one hundred percent correct and clear. She would check, and if it wasn't, she would rip the entire exercise book apart and mock and goad about how careless I was if I wrote a letter slightly wrong in her interpretation. It wasn't the daily homework she would rip apart, not a sheet, it was the entire booklet I had to rewrite again and again if I made a mistake. I remember sitting alone, holding my hands out in the air with no one around, needing someone to hold me while knowing well there was going to be no one coming. It's what happens when the parent who was meant to keep you safe is the one you need to be protected from. I remember the hopelessness, taking comfort in that physical pain that spread out in my arms because it was familiar, it was mine, it was reassuring and maybe easier to feel physical pain instead of mental pain. Even with my mother being physically there most of the time, I felt abandoned. It is not like I could confide in her when she was in a good mood. The narcissist only pushes their own agenda, they do not care about your fears, feelings or version of events. If she played with me, it was only to send the dolly to the shop to see how much change she will bring back – in other words, to test me if I knew my arithmetic. If she took me to the park, there would be no pleasure in it. I would be dressed inappropriately, would not be allowed to get dirty, it would be only for a few minutes on our way somewhere else and she would still bring it up later as a matter for me to be thankful for that she needed me to address as if to say, 'I proved I'm not the bad guy by taking you to the park!'

I learnt reading early too, long before school. You see, my mother would leave me instructions next to my bed before I woke up, in large, red, block capital letters. Those were my tasks for the day, things I had to finish before she got home, like dusting, doing the dishes, the like. The whole thing, it felt like being a puppet on a string. Of course I learnt how to read, I had to!

To top it off, she had a particularly hurtful way of finishing off her raging fits. After all the shouting, she would force me to hug her so that we 'part on good terms', delude ourselves. If at this point, I would object or say something along the lines of her accusing me for something that wasn't true, then she would laugh at me. Facts or logical thinking were jokes to her. Defending myself meant disrespecting her. I can still hear that fake 'hahaha', followed by 'I never said that, that's not it, you're lying,' when she just said it five minutes before. Or it would be 'what are you talking about, hahaha. Where do you think you can go? Nobody will want you. Do you think your father wants you? Good joke, hahhaha,' 'it wasn't like that at all. I'm the bad one? You're the only person who thinks that, don't you see?' Obviously, I was the only one, she presented a better version of herself to everybody else, if only slightly better in some cases and some got clues that there might be something hidden there.

It wasn't an anger management problem, not at all. She could control her rage just fine when other people were present, but was I terrified of the moment we were left alone. She wouldn't wait any longer for an outburst. I think that's the definition of evil, especially if they pretend to be good.

There was no Santa coming to our house. Not because I didn't get presents, because I did, but my monster of a mother couldn't stand not telling us she bought the presents. It was such an occasion where she had to be celebrated, she couldn't let Santa have that gratitude. Most Christmases were terrible anyway. Every time, she would find things to shout about, stress us out about because everything had to be the way she wanted it. Too much hassle for anything to be enjoyable. Of course, it is well known that the narcissist is prone to ruining special occasions like Christmas. This is because they cannot stand not being the centre of attention.

I should also mention the importance of the phenomenon of the narcissistic abuse technique called hoovering. Special occasions are also opportunities for people to enjoy themselves, but of course happiness, positivity and optimism are feelings of possible empowerment that threaten the abuser's control, so these need to be sucked out.

Without being heard or considered much, my spirit was dying more and more every day. By this point, I was afraid to talk, to express any inclinations, ask questions or simply share something that happened because I knew that everything could and would be used against me, if not immediately, then at some other point later. She would rehash it, throw it into my face as basis for blaming me for something. Any appearance outside the flat's walls was scrutinised to the extreme, as we were meant to look normal, holds hands, show affection, I was to sit in her lap, made to appear like everything was fine so nobody would notice anything was wrong,

Due to my underdeveloped identity based on having to disregard my own needs and inclinations, to this day

I find it hard to figure out who I am, apart from being a survivor, and apart from my ethos to life: never hurt another. I went to the university my mother wanted me to go to, I studied what she wanted me to study, worked in a job she wanted me to work in, at first. It was only later after I got married and became more independent that I started studying psychology.

Not even my extended family really know to a great extent who my mother is, or if they do, they pretend it never happened. No accountability. Move on, right? It's probably inconvenient to entertain the idea of seeing her in her true colours. Interestingly, it was mostly acquaintances who asked about my well-being, and noticed that something was off with my mother, people who had met her only once or twice. For example, my then boyfriend was warned about my mother from a friend who'd rarely seen her before.

Any friend I had, any boyfriend, was never good enough for her. I was discouraged to see them and if that didn't work, she would personally make sure it didn't by talking to the person, scaring them or their parents. If anybody who she couldn't challenge because of their position in society disagreed with her, she would just give them a blank stare. She would always have reasons why I couldn't see them or why they didn't come up to her standards. She faked having principles so she could look down upon people and her position on morality's throne wasn't affected, while in secret she would commit the vilest of vile acts, showcased by her lack of civility with strangers. These principles were solely for others to follow, she was exempt from them.

People in psychological circles talk about nourishing the inner child, supplying them with what they were missing while growing up. Only I get a panic attack any time I need to look at that inner child of mine, so lost and abandoned and in pain. I do want nothing to do with my inner child. It's probably associated with this phenomenon that I have huge memory gaps about parts of my childhood. I dissociate to avoid the tears, and do not remember some facts about myself. I do know that I spent years being someone else in my head, living my life as another persona because I couldn't bear to be me. I took on different identities in my head, pretended to be somewhere else, someone else, in different circumstances, disconnected from my own body and life. Shut up on the outside, I was speaking out loud in their voices inside my head, something like pretend play, but identifying strongly with the characters I made up; they were essentially me, living their happy lives, ignorant of mine. These guys, these figures, these saving graces, I do remember. I had nobody else to turn to, she made sure of that, but they saved me, I saved myself in a way, I guess. I would say it's a pretty useful survival method.

Dealing with such a minimising parent is exhausting, it tears you down to the extent it ends up affecting your fitness, your entire life and well-being. No wonder some of us survivors end up with chronic fatigue syndrome, depression and chronic pain.

Probably the first in a long string of photographs
all my life where my mother posed. No photo could
ever be taken without her pretending to
be doing something, being close to someone.
Here we have: the perfect mother.

I was about 3 years old here. I remember not wanting the photo taken and her grip on my wrist.

**My mother looking at me expectantly
as I receive an award for being a straight A student.
She wouldn't have it any other way, it had to
be or else. So no smiles from either of us.**

But this book wasn't written so I can feel sorry for myself. It was so that others with narcissistic mothers could recognise the pattern and stop blaming themselves for their current weaknesses. So I'd like to reassure you that I will try to limit mentioning my personal experiences. I will go into detail about my past only to showcase a point, such as describing my symptoms so that they can be understood more clearly rather than just giving a dry, impersonal list. Victims might have all, or any of these symptoms. What I hope is that people can find kinship, relate and realise that they are not alone with their symptoms or that I can maybe shed some light on what they're experiencing so they can go easy on themselves. Therefore, the following chapters might also be triggering for some.

The Narcissistic Parent

Understandably, my close family and I have little contact with my mother these days. I don't tend to talk about my childhood much either, so I was surprised that when I mentioned to my husband that I was trying to write a book about my narcissistic mother, he immediately agreed that she is, indeed, undoubtedly a narcissist. Perhaps it's not that hard to see it, from the outside, but too many people still get caught up in narcissistic webs. It's not easy escaping such a relationship, even harder if you're the child. As we have seen, the resulting clutches and claw marks can last a lifetime so the sooner we realise that we are dealing with a narcissist, the better for our escape route options and eventual recovery.

Narcissism is a kind of mental illness, not one the narcissist themselves would normally admit to. While it is more prevalently diagnosed in men, there still are plenty of women with the disorder. My mother is a prime example of the narcissist's behaviour in regards to accepting therapy. She was offered the chance several times and always refused. Her response was, also typically, that those therapists know nothing, have a lot more problems going on than her and that she shouldn't be talking to such lowly beings, belittling them in her usual fashion with whatever she could think of at the time. This is because narcissists don't listen. They don't see others as equals. They give no honest compliments. They don't take orders from others and similarly, they don't take advice, especially not that of the mental health professional because that would mean admitting there was something wrong with themselves. However, the reality is that even the healthiest individuals can improve and people who insist they don't need therapy despite problematic relationships tend to be those who keep causing considerable trauma in the lives of others.

The narcissist's most defining characteristic is that they are unable and unwilling to put themselves in another person's shoes, they are too self-centred for that. This is the state that their development took them to, and they cannot overcome this limitation. Arrogant and prideful, narcissists are individuals with 'an exaggerated sense of self-importance'[4], obsessed with having high status in society, appearances and entitlement, which makes them regard themselves as the best in the world and their opinion as irrefutable. Traditionally, it is commonly believed that there also is a somewhat perverted, cruel and heartless part to narcissists, it certainly has that effect, though the intention might not be quite as callous. A normal person can't just turn love off. But a narcissist can, like *The Vampire Diaries*-type vampires who turn their humanities off with a switch. It means the narcissist did not have love in the first place. Showing love is only a tool they use to manipulate and fool people.

Adversely, their type of childish behaviour of towering rage could also be a coping mechanism itself against insecurity and fears of abandonment and a lack of control stemming from childhood trauma, like neglect or bullying that makes them seek validation from others. They resort to vengefulness and manipulativeness to achieve this control and put people down so they can feel special and above them. To appear superior, these control freaks are prone to grand gestures that mean nothing but inflate their ego and force out acclaim and compliments from people. If it doesn't come, they will lash out with rage. Unfortunately, they keep this side of theirs in hiding so that only those closest to them will experience the fallout and everyone else will still only see their put-on personality. Thus, they have no real or healthy relationships, all they know is how to abuse, shame and manipulate to make you feel severely damaged, undeserving of love, apprehensive, drained and invisible. Their lies come so naturally to them that they even lie about things that don't matter out of habit. Ruinous, abominable acts, that is their game. They are out for control, of other's emotions, circumstances, options and decisions, everything, and they will keep manipulating everyone until their agenda has been met. They try to destroy others with lies because they can be destroyed with the truth. It shatters trust in human nature and makes you want to give up on yourself and life.

Their currency of love is money. As such eccentric individuals, they often break the law and don't conform to norms as they feel above those too. Everything has to be the way they want it to be. Abuse occurs because the narcissist will use whatever methods necessary to achieve what they want, they lie, cheat, take advantage of whatever they can. A lot of people have faults, problems, inappropriate ways to deal with situations, including inflicting abuse of course. Most of these people are trying to better themselves. Not narcissists. I never got any apology, for one. They deny their problems exist, they deny they've done anything wrong, they do not want to do anything different. What they want to do is keep their abuse secret so they can keep doing it. To achieve this, they need to silence you, usually by making you dread their anger. How dare you tell anyone what's happening in the house? How dare you ruin my reputation? How dare you shame us? In my case, that kind of talk would usually be followed with a good slap, meaning, how dare you have any initiative, do anything without my consent, how dare you have an individual thought? How dare you tell the truth? What a classic! Narcissists thrive on faking, especially when it concerns putting up a false front, looking like something they are not. And what better false front for disguising their evil nature is making it look as if they were charitable, caring, empathetic and connected. Their acting skills are spot on because they cannot attain what they want if the society they live in realises what they actually are. It is their survival that is hanging in the balance. Therefore, narcissists have this special talent of being able to mislead and delude the unsuspecting public. They need to be convincing in their ploy, they need the outside world to believe it, to think that their goodwill is true, that their fellowship with others is genuine and they get off on being apt at tricking people and leading them on too, something I've seen in action many times, along with my mother's glee at having achieved it. This illusion makes them achieve what they long for, be that a societal, a personal or a financial need.

When the narcissist invents a false self, some supreme creature beyond compare, superior to everyone else, it is to annihilate feelings of scorn and self-hatred originating in their own childhoods. They gain what they need out of life by inventing this false self. This false self being perfect, phenomenal, they would not have to work on themselves, improve themselves and they don't think they are doing phoney things, it is simply their coping mechanism. So they'll continue to gather 'evidence' that they are superior, in the form of subjugating others. Sadly, the easiest to subjugate is always their own child. They can assert dominance almost without an effort, terrorise the child, disallow objections to the maltreatment with the damage creeping in slowly in insidious ways. It is the epitome of domestic violence, a slowly dehumanising and purposeful soul rape.

Can you believe the arrogance and the idiocy of not understanding this is counterproductive in the long run? The child will eventually grow up and out the situation and then they will reject the narc* for what they've done, cutting their narcissistic supply. It is also why children of narcissists can sometimes become narcissists themselves. They identify with this false self because they can't face the truth. To be able to hold onto this false sense of self, they need narcissistic supply, people who will bow down to them, compliment them and lift them up with attention or funds so that this image can stay unshattered. Any reaction counts, a sign that they are important in life. The child's frustration, their tears, positive or negative, it doesn't matter as long as it makes the narcissist feel special, superior to others. A child's an easy target. 'Narcissistic supply is the oxygen that gives narcissists life.' – Maria Consiglio, therapist specialising in relationships and personal growth.

The narcissist often comes off as rude and derisive to strangers and this is because they are unable to take the other person's perspective and only see the wrong that has been done to them, however small, while thinking little of and dismissing the other person's problems and emotions. They are overgrown bullies who like to use threats, deception and coercion to control their subjects. They can never be held liable as they will never admit to a fault and they will do this with no sympathy or guilt. This haughty hypocrite will exploit every opportunity so that they can then act lofty from their forced position in an immature way and with a sense of entitlement, assuming the commandant's place whether required or not, to order people around and demand things they know nothing of because they are not willing to pay attention to anyone since they already know everything. They need this control because deep down they are so fragile they can't even admit it to themselves. At first glance, it sometimes may appear as if they had an appealing outward personality, but this mask tends to drop off when things don't go their way and they become angered. Sounds scary? That's because it is.

In the household of the narcissistic parent, all imaginable and unimaginable forms of power and control are used against the children from intimidation and physical abuse to isolation, economic abuse, threats, sometimes sexual abuse and so on. The menacing background, living in this kind of environment, makes it feel like the threat is always there, other people's presence will only delay the execution. It is impossible to forget about it. This controlling environment puts the child in a particularly dependent state as their moment-to-moment existence depends on someone else's mood or presence. This causes them to feel an extreme kind of helplessness which casts them into a state of frequent, if not constant, terror and upheaval. Another continuous feeling they endure is a chronic, overwhelming sadness that is hard to see the way out of. That was my reality.

Narcissists are self-obsessed, ignorant and lack empathy and remorse, which is why they are able to carry though acts that would be deplorable for anyone else. They do not comprehend or consider how their orders or actions might hurt other people so they see nothing as their fault. Sometimes I felt like disappearing under the ground in shame, not wanting to be associated with the way my mother addressed strangers, random people. The rudeness and lack of sympathy I found embarrassing, how could she speak to people with that little regard? There has got to be something wrong with the picture when the child finds themselves explaining to their mother the basic elements of human decency.

People with disabilities, regardless of whether they were physical or mental, were an absolute no-no for her; I was not to associate with any of them as she looked down upon them. It was only friends and specific other people she wanted to impress that she talked to in an acceptable manner, but behind closed doors, she would badmouth them too, criticising them with a sense of superiority, on her high horse with sanctimony and double standards.

My godmother, for example, was a devoutly religious woman and I have to assume my mother didn't think that my godmother, her friend Klari, would value her if she didn't go to church. So we went, occasionally, but only when we knew Klari would be present. Other times my mother would ask her when and where she would go to church and say we went at a different time and different place. This went on for years, while at home all I could hear from her how stupid her friend was for blindly believing in God. It was for this reason that once an adult, I studied and tried a number of religions to find out for myself what was true or good for me.

As it stands, I cannot blame my godmother either for not seeing through my mother's act. She was friends with her, she had her own emotions for her and it is hard to imagine a person without any empathy, so completely fake they have this other, made-up persona for the public. Another problem with noticing the damage is that the narcissist crushes the victim over time, little by little so that sometimes not even the target grasps it is happening till later. The narcissist always makes sure there's nobody around the victim who can open their eyes to reality.

Besides, there has, until recently, been a huge lack of awareness of narcissistic abuse. A lot of the victims themselves had not heard about narcissistic child abuse until they reach adulthood and it all starts to make sense. Most people think it must be very rare and others find that when they first encounter guidance on narcissistic child abuse, it all seems quite unbelievable so they simply disregard the knowledge. It is nearly impossible to change someone's mind using facts. They believe what they want to believe. This is because of the phenomenon of motivated reasoning, where, in the main, people tend to find the most insubstantial piece of evidence to be able to keep believing what they want, even if there are ample other pieces of evidence that contradict it.

During less rageful periods of time, it felt like living next to an empty barrel, an automaton with no emotions. It's your reaction that's their problem. They won't admit their faults and they won't change. Big warning there for the adult offspring: you shouldn't be giving them any more chances. They might appear changed to lure you back, but they do not change. Inside, they stay miserable as they despise the attention and success others receive.

They want to be the centre of attention and need to be in control of every situation, especially if it pertains to other people, making them feel smothered and powerless. Narcissistic parents have no boundaries, get into everybody's business as if it were their own. So I don't have to tell you what a mistake it was for me to start writing a diary as a teenager.

As you can imagine, being the child of a cold narcissist is rather problematic. These energy vampires try to make you accept their reading of the world and have a complete disregard for others. Being with them constantly is bordering living hell. I don't have to tell any good parent that 'because I said so' is not a good reasoning with a child at any time. Firstly, because it is a power play, and secondly, because explaining to a child why a certain action is necessary makes them grow in knowledge as well. Of course, this logical solution is not possible with a parent figure who can't regulate their emotions properly and is too bent on insisting on being in control rather than answering legitimate questions.

Mind games and abuse are a given, and then there is the pain and the second-hand embarrassment that comes with seeing that individual you're supposed to love deceive and lie to the world. There is also the wish that you could have parents who genuinely cared about you and gave you attention for the sake of spending time together and not to make sure you knew your prime numbers for the next day's lesson.

Narcissists make their own children their personal slaves without any scruples. They guilt their children for having emotions and play the victim, as opposed to healthy parents who help them learn to manage and express emotions. My narcissist was both violent and covert at the same time depending on her potential audience so while I feared for my physical well-being, every day I was also losing a piece of who I could have been. Especially when flipping out, she would expect me to pay attention and act on what she demanded, regardless of how unrealistic or impossible it was to achieve. For the reason that the narcissist wants and demands constant attention, they need to see people bowing to them on a regular basis in action. However, the child's needs are 'stupid, unimportant, undeserved and meaningless.' – Jill Wise, narcissistic abuse recovery expert and coach. It is part of their stonewalling approach, another tactic where the narcissist completely ignores the victim or their needs. They might refuse to have a conversation or make eye contact. As the child is forbidden from developing other significant relationships, what they've done in these cases is almost identical to cutting off someone's life support on a psychological level.

In this section, I have outlined some of the effects having a narcissistic mother had on me, before going into detail about each syndrome in the following chapters to clearly show how mental health deteriorates with abuse. None of it means we're crazy, we were 'just' abused.

The narcissist, unable to understand love, doesn't think a child should have their own personalities yet.

A professional manipulator, pathological liar and thief, people with this disorder don't see others as equals. The narc cruelly wounds and then soothes in maddening cycles that create extreme confusion, stress, mental discomfort and trauma in the child as they do not know how to categorise and relate to the parent any more. Are they Jekyll or are they Hyde for the moment? Stockholm syndrome might be the answer as the brain can't handle the two opposite realities the parent offers at the same time. This technique, this confusion is called cognitive dissonance.

On Cognitive Dissonance

The theory of cognitive dissonance originates from 1957 when an American social psychologist, Leon Festinger, published the results of his experiment where he tested the decision-making process[17]. In his conclusions, he noted that there is tension resulting from having two conflicting thoughts at the same time or from engaging in behaviour that conflicts with one's beliefs. The person then will experience discomfort. When this happens, people develop a motivational power within them to enable them to justify and replace their attitudes, beliefs, principles and reactions, and would basically do anything within these limits that helps them lessen or put an end to the jarring discordance they are confronting internally. It is a coping mechanism everybody uses from time to time to alleviate feeling uncomfortable when something disputes a belief we want to hold onto. Religious apologists use it to no end.

In the case of the crazy train narcissistic household, it is commonplace for the child to find themselves in the situation where they have no idea what will happen next. It could be good, it could be bad, or alternating anywhere between moments of kindness and violent rages. It creates a sense of unreality in the target. They become disorientated and come to not believe the perceptions of their own senses. The resulting cognitive dissonance is there, with all its discomforts, but not just any cognitive dissonance. As the situation is continuous, the presence of cognitive dissonance will also be, so in addition to the dangers of the environment, the child will also have to deal with this internal conflict and call forth some internal resources and defence mechanisms. According to the principles of cognitive dissonance, the parent can't be both Dr Jekyll and Mr Hyde at the same time, so the child will have to deal with this anxiety by unconsciously choosing one or the other and ignoring proof to the contrary to the best of their ability. This will then often result in lying to themselves to convince themselves of a false sense of security, bonding with the narcissistic parent or regressing into infantile patterns. It is a dangerous tactic of the narc's as it can make the victim hold compassion, sympathy and empathy for the abuser.

The Phenomenon of Infantile Regression

A baby, an infant, is clearly pretty helpless. Their survival depends on the caregiver and reaching out to the caregiver is their only option, no matter what. It is the case with narcissistic 'caregivers' as well. Isolated and alienated, as the narcissist's child often is on purpose, whether significantly older or not, the child has nowhere else to turn to and their unconscious survival mechanism will tell them what to do. It will be the only thing possible, which is to become docile and obedient without question, please the narcissist to the best of their ability, submit and bond with and cling to the caregiver the way the narcissist demands it as if their lives depended on it, which it most often does[18]. Over and over, I would put myself down, blamed myself for not thinking of better ways to avoid an outburst or confrontation. This regression is and was often seen in the history of prisoners. The phenomenon is also known as Stockholm syndrome and is very similar to trauma bonding.

The extreme terror the child is often experiencing will also need soothing, but the only person they can turn to for this, as with anything else, is the narcissistic parent. So they will do their absolute best to appease their tormentor so that they can reach the stage where their negative emotions are also soothed by the narcissist in their affection part of the cycle. It would be impossible to bear, divert or numb the pain without this important survival mechanism and thus becoming dependent on the ambient disposition and behaviours of the toxic parent like a puppet on a string.

Joined with cognitive dissonance, it leads to temporary denial of the narcissist parent's wrongdoings, a passage that ensures that the child can choose the alternative that leads to the least physiological, mental and emotional stress. Complying is, temporarily at least, the easy way out and it doesn't even need to ruffle one's belief system. As long as we can disregard the abuse, no struggle is needed. As long as we don't question anything they do and follow their instructions to the letter, they might just leave us alone. But challenging them, following one's own ideas, equates to the greatest misdeed that is committed against them. It's a personal attack so it will not go unnoticed and the victim will be punished out of vindictiveness. How dare anyone deviate from their ideas?

This behaviour pattern is often seen with domestic abuse victims and it's even more pertinent in the child's case. There is nowhere to escape to so why try? When parented by this skilled con artist, a thief of the child's self-esteem, the process of the fight or flight response becomes purposeless because the child is fully and literally stuck. Typically, the youngsters cannot get away from their homes or fight their parents and this is when the freeze response arises, once the subconscious has registered and is convinced, whether it's true or not, that there's no running away from the situation. This freeze response then shuts the thalamus down and access to sensory information is muted as if tranquilised; it is also why some survivors of narcissistic abuse experience a delayed realisation of why they are so different from others. Trauma causes disorganised attachment. When early attachments are dangerous, it generates an internal struggle between the impulse to attach and the need to be safe.

Trauma bonding, being a strong emotional attachment that can be hard to break, has clouded their senses and the dense cloud takes a while to dissipate, so it is merely after they've distanced themselves from the abusive situation for quite some time that they understand how unjust and immoral their circumstances have been while growing up. This is why developing a healthy outlook on life can only usually happen under the conditions of strictly no contact.

Opportunities for education on the subject are pivotal too, which I am hoping to further facilitate with this book. Signs of trauma bonding include thinking that the abuse was deserved, justifying it or accepting blame in any way, making excuses for the narcissist parent or believing they can change or be useful to the abuser, taking responsibility for keeping them happy and healthy. 'When you are not fed love on a silver spoon you learn to lick it off knives.' – Lauren Eden.

In most cases, the abuser sometimes helps the victim, gives them things, even shows kindness in certain circumstances. They love you, right? Such concepts are hard to navigate for adults even, what chance does a child have? Once I was cognitively old enough, my narcissistic mother used to tell me sob stories of her own, the same ones she would tell others so she would be seen as the victim and felt sorry for. For a while, it worked on me as well. It was only somewhere during my teenage years that I stopped believing them, once I had proof that many of the things she circulated were lies.

It was at this point, however, in my early teenage years that I became acutely aware of how different I was to my peers, of how much my well-being depended on the internal fantasy world I created as opposed to their contemporary interests in boys, make-up, gossip, the flavour of the day. While these fleeting interests of theirs were and are not necessarily useful in the long run, my lack of interest certainly alienated me more from other teenagers and made me a target of bullying and exclusion. Pair this up with my mother not allowing me to wear what was fashionable, instead making me wear quirky hats and decades-old styles so I looked more like a mini-her than a child, you can see how impossible a social life became. The younger me did reach out to other children, trying to complain about my home situation and I did achieve some sympathy, if nothing else, but the older, teenage me felt like I had to conceal my home situation because it made me stand out more. I tried to be normal as much as possible, avoiding a peer's contact with my mother as much as it was practicable, as I was ashamed of her, of her behaviour, of how she treated me and others, of how she dismissed any association of mine and gave them no importance, of how I was rendered nothing in any interaction with her. I didn't want people to see that. I was in a no-win situation then, with my mother, and with my peers as well. It is a lonely life, that of the victim of narcissistic abuse. This, of course, led to continuous anxiety, a feeling of helplessness and low self-esteem.

The 'narcissist's number one tool is neglect. What better way to crush a person's spirit than to treat a person like they don't matter. What better way to invalidate a person's existence than ignoring them, their needs, their wants, their words, what is most important to them and what means the most to them? What better way to take a person out of the equation and make them feel invisible?' – Maria Consiglio. Relatively, though, the nicer periods were when my mother was too preoccupied with herself, too engulfed in some problem, too preoccupied to bother with me. These were the times of relative peace. I only had to look out for her tension-induced temper, not the overly unrealistic demands that were put on me other times.

Another side effect of my terror was an aversion to sleeping in another person's company for the vulnerability this put me at. Thankfully, I had my own room at home, but I was virtually unable to sleep in public for much of my life, times others can spend resting in the commute, napping at home outside of their bedrooms. Similarly, I still sleep very aware of what is going on around me so it is very hard to catch me unawares. I will open my eyes before anyone can surprise me. All this comes from a lack of sense of safety, not being certain of when my mother would burst in, shouting about something I'd have no idea about, producing another of her senseless outbursts aimed at me or someone else. They seemed to come out of nowhere, very loud and unexpected. They shocked me into a state of stillness, fright, and then they usually confused me. What was she on about? What was the big deal and what did it have to do with me? I still had to listen to it, agree with it or else, so this was my survival mode in action.

I have recently landed in some further trouble in connection with sleeping. Writing this book and thinking back on memories I've spent most of my life suppressing caused me some nightmares featuring my mother. I decided to take a break from writing when needed and pace myself more.

As an example of unrealistic expectations, I remember having to write a 'diary' during the summer holidays after Primary One so that I could practise writing. Of course, this was mostly dictated and on one occasion, I had to write about how I was supposed to be ashamed that I accidentally broke a glass while doing dishes. A seven-year-old! She often brought this up afterwards, reminding me of my 'wrongdoing' in tirades that often left me devastated and crying. I did at first feel it was wrong to blame me for that, but it didn't occur to me until many years later how it was wrong to make me do the dishes and the ironing regularly at that age to start with! I had to be good at everything. At school, I had to constantly compete with the best of the students, report back to my mother what their exact achievements were each day and match it at least. Everything was a competition and I could only fraternise with the best. The same applied to outside of school, no matter what, or suffer the consequences, criticism or being called names at the very least. Due to this, I fear talking on the phone to this day, as my mother was always listening and calling me out if I didn't greet someone correctly, tell them the 'right' information, which oftentimes was a lie she wanted circulated. I get the shivers when I remember her shouting on these occasions. Not to mention that the exact lie was not something I found easy to guess at times and yet I couldn't ask in advance in fear of her reaction. How would I know what to say? I did not consider truth as an abomination and I wasn't the same kind of charming con artist to the public that she was! It was a weighty issue, however, as consequences were harsh with her reputation at stake if I accidentally revealed her to be the pathological liar she was.

Unrealistic expectations then of course lead to the child being disappointed in themselves as well, along with shame, frustration and humiliation from the parent. As if they were puppets, narcs manipulate the child's emotions so that then they can feed on the pain, feel their power. Infantile and petty, they are self-absorbed, blatant, stubborn and uncontrollably defensive. They don't know any other way to be, this is who they are. She would say, 'you think that way, I know what's right,' and the scornful tone carried the meaning that I could be nothing else but crazy. In some strange way, they seem to show no recognition that other people would even have feelings. It feels surreal.

It would have been a joke for me to have emotional needs or my own thoughts, a mind of my own, nothing was about me. So to this day, I'm terrified of picking up the phone, self-conscious of doing it to the highest degree and she's not even around anymore. I experience the feeling of sheer terror every time the phone rings or someone mentions calling me, with little regard to who is on the other side of the line.

Also as a result of fear of criticism and retaliation, came a tendency for perfectionism and people-pleasing. I couldn't just keep it in one box, though, in relation to my mother. I developed extreme anxiety if I felt I could not please someone, a family member, the most random person I came into contact with. To some extent, most people have been conditioned to the myth that how others see us is important to our self-worth and this makes people want to please. Victims of narcissistic abuse take this on the next level. They have to be busy and useful all the time or they'd feel guilty. If I did anyone wrong in any way, I had to make it right, spend extensive time fixing some mistake they would have hardly noticed, if at all. I would stress out about fixing it, rushing to fix it before they saw it. Writing a greeting card, for example, took me hours. I had to have a perfect quote for the occasion, the perfect set-up. Anything less than that and I wasn't happy with myself.

I would say I lost myself in those times, but that wouldn't be correct exactly. People often talk of rebuilding, scraping together the pieces of who you were before a trauma, but I did not have an identity before the trauma, that was what shaped me into becoming who I am. If not for my father's regular appearances in my life (something like fortnightly, but not quite as regular as that), I doubt if I would have known what was real and what was not, what is right and what is wrong. He also assured me that I wasn't just imagining or misinterpreting things, that my mother was really an abuser. However, I don't think he quite realised how far the abuse and shouting would go in his absence, how she'd throw temper tantrums worse than a toddler's, especially if presented with the naked truth in the form of proof of something they undoubtedly did that was hurtful. But with no adults there, she didn't have to be ashamed of any behaviour so she'd simply let her temper fly.

While our financial situation was often lacking, I was discouraged from taking a job in my teenage years and while I was at university. I think this was so that I remained dependent on her, so she could still keep me in as much control as she wanted. 'Where would you go, do you think anyone cares about you?' was another of her favourite phrases. She would often state how she was better than everyone, would never utter a good word about anyone, and would talk negatively about people behind their backs instead. She would threaten to tell my 'humiliating' secrets to my friends, something that was terrifying to me at the time, but only because I didn't see how it would have only put her in a bad light. There was nothing humiliating about my behaviour, it was simply just the typical behaviour of a child.

Money was a tool she used consciously to alter how people saw her. Despite not having much to ourselves, she would often give presents to friends, family members, acquaintances, whoever she wanted impress so that she could be seen as a do-gooder. This was even more so in the Socialist Romania where I grew up, as oftentimes you needed connections to get your hands on specific luxury or less common items that were not in the shops or came from abroad. She enjoyed being perceived as all-powerful, well connected and successful. It was easy to see how she fed on it, this feedback called narcissistic supply, while I sometimes felt like she was in fact humiliating them with her gifts, like they couldn't fend for themselves. This gift-giving also put her above suspicion, she couldn't be the cruel abuser I complained about to her friend, my godmother, could she? They do tend to have 'friends' like that, people who are quiet and wouldn't question them. They need this, the unreserved acceptance, as they cannot take any form of criticism.

And she still uses money and presents as a hook, and do I fall for it? After having my own family, I operated a no-contact policy with my mother for many years, for the good of everyone. It worked pretty well and I am proud to say I withstood my brother's pleas to stop it, but what I felt I did not have the right to stop was my mother sending presents or money to her grandchildren, my children, on birthdays or Christmas. You see, it wasn't my place to take that away from them. And then gradually, little by little, she would ask questions about what to buy for them, practicalities about sizes and I found myself picking up her call a few times a year. I still do, even though I'm starting to recognise the conversation pattern, the checking up on me she dares more and more now, the criticism she has no intention to stop, the badmouthing of others I hear. My father has been buried in the ground for many years now, and she still finds bad things to say about him, and ways to covertly put me down, criticise my actions as she knows now that I don't accept direct insults anymore. She also brings up her saintly quality, how she suffered for her family. While her actions rarely matched her words, she would wear me down over time with lies and using whatever sprang to mind, to the point where I argue no more.

However, these days I can put those down as her faults and her faults only, nothing to do with me. It is the darkness in her. I don't argue with her, there's no point, and besides, it is hardly possible to get a word in edgewise. You need to speak over her if you want a shot and even then, she would not hear a word. There was a time I wished for an apology, a chance to forgive. I now know this isn't possible. The callous narcissist will never see their own faults, this would break their flawed illusions of entitlement and grandeur. Most importantly, they cannot change and they will not seek help. So I can't stand around waiting for something that isn't going to happen. I didn't exactly forgive, but I have accepted my situation for what it is.

I am aware of the fact that other parents and teachers were mostly 'strict' too and corporal punishment was not unusual in schools. Unfortunately, during the 70s and 80s, and partly still in our times, some parenting and teaching techniques can only be described as socially acceptable bullying. I got wind of the occasional slap another child received so, to some extent, I wasn't certain that my experience was all that different from others'. On the other hand, I was too desensitised to the abuse to recognise how much deeper my being abused went. In a lot of ways, it was only after escaping the household and seeing more of the world, experiencing other relationships, that I truly understood how wrong my childhood was. This scenario is not unusual with narc victims. First of all, because their world is controlled by the narcissist, and second, that the abuse is done in such a manipulative manner that the victims question their own selves foremost.

Moving house in my teenage years happened from one day to the other. I was not consulted, I simply had to sleep in the other house the next day. While this experience might have been commonplace in those days, I would have appreciated a little forewarning. I did not know it was going to happen till the day it happened! Anything good in our lives, we had to flaunt. She took many photos of our holidays and achievements and made sure to show them to obviously bored individuals, bragging and forcing praise out of people with pointed questions, while I tried to sink into the ground, ashamed again. Needing validation, she would have been a prime candidate for Insta fame if those were the times[69]. Either way, the Oscar for best acting performance goes to the narcissist!

So in matters like this, I've grown enough to see, she could not deceive me anymore. Cognitive dissonance was still a factor in other matters, such as her telling me I cried too much, that I reacted too much, that I was too sensitive. I still believed that I was, that there was something wrong with me, instead of reacting like I was a victim of narcissistic abuse. Because other people didn't cry as much as I did, did they? Other times I got chronically confused by lies, second-guessing myself that maybe I didn't remember it well, that maybe she didn't treat me wrong that time. Was I losing my mind? Cognitive dissonance is also why the gaslighting they do is so credible.

On the rare occasion of trying to stand up for myself against the depth of her cruelty and pointing out something I found hurtful, the whip was immediately turned on me. Instead of addressing something I dared to say, she would criticise with whatever would jump to mind at the time. I was the one to blame and she would have zero accountability. So, of course, you learn not to do it, trying to make them see sense, there is no point, only more suffering. She would always find what hurt the most and spit it back at me. There is this dark truth that everyone dealing with narcissists has to eventually accept, that expressing emotion, frustration, is like giving the narcissist more power. When this compulsive pathological liar sees the other person bothered, angered, exasperated, their crying makes them feel all the more powerful, like they can play you to their heart's content. It is all futile because the 'narcissist has all the rights and

THE IMPORTANCE OF ACKNOWLEDGING CHILDHOOD TRAUMA

you have none. The narcissist doesn't follow orders from others, they can do and say whatever they please, and you can't. You are expected to abide by high moral values, and guess what? They aren't! And when, and if, you finally try to assert your rights, or decide to leave, then they play the victim, and you are the villain. The only way you can win is by actually not playing the game. And getting the hell out.' – Maria Consiglio.

Again, I was the one to blame, and this time I blamed my own self for trying. One good that could come out of this at times, though, was the silent treatment I received.

People talk about the narcissist's silent treatment as their punishment, but personally, I kind of liked that. She would punish me by not responding, not talking to me for days, but to be honest, this was simply a holiday in my head. I knew her routine, I knew the noises, I could stay out the way and not even see her for days long, no need for hypervigilance beyond escaping her sight. No excessive shouting over something trivial for a change. Peace – that was great.

The Gaslighting of the Soul

By this point, does it come as a surprise to anyone that the narcissist doesn't play fair? In short, gaslighting is when someone hurts you and then blames you for it, yet another harmful manipulation scheme narcissists and other toxic personality types use to have us questioning our own sanity. It is a ploy to avoid responsibility for anything they've done. With the many systematic lies, the victim loses their grip on reality, they might not know what is true anymore, what has happened and what has not. It sometimes takes years of stepping back after the events to bring clarity in these matters. On the narcissist's part, this is an intentional undertaking, they tell so many lies to confuse you and make you believe their version of events. As it happens, I was a firsthand witness of these lies she told to others – my father, random acquaintances, office workers she wanted to acquire a document from. She apparently had absolutely no scruples in lying, deceiving. I guess it was somewhat easier for me to see through the deceit, after all, I was made to take part in it intentionally on occasion! If the trick didn't work on an outsider, she was 'just joking'.

I have had problems with jokes ever since, as I fail to find many that do not have some sort of hurtful hidden meaning directed to at least at some strata of society. I tolerate teasing even less. I don't see the value of pointing out others' faults or ridiculing someone's actions in this manner. If people laugh at it, it's all in good fun. Really? In my opinion, it should not be acceptable.

Either way, the gaslighting method hurt me as well at times, like when she would flat out deny something I knew had happened, proof be damned. She made that chilling, deprecating laugh that makes my blood freeze in my veins when echoed in my mind, 'Hahaha, it wasn't like that.' It was a stone-faced, cruel, derisive sound that only mimicked laughter. She would say, 'you are insane!' Or a derisive 'you'll never get what you want from me,' alternated with 'you'll never get what you want this way, I just made sure of it!' With those exact words, no sugar-coating from my mother. But in most cases, I knew I wasn't insane, but constantly defending yourself is arduous, so on many occasions I would just leave it. Narcissists won't let others prove them wrong and can also make you feel like others are a threat by lying, or they lie about past events so you constantly feel like you're maybe forgetting the way things went down and start questioning your own credibility and sanity. Resolving a conflict with a narc using rational arguments or discussion is not possible.

Narcissists have other trademark favourite sayings, such as 'you didn't let me finish what I was saying,' 'you have to be tougher in this world,' or 'that's not what happened.' These red flags are to stop you being able to think by shocking you with some further emotional abuse first. Another is to give no credit and value to your emotional reaction by 'just because I didn't do what you wanted,' also characterised by being said derisively. They are angry you reacted in some way that revealed their cruelty and they want to negate it, deeming it improper. They will try to bounce your issues back to you without as much as acknowledging or addressing or even admitting their unacceptable behaviour. So they quickly bring up something else, something they can find fault in, so that this countering can prevent every chance that the narcissist's culpability will be discussed.

Another classical one is 'why do you have to make things so difficult?' or 'what more do you want from me?', as if there would be a plethora of goodies we would need to thank them for. In the end, as a child, you end up having to try to calm the narcissist down because they got mad and you feel threatened, instead of achieving anything by bringing up a subject. 'I'm not going to argue with you,' means they will have it their own way and there's no point resisting it. They have to be right, no matter how that makes anyone else feel. To make matters worse, they have shut you down. The conversation is over because they said so. It is a show of power and control, the most important issue for them.

'I don't know what you're talking about' is another one. It is a variation of the usual discrediting behaviour and it could refer to something that literally happened in the conversation a moment before. They will deny they ever said it. Voice recordings are really necessary in conversations with the narcissist! They don't admit to having feelings either.

If you somehow manage to catch them out on a lie, they will pretend they forgot about it, play the innocent and stupid. They might even say that you presented them with the facts wrong and that's how they got confused as projecting blame is what they do best! The narc blames you for everything owing to the fact that if the target is too busy thinking about how to do better and be better at anticipating the narc-parent's needs then it will not become obvious to the child that they have been abused. The irony of that literally hurts. Sick, sick, sick! The sole purpose is to create a sort of brain fog in the victim, leading to self-doubt and a feeling of having lost one's mind or memory, in turn resulting in difficulties making judgements or decisions. I've heard 'I'll give you something to cry about' often enough as well, though I think that's more commonplace than being mainly restricted to narcissistic abuse. Ironic, however, is that when hearing that phrase it is the physical punishment we fear, but instead, we end up with a plethora of mental afflictions.

Some other classics are 'why can't you just get over it?' And 'you're the only person who thinks that' – both meant to make you question your sanity and reality. Or, 'it's your fault, you should have known that was going to upset me'; 'stop taking everything so fucking seriously'; 'why are you bringing this up?', 'you have mental issues', 'you're crazy', and 'you're so perfect/sensitive/emotional', 'don't complain, you're not perfect' and 'now look what you've done/look what you've made me do/look how you wasted my ...'. 'I did the best I could' is another common excuse. But no mother should be in the habit of putting a child down like this while they are already down, sad, hurt, unwell or going through something emotionally difficult. A poisonous, controlling, narcissistic one, though, lacks empathy and doesn't give a damn about how their actions or words affect others. They would not go as far as thinking about that because every situation, all the interactions and every moment, is about them.

Alternative put-downs they use are: 'how do you imagine you could do that on your own?'; 'you are useless/ know nothing'; 'you are a big fat zero', all forcing the child to see their caretaker as omnipotent and themselves incapable so that they remain dependent on the parent. While the developing child is desperately wishing to become free, their mind remains tethered to the narcent, conditioned as if they were dependent on the parent.

The narc loves drama and feels like they are entitled to everything, and the child, the closest person around to blame, becomes the basis for not having it all. These superficial people think they deserve everything, for no other reasons other than that they want it. 'They are deeply flawed and abnormal human beings, who will forever think the world owes them.' – Maria Consiglio. They are extremely bitter and spiteful too. They will deliberately try to get you to react negatively by probing and prodding and doing things they know will upset you or set you off to put you in a less favourable light, appearing hysterical to an outsider.

The narcissist is unerringly correct and never mistaken and they suppress who they are. An attempt to confront the narcissist typically results in them providing you with their regular routine 'word salad', a version of an abusive contention they are very good at. This consists of going in ludicrous circles with no intent for a resolution till it makes your head spin, as it is meant to, for its lack of logic and conflicting, confusing arguments, seasoned with denial, gaslighting, projection and further criticism. Meanwhile they bring up your past that has nothing to do with the current issue till you realise it's all pointless because the narcissist will never admit to a fault. Its purpose is to change the subject and divert you away from concrete facts and their blameworthiness by dragging the you through the mud and accusing, humiliating and frustrating you, with the purpose of forcing an argument. Using their well-oiled, self-centred pretentiousness, their word salad farce is a thorough deflection to transform the conversation into holding you liable for something related or even unrelated. It is supposed to turn them into the injured party and sometimes into an incredible, irreproachable, shiny paragon of the perfect parent as well. It is supposed to cause you to lose focus, forget the actual problem or stop you from having or expressing a position or any independent thought. Another way of appearing to be the injured party is by treating the victim with such a lack of respect that they will have a hard time holding back and explode.

The narc will not take no for an answer. I prefer not to think of the amount of second-hand embarrassment I endured as a result, the worst time being when she left me with a barely known family for three weeks simply because she got it in her head that they should be able to keep me because they were richer.

Narcissists treat strangers better than their so-called loved ones, they twist everything with lies, everything that matters and everything that doesn't. They will make you undeserving and invisible and destroy our trust in human nature. They make you want to give up on yourself and life and leave you with a paralysing amount of damage and debility. They also devalue, denounce and reject everything they were ever given, maybe excluding money and other significant material gains. In denial, they avoid emotions and stonewall during conflicts. In a childish way, they rage if anyone challenges them and they accuse you of things you aren't doing, chronic liars as they are. Narcissists lie because they're so conceited that they feel as if they have a right to whatever they want, whenever and however they want it. They lie to ensure they're able to control, use, take advantage of and silence others. They lie to conserve their fake identities and because the truth inconveniences them.

They use guilt, duty, terror and spread uncertainty to get what they want. They aim to distress the victim, provoke them and swear, and subsequently pretend, with no remorse, not to know why the other is perturbed.

A type of manipulation not mentioned enough, but utilised frequently by the narc is blackmailing, especially the emotional manipulation that places demands on and threatens victims in the form of, for example, 'I will tell your boyfriend you've been a slut,' or a more simplistic one, 'you get nothing from me for the foreseeable future if you don't shut up right now!' Though any form of blackmailing has an emotional undertone, these imply that if you do not comply with the demand, you will be subjected to pain in some way. This is because the narc processes things differently to other people. In the moment, they don't see what they do as abuse, it is their instinctual reaction and nothing more. Sadly, they are like a child, they use this method because they don't have healthy ways of communicating and reacting. They resort to what they have, which is stonewalling, destroying things to convey an emotion, blaming and ultimatums. I've even heard the ultimate one: 'If you leave, then I'll kill myself.' Their world is black and white. For them, most people are either convenient fools they can play to their heart's content, or they are an adversary. They prey on the weak, and will mow everything down that stands in their way. Their fake self frolics in their fake world of fake relationships and prizes to secure. Recognising the pattern is half the win because then it is clear that they do not change and that being around them denotes being in terrible danger.

Narcissists are very conflicting, the archetype of hypocritical. They want control without taking responsibility for their actions. They want to be seen as exceptional, but not scrutinised enough to be found broken. They want to be able to do what they want, but they don't want to be alone. They want to be needed, as it suits them.

What made my mother like that, I don't know, and frankly I'm not sure I am able to care enough, not after all that, though we do know that violence runs in the family. While some genetic origins have been linked with narcissism, I know that she didn't have a great childhood herself, but she also didn't talk about it much, as I assume it wouldn't have put her in a favourable light. I know she despised her mother because she was 'only a cleaner' and would beat her up in front of me, kick the poor old woman till she was down on the floor. This happened regularly, she pulled her hair, she spat at her.

I did not meet my grandfather as he died before I was born. Even his death is shrouded in mystery as he died either of cancer or heart failure, depending on the day you asked my mother. In most cases when she talked about him, she would idolise him and give him credit for all that was good in our lives, but other times she would say that he was an alcoholic who beat them and my grandmother had to hide the children from him when he came home drunk. She also had a brother who would beat her up to the extent of breaking her ribs, he beat up their mother to the extent of landing her in hospital. He was a thief and expert racketeer, spending years in jail for it. So I have absolutely no idea what to think, the whole situation is confusing to the level it hurts to think about it. You know how our psyche hates cognitive dissonance, right? I only know that my mother will never tell the truth, admit that anything would be wrong with her or seek help to achieve healthy relationships. You will never get the truth out of a narcissist, they make you intentionally misunderstand things, omit the most important detail. I have to assume that they lie to themselves even, so much so that they don't know the truth either.

Another exculpating circumstance is the fact that the narcissist desists from any self-analysis for fear of what they would find. So they don't know who they are, they don't know why they do the things they do, they simply feel compelled and are not interested in the reasons for their impulses. This makes them unable to talk about deep, radical, heartfelt subjects, they only know gossip, criticisms and platitudes.

One thing for sure, I was going up against generations of trauma. What I can also bring up for her defence, to the defence of any narcissistic person, is that they don't know what love is. I know that excuses don't need to be made for these kinds of people, but I also don't think they mean to be evil, they're simply unable to live any other way and they don't know that being unwilling to say sorry is a sign of cowardice, not strength. But I would like to stress that while they're not governed by evil, they might as well be, because the end result is the same. Narcissists are destructive and it is decidedly dangerous to be in denial of that. They wilfully choose to be reckless, thoughtless and unreasonable. They decide to hurt the child because then they'll feel in control and that feels good for them, addictive, even, like a drug. They know it is not healthy or moral, they could stop if they wanted to. They are not at the mercy of their pathology or at the whim of their disorder, so there's no need to feel sorry for them. They can be so chaotic and their behaviour baffling. There isn't any dependability or reliability. You can have a good day or a really bad day, depending on what they want in the moment, how they want it and with whomever they want it.

The narc will ruin you all the same with their selfishness, their superiority complex, their lack of empathy and a proper sense of responsibility, their accusations and lies. Narcissistic personality disorder is the only mental condition where the patient is left alone but everyone else around them needs treatment. Of course, the questioning of the legitimacy of the abuse based on apologetic factors is also part of a relationship with a narcissist. After all, they have been misleading and gaslighting you all your life. It is major eyewash, is what it is. Were they really unable to control their behaviour? Can I blame them? Were they aware what they were doing was wrong? Were they aware of how much damage they were causing? Are they capable of love? Was some of the love bombing real? Can I ever have a proper relationship with them? When were they lying and when were they not? Am I paranoid? Am I insane? Is my parent stark raving mad? Can they be considered accountable? All these and similar questions are completely normal and all of them lead back to one thing: Remember what was done to you, so your anger is legitimate for those childhood years stolen from you, for all the handicaps you suffer from as a result, for being behind peers in careers and relationships.

I know it is easier said than done, but the only way to deal with this kind of person is by removing them from your life as soon as possible so that further damage can be averted. As a child, that is even harder. All I could manage were small stints at my grandparents' or my brother's house. As a breather if nothing else, those were okay. Getting ourselves independent, able to soar on our own, should be the next step. No contact. Don't let people guilt you into a sense of obligation and loyalty to a parent. This is not just any parent. Give no information that can be used against you because if there is one thing you can trust, it is that the information will be used against you. Unfortunately, dealing with the damage is rarely possible while still in the clutches of the narcissist, because of the cognitive dissonance I've described.

A certain time needs to pass in the absence of the narcissist till we can trust our thoughts and feelings, learn how healthy relationships work, know what exactly needs done from the outside perspective. These things take time, sometimes a lot of time. It can also take months, sometimes even years of no contact with the abuser to develop a rounded sense of self, to know who we are without the constant pulling and pushing into whatever direction the narcissist shoves you in. It can also take a long time to shed all the misguided, misdirected guilt, shame and continuous hurt, and properly cherish what it is to be free to act as one wants without the constant looking back over the shoulder for whatever punishment is incoming.

The main thing, though, is that we are away from further harm, our reality cannot be hijacked again and we can contemplate our own behaviour consciously, find the road to happiness. Respect yourself. Put out those boundaries you were never allowed to have. These might be too wide at first, but you'll get there. The moment the narcissistic 'person crosses your boundaries, be very clear that that behaviour is unacceptable and should not be tolerated. And if it continues be prepared to walk away. No one is worth disrespecting' – Maria Consiglio.

Once left, the narcissist will generally try to win you back, bring you back into the fold of their narcissistic supply. They might appear changed, say different things that have you questioning your memory again, blackmail you with their rights to see their grandchildren, like mine did. But regardless of how cordial, unhappy or on the rare occasion, if you're lucky, apologetic, they may appear, we can never disregard the fact that it is all a show, the same kind they would put on with outsiders before we became one ourselves, that they never change and that they are secretly angry with you for seeing through them. They already have their next insults or undermining games set out, be sure! A genuine apology will never come and you don't need it. You don't even need to apologise to yourself for thinking you were not good enough, unworthy. It is important to remember every time when confusion raises its head that it wasn't your fault, it was a reality you were fed, you didn't have any other frame of reference.

It is understandable that some people would want some kind of closure, a solution to how to approach the relationship. Again, we have to acknowledge that this will never come, for the same reasons why we will never get a real apology. They are unlikely to give any kind of apology, though some might go as far as 'I'm sorry if you feel disappointed,' but that isn't a real apology because they haven't accepted responsibility, they're simply throwing the blame back at you. Sounds immature and toxic, right? Mature people have the strength to accept liability and change their actions accordingly.

So this is the closure, the awareness that there won't be one. If there is any doubt about this, simply take note of the treatment you got every time you tried to achieve a more balanced relationship as a teenager or an adult.

Now let's take a moment to appreciate that you know all this now, you're at the other side of the ordeal and that you are a survivor! Of PTSD, of trauma, pure evil and abuse and whatnot, as it will be described in the rest of the book. You rock! People might not see it first off but you're amazing, you're strong! You lived through it and got to the other side of the horrific experience and you kept standing up, you kept going. You are not broken, far from it! Your survival skills got sophisticated to keep you alive, to keep you sane. Yes, you are sane and self-aware! You are paying attention to your needs, seeking help and will not live in misery forever, not like those narcissists who are unable to admit their internal world even to themselves. You are powerful and it's not your fault you were treated like that, none of it is! If someone hurts you again and again without guilt, it is because of who they are and it has nothing to do with you.

And, to come back to cognitive dissonance, you are now also aware of the ways your brain deals with new input when something makes you uncomfortable. You won't fall for it again!

Another side of the narcissistic parent's needs is intentionally keeping you dependent. If you're dependent on them, they will stay in control. It's not just about making you keep your mouth shut by allowing very limited contact with the outside world, but also they need you to feel thankful for what they're doing. It is like saying 'do you see what I am doing? Why aren't you grateful? You should be filled with gratitude. I suffered so much because of you.' Sometimes with these exact words. It's a confusing message for a little child, especially as the narcissist's acting skills are so great they seem to believe their own words when they say the abuse didn't happen. And that's what they're banking on, that you were too young and may forget or that you question your own memory of the events. But everything they say is constructed on deception and charades.

Narcissists themselves cannot deal with who they are deep inside, so they lie to themselves as well so they can live with themselves in a reality they can accept, which means that they are a fraud. They imitate others' altruistic behaviour, but they are without doubt fakers for the duration of their whole lives. They are even better than skilful method actors because they live the lie, every minute of the day and night. They will often attack and deprecate the person who is being critical instead of dealing with the points the person is making. They usually have to resort to this because they have no defence against the criticism. They don't want to be found out so the way to go is to damage the reputation of the critical person instead.

What we need to remember in these cases is that the truth doesn't mind being questioned. Lies do and the narcissist parent does very much mind being questioned! So much so they would rarely answer, or deny the whole thing happened. Again with that contemptuous laugh that I find hard to shake from my ears. I'd get angry, but mostly, I'd just get sad, yet she would not tolerate such justifiable responses either. Someone who uses your emotions caused by their own dreadfulness against you is devious to the core.

All that evil has to be compensated with something to keep you attached. A lot of times, a narcissistic parent would indulge you with money, promises of amazing holidays, giving you your favourite foods, the like. They will constantly remind you that they'll do everything for you. Any time we were given a present, my mother would ask us, 'am I a good mother then?' Obviously, she would only let one answer stand. Of course, this demand to proclaim her 'goodness' is only another way to minimise the effects of the abuse. 'There are some narcissists who literally believe their own masks. No matter how many lives they destroy, no matter how many people they hurt along the way, they literally find a way to justify every horrible thing they do. What's worse and what completely baffles my brain is, they not only justify what they do, but they believe they are good people.' – Maria Consiglio.

I don't remember one moment of genuine love; the good moments were moments of gratification for her where she literally pushed her chest out in pride when she or I achieved a goal. Ice cold she was, literally. No wonder, as the narcissist is always frustrated by someone whose time is spent on bending over backwards to try to make them content.

They seem to think of themselves as the power that controls the very folds of reality itself and, unfortunately for the dependent child, that is exactly the case. Being sadistic and mean gives narcissists' self-confidence a boost. It makes them believe that they are in charge, that they are the dominant and the finest specimen of the species. Only this can make them happy with themselves because, of course, thinking themselves superior, they believe this is what they deserve so a resilient subject vexes them to no end.

The narcissistic individual hides in plain sight and likes to be the centre of attention and, depending on the person, will achieve it in different ways. Some use fashion and expensive clothing, jewellery, unique appearances, others with being loud and having an opinion about everything, whether they have any idea on the subject or not. It can be seen as a sort of addiction, with the 'substance' being the need to appear significant, validated and acknowledged. Narcissists will do anything to get this, the narcissistic supply, the same way as any addict for their own drug, regardless of the consequences. They achieve it with tactics such as inconsistent overprotectiveness with no empathy, hysterics, withholding validation, the non-stop playhouse drama with no remorse, creating intentional uncertainty with no conscience, double standards, financial abuse, triangulating, mistrust. They will constantly commandeer, try to shine with their culinary competency, or overemphasise and fake ailments, grievances or injuries. As a result, I suffered from second-hand embarrassment every time my narcissist mother overexaggerated, to the extent that I feel shame when I have a real illness and try to deal with it myself without discussing or disclosing it.

Try to set rights and boundaries when older and they will make you feel guilty for trying.

In my case, as a young child, for example, she would brush my hair and style it every morning, then as a punishment she would refuse so I couldn't go to primary school, till one day I sauntered out, backpack on and ready to go, my hair done by myself. Oh, what a moment that was! At some level I think she knew that school was my heaven. I wouldn't exactly call it safe, as I was bullied there too, but it was a great breath of fresh air in comparison with being at home. But that time she was so shocked, she just stood there and let me walk out the door.

Trust me, she never did otherwise. She had to always explain in the greatest detail what I was meant to do, she monitored where I went and who I spent time with, and I'm talking about when I was over eighteen years old, too.

Unfortunately, keeping you dependent like that will make you end up with serious handicaps compared to your peers, starting from mundane skills such as we're seen with arranging hair. She never taught me about make-up, cooking or filling out a form either. Official documents were always her department, of course, my independence was at stake! For making those arrangements, again, you had to be thankful. But it also meant you were never given the chance to accomplish something on your own.

As you can picture, codependency and a lack of basic skills will lead to a further lack of self-confidence and then significant negative self-image issues, along with being unable to handle formal situations such as going to the doctor's or opening a bank account. It is a form of withholding, not letting us practise independence.

'You're crazy,' my mother used to tell me, or '*bolond vagy te, fiam*' in Hungarian and it was the tone of voice and the way she implied I was despicable with it and that she was superior that hurt the most. Being told similar things on a regular basis till the mind takes it as fact, it is not unusual for the victim to spend half their adulthood trying to get rid of unfounded beliefs and patterns from their childhoods.

I often wondered if my mother had any shame. Narcissists cannot stand peace and harmony. They never listen and they overstep boundaries till the child loses self-respect or starts pushing back to defend themselves, in which case they will be labelled unstable and mocked for their reactivity. In effect, they're unseen and unheard because narcs have learnt how to make the victims look insane for questioning their hurtful experiences.

'Pathological people will do things to get a reaction from you. They will sometimes antagonise you so fiercely that you end up losing your cool, and then you start raging at them. Then they point the finger at you and accuse you of being the abusive one. This can happen so often that victims start to feel like they are abusive as well. Everyone has their limit, and some people can blatantly overstep your boundaries, in such a way that it prompts you to fight back to keep any semblance of self-respect. Narcissistic individuals use that to convince you that you are the problem, and you are the one that is crazy and abusive. Do not let them confuse you, you are reacting to the abuse; you are not the abuser.' – Maria Consiglio.

The narc wants to feel powerful and this is very easily done if you attack a small child. They love that they can get angry without consequence. As Maria Consiglio says on her Instagram, it 'is about control. Narcissists are very self-sabotaging and destroy anything good that comes in their path. Deep down they know they don't deserve it. It is deep down and unconscious. On the surface they are egotistical and they think they are the best things coming and going. Toxic people never acknowledge their role in a situation. They refuse to look into their own behaviour and so are unable to see the wrongdoings in their steps, yet, they will look for opportunity to point out faults or perceived faults of others' or focus on others' responses to the situation they've fabricated. They will create chaos and turmoil. They push your buttons. And when you finally respond to what they've done, and get angry, they end up telling you and everyone else YOU have anger issues. They manipulate every situation to their benefit'[5]. They drive you to insanity, they treat you like an object without feelings, they make sure the way you see the world is the way they want you to see. They cause so much scarring and havoc in the meantime, even your functioning is reshaped to play the way they planned it to perform. If they ever say 'I love you,' it means 'I like how I can keep you under my thumb' or 'you've done well as my puppet.' The rest of their love language is even worse. 'You're stupid' means 'I'm scared you might be more intelligent than I am so I need to make sure you don't think so.' They tend to act in this passive-aggressive manner when they don't immediately get what they want as the word compromise is not in their dictionary. The target attempts to fight the manipulation, but they are made more unsure of what to think by being called names or being told that they're 'too sensitive', 'crazy' or only 'imagining things'. Most narcissists don't think there's anything wrong with them. Instead, they think everyone else is causing problems, including for them.

The narcissistic parent sees their child as an extension of themselves, a way to gain more attention and accolades. This is why they get so upset when the child doesn't exactly follow their ideas. They would want to parade the child around proudly, shout 'look how perfect they are.' Of course, it seems like a crime to them when we are not perfect and others see it.

They don't give real compliments. Therefore, cold and cruel and gruesome, they demand you are perfect as well in the ways that they judge perfection to be. Just how they judge themselves to be perfect. I don't need to tell you how hard that is for a child to achieve. This also means that the child can't have their own opinions, needs and impulses, rather they are marionettes handled by the parent.

Therein comes my brother, an older sibling, the typical golden child in the family unit, an extension of our mother, an effigy that performed better and it was decided somewhere along the line that they will therefore be hailed by my mother as the personification of perfection to torture me with. Another strategy where she made me feel little and insignificant was when she compared me either to him or to someone else who did better than me at a specific task, no matter how different their circumstances were. And then comes the oldest trick in the book. Turning people against each other, talking behind backs and sharing negative, largely fictitious information so that they become doubtful and cautious with one another, generating envy, antagonism and discord. It is a recurrent manipulation theme that puts the narcissist in a position of power. Words not matching actions is called manipulation though.

Other emotional manipulation signs and tactics include: trying to make the child feel guilty for 'not honouring' their duties to respect the parent in a power play where they play the victim, rigid rules, not giving any value to the little one's views or feelings and refusing to listen to them, making them feel little by degrading or shaming them and putting them in a bad light. Sometimes the narc will act as if they don't understand what you're talking about or twist words, as a method to avoid all responsibility and make the victim feel out of their mind and uncertain in their view of reality, ridiculing and trivialising the issues the child might bring up. Worse than what a bully would do. You name it, the above all happened to me. Who would do such a thing? Only some alarmingly aberrant, unbalanced, dysfunctional individual with a personality disorder.

The Conformer/Golden Child Syndrome

There is no doubt that all children of the narcissist parent suffer because they lack empathy and the ability to nurture their children. The narcissistic parent uses the golden child to manipulate their siblings. Typically, the only boy in the family becomes the most likely to be the golden child, while the second-born daughter is earmarked for the role of the scapegoat, but other considerations as unpredictable as appearance or intelligence might sway the narc parent to put a sibling in the scapegoat's position, with designations even changing over time, with more devastating results for both children.

As I have never been in the golden child's position, I would like to state in advance that I do not claim to know all their troubles and experiences. My description is subjective again, this is how it looks from the outside.

I would be lying if I said I had never been jealous of my brother. From afar, it always looked like he had it easy compared to me. I have to admit now that this is only partially true because we were manipulated in pretty similar ways. While the golden child undeniably suffers, being brought up by a parent who doesn't understand all the essential warmth, care and considerations of love, they wouldn't be called names or criticised as often. This only happened because they met the mother's expectations, not as individuals, but as moulds shaped by the common parent, who saw them as a way to accomplish their unrealised need for flawlessness, power and triumph. They were clones of the narc, who didn't consult the child on their own perceptions, plans and intents. As such, the golden lives are hijacked with weapons of high toxicity. They are fully controlled, micromanaged and run down till they perform to the expectations of the narcissistic mother. Already brainwashed, these golden conformists lose some of their sense of self before it is even formed. They might not know what their real characteristics are, what they like or what their goals would be, and at this point, they don't want to find out because, while they are their false, compliant self, they are not only protected from the narc's anger, but receive the benefits of the only kind of nurturing the narc parent is capable of.

The conformist child type tends to be creative, and loves school and studying. They want to make the parent proud and happy, and they wouldn't just be exceptional at a few areas and topics, but would excel at all, including specialised subjects such as foreign languages, sports and music. They would of course never need to bother the narcent for help with homework and would in most cases also be popular with other classmates, showing off their leadership skills by helping out and teaching people random new facts to do with their hobbies.

These children are often so ensnared that they don't realise it, which makes it questionable if indeed the scapegoat or the golden child is the more damaged one. But they do tend to grow up mentally unwell as well, with confidence, anxiety and paranoia issues, terrified to make their own choices because they know praise to be conditional, but they manage to please the parent so often that they don't mind the criticism. After all, the narcissistic parent does need someone to look after them in their old age, they can't alienate everyone. They can't complain about them openly in front of them, but they will find plenty of opportunities to criticise them to other people, such as the scapegoat child. The regard offered to the golden child is conditional as well though, and the conditions are in abundance because the parent tries to mould the child into themselves or their idealised self. They are simultaneously overvalued and undervalued, which causes confusion. Similarly, to their other children, the narcissists instil shame in the child through deprecating their weight, hairstyle, fashion choices, personality traits or views. They say 'what do you look like?' in a demeaning kind of tone, implanting either the seeds of eating disorders or showing that being judgemental is a model to aspire to, or both. Used and brainwashed like this, they would be too upset not to conform at the same time as, deep down, every fibre of their being would scream the muzzled fury of false imprisonment and the solitary confinement of the self, a stage that tends to raise its head during teenage years or later unless they remain overly afraid to live and think autonomously of their narc-parent. In some cases where the narc-parent has achieved their goal, they don't even have their own objectives as they are unable to imagine differently from their dominant parent. In this case, and without healing, their actions throughout life will be controlled by the fear of being condemned or criticised rather than their own moral code.

This is why they also tend to reject looking for the reasons they do things. For the golden child, it is easier this way, while they are still children at least, but sadly, in many cases, afterwards as well. At a younger age of course, they might not even know that the parent also manipulates them and that they 'would quickly be cast aside if they ever stopped conforming.' – Tina Fuller, author of *It's My Turn*.

The rewards themselves are often monetary or physical since the narcissist is incapable of real love but they are capable of creating another version of themselves in the child because they don't see them as individuals, but as extensions of themselves, often turning narcissistic themselves as a result. And there you are, dealing with two narcissists in the family instead of one and a situation of intergenerational trauma that will get passed on one more time!

But even if the other child does not become a narcissist at this point, they do not have other, healthy models of behaviour they can learn to deal with relationships and might replicate the harmful behaviour till life can show them other options.

Unfortunately, this also applies to the other child. In young adulthood and for some even beyond, it is hard to shed those behaviours we copied from our parents, not having any other model to shape ourselves on. Because of these copied behaviours and traits, I'm sure it has occurred to you, am I following in those footsteps? Could I even be a narcissist myself?

I have good news for you. If you wonder, if you analyse yourself day by day and understand the basis of your own reactions and words, you probably aren't! Everybody has some narcissistic characteristics and it is fathomable to have more than others after suffering narcissistic abuse.

Despite that, if you recognise them, admit to them and change them, actively and on purpose to become a different person than you are most certainly not a narcissist as they point blank refuse to change any of their toxic behaviour – the insults, the reproval, the accusatory spectacle and the lies.

Another way to tell the narcissist from the victim is knowing that the victim will talk about their painful experiences and share their deepest feelings as part of their attempts to heal and grow emotionally from past trauma and search, to ask for answers. The narc will ridicule and try to censure the victim for this in their attempt to silence them.

Our reactions to abuse beggaring description does not necessarily make us narcissistic either. The narcissist calls our reactions unnecessary drama, but all the tears, verbal explosions, screaming and swearing are entirely understandable reactions to being shockingly abused and pushed to the breaking point on a regular basis to get a reaction. These reactions arose while being stuck in and made to survive in an oppressive situation, an intense and deviant environment.

Given the above situation and how the golden child attributes some of the narc-parent's characteristics, they might also fail to understand the necessity for boundaries in relationships without becoming a narcissist themselves. They may have an endless need for approval in relationships and thus become hypersensitive with anxiety disorders or may have difficulties making decisions or with the concept of good and evil. Some others become completely emotionally detached as a coping mechanism.

After growing up, the narcissist parent will frequently make the golden child the focus of their life without ever really listening to them. In my mother's case, this was through exaggerated illnesses and financial emergencies. As a result, I am forever too ashamed to ask for help, both health-wise and financially; thinking about how my mother used and still uses those situations makes me feel sick. I underplay my illnesses, I persevere on my own.

She spends months at a time, year after year, at my brother's house and involves herself in their family matters unprompted, such as how long my nephew should stick with piano lessons or where they should buy another house. And lies, and pushes that lie till it's believed, even if the lie is a blatant one. The influence they have on the golden child's family becomes more and more important as the narc-parent ages and thinks they have a right to it, because the way they see it is that they have dedicated their lives to the guidance of the child. They will continue to manipulate the golden child for money and other resources, lying about where it goes.

As we know, narcissism is a mental disorder and narcs don't like not being entirely in control. Ageing and the process of dying puts everyone in that position, a situation the narc finds harder to tolerate than the average person. As the narcissist ages, their social circle dwindles as one by one people are lost, they depart, retire, pass from sight, no longer finding the narcissist worthy of their time. Towards the end of life there is often not one person who cares whether the narcissist lives or dies.

At this point, the power dynamic is likely to shift. Possessing all the resources for their support, the golden child is in the position of power. The narc-parent has no other place to turn to for the alienation of the rest of the world and becomes entirely dependent on the golden child, a scenario not comfortable for either and pitiful for the narcissist.

Never seeing the naked truth, the golden child is not likely to truly support their siblings, they are too entangled with the narcissist and this havoc the narcissist dealt out between siblings is too profound to sort out.

There is a special relationship between the narcissistic mother and their son, to the point of a reverse Oedipus complex at times as they apotheosise* the son above their fathers, cogitate about being with them often and see them as partners, rather than children who could give them what the father 'couldn't'. Some boys then take on this role to please them, or out of fear that the mother's conditional love will cease for them if they don't comply. Either with resentment, or not, they will then have to subdue their own real characteristics to achieve this. Therefore, sons of narcissistic mothers face damage to their capacity for self-determination, self-worth and relationships with women. They've been trained to consider their mother's needs first and foremost and it is therefore hard for them to consider their own needs without feeling egocentric for doing so. What they fail to note is that narcs don't have proper relationships. They only have servers chosen on the basis of functionality who can give them what they need, from money and shelter to attention and contacts, opportunities and validation and the golden child can at times provide all the above.

My brother and I, we have never been close and barely have anything in common to talk about when we meet. For this, too, I'm afraid I have to blame our upbringing. From day one, we were placed in a competition neither of us wanted. We were also put in constant competition with anyone who performed better than us at some skill, always urged to continue in their footsteps. Neither of us has seen healthy relationships growing up, acceptable ways to behave. What I felt was usually a bout of victim shaming from him when I broached the subject of our mother being an abuser. That my behaviour was the problem, current or past, not hers.

When meeting someone from the past, some people, family members in particular, choose to call to and uphold in their minds the model of us they have held the most power over, no matter how much has changed. This is how it had always felt with my brother. I was never a fully-fledged person for him and, in his eyes, I was holding onto a grudge.

Having such a perfect child in the family also means that somebody has to take the blame for things that go wrong. We already know that no narcissist is going to do that so liability has to lie with the scapegoat, who has to be reminded of the golden one's achievements on a regular basis. The narcissist will boast about their accomplishments in public, as well as that of the golden child, looking for admiration, commendation and attention, but above all, feeling superior to others. To this very day, on the once-in-a-blue-moon occasion I do talk to my female parent at my current seasoned age of forty-seven, she somehow always manages to bring up my brother's recent or long past accomplishments as if she just wanted to make me feel and look bad in comparison. It is a matter for another part of the book why I still talk to her sometimes when I know there will be no closure, that she'll never acknowledge the damage she did, no matter how many times I confront her.

After all this, it is no surprise that I ended up feeling like I'm never good enough and I forever bend over backwards to please others. I become uncomfortable and anxious if those around me are not happy. I have big issues with seeing people crying. I either join in or do everything in my power to stop them, including children. Probably how I've spoiled my own.

Who would've thought that a developing child who's being criticised often might become a validation-dependent adult with low self-esteem and a paralysing fear of failure that manifests in self-sabotaging perfectionism, right? This is the technique of devaluation used by narcissists, the act of breaking the child down by never-ending criticism, slander and subtle or not-so-elusive insults and humiliation, at the same time as not being able to accept any criticism themselves as the false self they cling to can't be anything less than ideal, anything less than amazing. They are incredible all right, in their own way. They typically react to anything negative said about them in an almost vicious manner, with loud, scandalised denial. They have to defend the grandiosity of that false self.

Astonishingly, new research shows that by the time they turn five, children already develop a sense of self-esteem as strong as an adult's. This suggests that a child's first five years are extremely important for developing their self-image, which is a further basis for how they form relationships and establish their identities.

So, not surprisingly, I have no idea where the boundaries are, when I should say no to any request for the sake of my own health and sanity, thus losing the ability to communicate authentically. I make mistakes with boundaries both ways, sometimes I leave myself too open, sometimes I refuse all contact. Some of it is because I can't judge where the healthy boundaries should be in different cultural contexts, and other times I know I bend the boundaries, but I feel unable not to. Completely lost at it, navigating boundaries can seem like a paradoxical task for a trauma survivor because of what they've been conditioned to. This could appear very strange for an outsider; they might judge us as weird or they might take advantage of it.

In other words, I'm fucked up all round, royally. My tainted self-concept damages relationships and my ability to thrive personally and professionally. My anxiety levels will make me overthink everything, and lose the confidence to try. Being always busy in my head applying personal coping strategies, including OCD, sounds like doing nothing, but in fact takes all my energy before I can use it elsewhere. Overwhelmed, I appear quiet and I'm engrossed in replaying stressful moments in my mind, either missing social cues or deciding not to bother people with my needs since I deemed my own needs less important. It would be too hard to put them forward with this amount of social anxiety.

To keep this account balanced, I feel like I should mention the positives of a narcissistic parent. As mentioned, they are fiercely possessive and as a result, heaven help anyone who tries to inflict real or imagined plights on the child. Only the parent has the right to do so, or someone they may have authorised to commit it by abuse via proxy. As a result, I always knew that whenever I bumped into difficulties, with official affairs, at school or with another child, all I had to do was let my mother know and she would go with her usual uncaring and dismissive attitude towards her victim, and threaten or force them into submission. Nobody would dare to mess with my mother.

The other positive I can think of is her compulsion to have everything appear in order. Therefore, again, she would not let stand any criticism directed at me from outsiders and would lie and cheat as well to make me appear as she wanted me to appear. Criticising me, that was her right, and at times, my brother's.

Ultimately, I'd like to touch on the naked truth that there are other kinds of toxic people not fit for parenting who can also certainly screw up a child for life through emotional abuse. Having toxic parents or a toxic family is more challenging than relatively functioning families can imagine. Nothing is ever a simple conversation but a literal minefield as nearly every sentence is full of passive aggression or hidden meanings. A core characteristic of a toxic individual is that they never change, but try to change the other person instead, mould them for their use, whatever that may be. They tend to reject blame and they can also be hypocrites, selfish, draining, unsupportive, judgemental, envious, demanding, drama magnets or pathological people who will do things primarily to get a reaction from you, or an emotional wreck themselves, unable to take on the problems of another. As another example, there's the emotional moocher[41] who always has something gloomy, cynical or alarmist to opine and there is the soul sucker[42] who drains all the energy in the room. Some don't understand that not everyone can charge around doing things and achieving with the same amount of energy they do because not everyone has that amount of energy. These people don't understand that parenting isn't supposed to be about exercising control over a child and forcing them into who they want the offspring to be, but about understanding who that person in the making is and helping them become the best as possible, for the child's sake and for the people they will meet along the way.

You wouldn't want this person as a friend, but you are cursed with them as a parent. The toxic parent frequently makes something out of nothing to pounce on the children and uses emotional blackmail to keep making the child feel guilty, a classic example being victimising themselves and frequently mentioning how much they're sacrificing for the child. They can be begrudging the little person's attainments or social life, they might not ever say sorry, they might force the child into a cult or enforce religious doctrine, or they will pay no attention to their children while demanding blind obedience and gratitude no matter what, with dire consequences for disobedience[43].

There's the accessorising parent who treats their offspring as a trophy; the lawnmower, the helicopter or the drone parent micromanaging every aspect of the child's life and prospective future and not giving them chances to grow or express themselves and their desires without sounding disappointed. The butler parent limits their children's ability to achieve anything for themselves, or there is the perfectionistic parent[44]. And I haven't even touched on substance abuse. 'One doesn't have to operate with great malice to do great harm. The absence of empathy and understanding are sufficient.' – Charles McRay Blow[45], commentator and op-ed writer for *The New York Times.* These toxic home environments lead to levels of anxiety akin to those of children in war zones, only they experience the trauma within their own homes.

Regardless of what toxic category the parent comes from, none of the children in these families emerge undamaged. It is important to remember, however, that in most cases, this damage is not a fatal disease, nor do we have to repeat the mistakes of our parents. For this, it is essential to understand and work out the dynamics of our own minds as it is the only way to make real progress with shedding ingrained behaviour and accomplish healing.

This list is, of course, not complete, but it does suggest two things. One, that it is pretty hard to get parenting right, and two, that childhood has a much greater effect on adult life that most like to acknowledge. I hope I also showcased why it is so hard to recover from narcissistic abuse. Because of a lack of a rightful apology for the things they did, the adult child remains hurting, with no chance for closure. Especially if they haven't realised the parent was narcissistic, they will have many questions that remain unanswered.

Abuse by Proxy

I can't say I experienced this phenomenon often myself, but I should probably touch on it as it is a regular feature of some narcissistic households, and because it can harm victims to the same extent as direct narcissistic abuse, leaving them feeling alone, beaten and unable to think clearly.

Generally, narcissists surround themselves with enablers, people who can't detect the abuse and thus remain loyal, people who fear them and therefore intentionally disregard the abuse, or those who they think could help in some way, be pumped for money or influence. The latter group might have to be kept in the dark about the abuse. 'They positively despise anyone who goes against them or their agenda. They will try to destroy anyone they feel is a possible threat or hurts their fragile ego.' – Maria Consiglio.

As the title suggests, narcissistic abuse via proxy happens when the narc manages to convince another person to hurt or have power over the victim. There are many ways to achieve this if the targeted family member or friend is not immediately willing to criticise the victim as well. The narc can say the child committed things they haven't or exaggerate their misdeeds so the other parent or family member will react in a punishing way, from disapproval to denunciation and physical punishment. Unfortunately, there are many cases when the narc parent alleges the child has done certain things to authorities, counsellors, neighbours, teachers, even the police and other arbitrators to punish or intimidate them, with grave consequences in some cases, using the third party to pressurise, persuade, pester or control the child.

Or they can even manage to make the child themselves say or do things that will anger the target and suffer the consequences that way. These days, it can also happen through social media attacks. In some distinctly dire situations, the victim might go as far as believing that they themselves are at fault, resulting in the narc having the sway and power over the victim and the relationship.

An art form of manipulation, if you will, but it has been seen way too often in seemingly normal households. There is a term psychologists use for the target friend or family member they use for the abuse and that is the rather cheery flying monkey[48]. It is, of course, a little harder to spot in some cases than a direct approach from the narcissist, but the practical experience of it is pretty much the same: boundaries being constantly disregarded, a sense of being stuck as everything turns out in a different way as intended, a loss of control over one's life.

Such typical abuse situations happen in cults or during religious indoctrination, where the social group convinces the members that the abuse is in the child's best interest. Often, these children have nowhere to go for help, as everybody they are in contact with is part of the affiliated group and there is also an abuse of information limitation. These people intentionally keep the victim looking and acting unreasonable, disruptive and with mental health problems as they try different approaches for self-defence, compared to the narc's put on, calm persona they use to ooze confidence and reliability. The group then decides on some form of punishment for the victim, sometimes public ridicule because the flying monkeys are so wrapped up about the lies of the narc that they can't see clearly through it. Furthermore, if these people are aware that the narcissist has been abusive towards you and they are still in a good relationship with the narcissist, then they're simply toxic themselves.

Clearly, the only option to stop this situation is to flee, but the child is unable to, due to legal and societal constraints. So the next best thing is to force calm and try to refute mental health claims by not giving the abuser the satisfaction to react in an emotional, and especially hostile, manner. Not reacting in an out-of-control way, they cannot point the finger and say, 'there, you see it, don't you? She/he has gone insane.' What's more, they will tell their community that the victim should be thankful they still care for them as they are only trying to help. So responding with class, rather than reacting, is more likely to subtly steer the unsuspecting flying monkeys in the direction of the truth.

It is often said that in abusive situations, there aren't two sides of the story because one of them is a lie. Still, all too often, this lie is believed by outsiders because of the exact nature of the abuse, relying on a power imbalance. So it's worth asking, who is the one with all the power? Which one is playing the victim and which is the real victim? The answer will be easier to see once the shading can be removed and all is looked at are the core truths. Unfortunately, even the victim falls prey to such shaded thinking, blaming themselves. Delayed realisation is common in these cases as well. Some don't realise how wrongly they've been treated till after they've distanced themselves from the abuser for a time. This is why the no-contact strategy is so important, severing the trauma bond, which then, with the right education, can mend the shortcomings of our upbringing. The abusers are thieves and they steal so much from us – our childhood, our health and well-being and the financial security with it as a result of our afflictions, our hopes and dreams, family and friends, our self-respect, confidence and decorum and sadly for some people, even their lives. The gift they give you is when they leave. You have to accept that this background was not your fault, and that this is the way they relate to everyone. 'They are broken people, who are angry and resentful and want nothing more in life than to make sure they break other people too. It's a sick way of looking at the world but that is the way they function. They are sadistic people who can't handle anyone being happier or better than them. Get out, go, no contact. You didn't break them and you absolutely can't fix them. But they definitely could and will break you if you stay.' – Maria Consiglio.

Everybody will respond to childhood trauma differently, but there are some predictable commonalities we can talk about. Going further, I will try to outline the main symptoms and syndromes that can emerge as a result of toxic parenting.

Part 2: The Effects of Psychological Abuse

1 The Dissociation of Living in a Fantasy Worlds

Although it is not the most detrimental consequence of long-term childhood emotional abuse by far, I am going to start with this one because it was the first coping mechanism I used, starting from as far back as I can remember and increasingly during my teenage years, and well into my twenties and thirties. It continued until I was actually ready to face my past and not run away from any memories that might pop up in the form of escaping into an alternate reality of my choosing.

As I have mentioned, I spent years imagining being someone else in my head, someone who had it better than me. It wasn't me who got up, it wasn't me who did the homework. In my head, our house was transformed into somebody else's, usually a made-up character, but sometimes a real person I knew of. I was so disconnected from my own body and life that I didn't hear what atrocities were thrown at me, didn't feel the sting of the abuser's palm on my cheek. I simply wasn't there, not in my head. It was as if I were speaking out loud in the character's voices, but inside my head, doing things like swimming in the ocean, running about, whatever pleased me at the time, my senses providing me with fake experiences. I completely identified with them, even made up some problems for these imaginary characters because who doesn't have problems? But these were, of course, totally under my control, the problems as well as the characters. It was a consciously built world and not some sort of schizophrenic disconnection from reality. I picked and chose who I wanted to be that day. I was happy being someone else, sometimes ecstatic even, appearing strange to the outside world as I had no reason to be ecstatic. I was not hurting, I didn't exist, I lived another, elaborately detailed life, almost like videos in the mind's eye. I could ignore problems. As a result, writing essays at school was never a problem, my imagination was not just endless, but it was already well-oiled and I didn't have to come up with a new story, it was already there inside my head, I only had to put it down on paper. I was never bored, I did not understand how anybody could be bored as I could always just create my own entertainment. Sometimes, hours would pass and I honestly couldn't give an account of where the time had gone. Revelling in an imaginary happy moment cannot take that long, can it?

From my psychology studies, it turns out this disorder is called maladaptive daydreaming, now recognised as a psychiatric condition, typically making the individual get lost deeply into their thoughts of their fantasy world. It is caused mainly by childhood trauma, consisting of an abusive or toxic environment where the child cannot cope with their situation, or where excessive stress and a lack of emotional support discouraged interaction with others and prevented the child from asking for what they needed. Research by Deirdre Barrett at Harvard confirmed the characteristics of fantasy-prone people by identifying highly hypnotisable subjects who had had traumatic childhoods[14]. They also tended to have out of body experiences and other similar escapades that can be seen as extrasensory, parapsychological or other-worldly[15]. Another characterising tendency was the subject's exposure to severe loneliness and isolation during childhood, such that fantasising provides an escape mechanism. Freud even said that 'unsatisfied wishes are the driving power behind fantasies, every separate fantasy contains the fulfilment of a wish, and improves an unsatisfactory reality'. This points to how childhood abuse and loneliness can result in children generating a fantasy world of happiness to fill this need.

It is also a type of addiction, with 'great activity in the ventral striatum, the part of the brain that lights up when an alcoholic is shown images of a martini'[6]. Now I know why I couldn't stop unless I was forced to by outside factors. It was partly what first made me develop sleeping problems, these structured daydreams were so intense and comforting that I never wanted to stop immersing in them, not even when I was supposed to be sleeping. Often, I couldn't overpower this profound desire to continue daydreaming, even when I was supposed to be going somewhere, doing homework, crossing the road or even driving! I was driving as someone else in my head, with their thoughts, their conversations. I would neglect my studies and, when alone, I would always act the plot out, what the character would do, what they would say. I would have a number of comfort scenarios I would act out over and over besides new ones I regularly tried to come up with. I would get distressed in an obsessive-compulsive way, with physical sweats, agitated behaviour and shaking hands as withdrawal symptoms if somebody interrupted me and hindered my ability to daydream. It was a natural high, one I needed no drugs to achieve. Needless to say, I was not interested in real life anymore, even when it was pleasant. As a child, daydreaming was usually the highlight of my day.

The true motivation behind watching or reading anything was to find new inspiration for the daydreams. I had to gather information for the details of somebody else's life. The right scene or character could keep me going and happy to elaborate on for months, keeping me safe from feeling much of the real world. I didn't have many toys besides the ones my grandmother dug out from other people's trash for me, but that didn't have to stop me either, all could be achieved through fantasy.

I'd rather not imagine how my acting performance would have looked from the outside, if anyone may have happened upon me during the middle of a plot, with random whispered words, some in made-up languages and with repetitive movements in the air, sometimes singing and dancing to no apparent sounds, accompanied with respective facial expressions for the dialogue between characters. Crying, kissing the wardrobe as a character and laughing was also on the table. When I was five-six, it would have been okay, children do that, but not when I was twenty-five! Yet I had to remain in this world well into my adult years, venturing out felt too dangerous.

If I could have, I would have stayed in this imaginary world indefinitely. I haven't ever been happier, this is why I don't call my childhood a complete waste. It was, and always has been, easier to interact with these characters than with a real person. I never had much experience with that side of the world as seen from my childhood and after this, even less so, as I preferred them to real-life relationships and responsibilities. Often, I would have to panic and rush about to finish a task in the real world as I'd wasted too much time in fantasy – hours, nights, days, when I really got going. Other people would be interested in boyfriends, I tended to be bewildered as to why as I always had my male characters to play with as well. Who needs real-life boyfriends? Thus, I often found it hard to keep up with conversations, tune in, say the right things, oblivious to my surroundings, alienating me further from reality. I could also rarely tell people what I was thinking about, what had prime importance to me at that moment, not till I eventually found some similar people.

Studies show I'm not alone with these intentionally generated fantasy narratives[8]. It is a coping tool, but not a particularly productive one when it comes to solving the problem of dealing with psychological abuse. Daydreaming or zoning out is often a coping mechanism for people who are lonely or don't receive the amount of love necessary in their lives so they make up people inside their heads that will love them. Love is invented in the fantasy world. Lack of motivation to engage in the real world can be a sign of trauma as well.

'Daydreaming can help solve problems, trigger creativity, and inspire great works of art and science. When it becomes compulsive, however, the consequences can be dire'[7]. Which leads me to how I became numb to abuse.

2 Further Dissociation – Emotional Numbness

Do you ever watch people doing things but you just can't seem to join in, despite several tries? Then, when you can't connect, you give up and it doesn't even bother you much? This and similar emotional numbness is another coping mechanism to trauma. It is pretty obvious how it can come in useful in crisis situations. I did not care anymore, I could ignore some situations that otherwise would have been upsetting by being elsewhere in my head till I grew up and could physically be elsewhere, free of my connection to my mother. Much better than being overwhelmed by terror and nerves, right?

Dissociation is a common trauma response where we check out from some moments of our lives in order to feel safe. While at first it may also sound like a good idea to avoid pain and misery, using emotional numbness for extended periods of time can have even more long-lasting consequences. For example, it taught me how to distance myself from others, a hindrance that still exists in my involuntary arsenal of self-protection, often causing me to be unable to fully participate in life's events. Sometimes just being in a room with someone without interaction feels overwhelming as little gestures and sounds can give me a view into how they might be feeling. After spending a childhood dependent on whether I could anticipate an outrage from my mother, and being able to get out the way in time, getting feels on somebody else's emotions can be overwhelming and I need to escape into self-imposed isolation because I don't want to feel any of their emotions, especially if it has anything to do with anxiety.

Feeling emotionally numb can also happen after being wronged and crying for a long time and it happens more often during times of great stress. After great emotional upheaval, feelings mingle into a fog and then a heavy, but steadying, sensation comes in its place where nothing matters anymore. Numbness is safer and it has become an automatic mechanism to help myself. It really works like how the vampires in *The Vampire Diaries* turn off their emotions when it all gets too much. When we feel too much, we sometimes turn our emotions off, only a lot less consciously or deliberately than those vampires do.

The most widespread cause of why people go through periods of emotional numbness is indeed childhood trauma[16], any of the principal abuse types. For example, sexual abuse can make grown adults detach automatically during intimate situations while operating as normal in other settings. But there's worse – as patients have said, some manage to dissociate so well that they cannot even recall what happened during the time of the abuse[96].

Remember also that, as a child, we had to teach ourselves how to conceal our emotions to avoid attacks and confrontations. So numbing them down comes pretty naturally. And if the abuse brought anxiety or depression with it, then emotional numbness can simply be a symptom of one of these as well.

Dissociation can manifest in many forms, including feeling like our surroundings are not real (derealisation) or a sudden moment of not recognising our surroundings, feeling detached from people, the body, the mind, emotions or the self, or as if we were looking out at reality through a filter – out-of-body experiences.

Just like living in a fantasy world, emotional numbness also disconnects you from the self, your identity and the environment. Being punished for revealing our feelings during childhood can also cause emotional numbness. Having not been able to share my emotions, I could never learn how to deal with them correctly. I couldn't have a temper tantrum, like my mother had regularly, so I knew how to keep myself in check, but that doesn't mean I knew what to do with my emotions apart from burying them in confusion. It's not as if I had a role model to show me what to do either. Studies show that people who, as children, experienced emotional dysregulation, including emotional numbing, are more likely to experience it as adults as well[10]. It happens more during stressful times. Feeling burnt out, emotionally or physically exhausted or overwhelmed might lead to feeling detached from our feelings[11].

I have trouble faking emotion as well, so I fear opening presents because I'm not good at looking excited about something when I'm not. Chunks of time can go missing through the day, some could have trouble remembering day-to-day events. I often find myself disconnected when someone is talking. I zone out, too distracted to make sense of what's being said. I'm physically there, but mentally I'm daydreaming. Appropriate reactions to things good and bad are a problem, it leads to rather uncomfortable moments when friends and family don't get the responses they were looking for, but I have gotten a little better at it over the years.

Adding depression and PTSD as a result of emotional abuse, numbness makes even more sense. 'Higher levels of depression and mood dysregulation result in a greater propensity for emotional numbing. While emotional numbing blocks or shuts down negative feelings and experiences, it also shuts down the ability to experience pleasure, positive interactions and social activities.' – Mayra Mendez, certified group psychotherapist and certified supervisor for the California Association of Marriage and Family Therapists[9]. It all interconnects and causes further complications such as, for example, spiritual emptiness, the inability to enjoy life, the inability to form close and fulfilling relationships, irritability, fatigue, addictions, chronic and somatic illnesses[12].

Part of being numb is often having surreal moments of feeling as if we were looking at ourselves from the outside, as if life were a simulation in the matrix, feeling distant from others, a lack of interest in things other people seem to find enjoyable such as chatting or sharing a meal, emotion-dependent illnesses and a tendency to avoid friends and family members, especially the presence of those who are emotionally intense. I find them too much to handle. It is also hard to get excited about some future project that depends in any way or measure on another person because I don't trust them, I don't trust anyone. My default is that they will disappoint me so if they don't, then that really is a great surprise! Which is why I make sure that whenever I say something to someone, I stay true to my word, no matter how little or big the matter is and how much inconvenience it causes me. I don't want to disappoint anyone the way I've been disappointed because I know how much it hurts. This inability to say no of course then leads to unhealthy levels of overcommitment and the stress that comes from it, but more about that side of the disorder in another chapter.

One of the major pitfalls of using numbness as a coping mechanism is the tendency to have an enormous number of feelings lying suppressed like a ticking time bomb. The anger against the narcissistic parent is valid and it is safe to express it now. These emotions will eventually need a release or they will contribute to more mental illness and symptoms such as depression or addiction, over-accomplishing, the need to stay busy at all times, being overly nice to everyone, resentment, impatience, fatigue, paranoia, perfectionism, mood swings and isolation[13].

What is important to remember is that our emotional numbness doesn't mean the loss of empathy as it presents in our narcissistic parent, we did not become a copy. It is only because we feel too much and too intensely and have to file it away for later processing. So it is reversible. We can learn how to deal with our feelings properly instead of completely avoiding situations or using emotional numbness as a defensive mechanism to push them out of sight, out of mind again. Of course, avoidance sometimes is the right way to go, such as cutting toxic family members out of your life, especially if they do you out of your cardinal positive emotions too. We should only keep the kind of friend and family member who lets you feel like you can be yourself with them, but I will come back to that later as well.

3 The Neurodivergent

After trying to live and work amongst different groups of people in a variety of circumstances, I eventually came to the conclusion that while I do find a friend here and there, I don't fit into any particular groups no matter what country I am in. I will always be different from the majority and after the initial feeling out that people give to the newcomer, I will always be ignored because my thoughts, ideas, ways of being and topics of interest will never match the majority's, the 'norm'. This is partly because of my childhood, that I don't share a conventional upbringing with most people but mostly because of who and what I became as a result, the conditions that cripple my everyday life. People like me think differently, act differently, feel differently, arrive at different decisions, and no wonder since our experiences wired our brains to work differently. In other words, many of us became neurodivergent as we developed as children with trauma.

It can hurt of course, not belonging somewhere, feeling invisible, especially if you have to spend a lot of time in that place, but this doesn't bother me too much anymore. I am tired of explaining myself to neurotypicals, who have the brain function and processing considered standard, and who will never understand how I am the way I am through no fault of my own. Having found people akin to myself, other neurodivergents, I can belong with them. In any case, not being invited, included or considered within the general population doesn't usually bother me, in fact,

I prefer it because I do not have to fight with my social anxieties to take part. It's easier that way. For example, I tend to use my Twitter as a sort of dumping ground of ideas, write whatever occurs to me, some of my own truths, so most of the time I in fact get offended if someone responds. Liking it, retweeting it is fine, but I didn't write it to result in me having to interact. I'm trying to avoid that.

Neurodivergents have more trouble than the average person with identifying inauthentic social cues, such as fake smiles and small talk. These can be puzzling as they are of no significance and value to the neurodivergent in their quest for truth. It is confusing because we can feel a contradiction between what the person is saying and what our neurodivergent senses are telling us, for we can't in good conscience be comfortable talking about the weather when there are so many things we deem more important.

So people with brains that function consistently differently in one or more ways than what is considered typical are called neurodivergent. Some neurodivergence is minor so it is not immediately noticeable and some syndromes are more obvious where the individual's behaviour starkly differs from those around them. Obvious examples would be autism spectrum disorder, Down's syndrome and attention deficit hyperactivity disorder. Less known ones include dyspraxia (a physical coordination disorder), Tourette's syndrome, epilepsy, synaesthesia (a perceptual phenomenon in which stimulation of one sensory or cognitive pathway leads to involuntary experiences in a second sensory or cognitive pathway) and lifelong chronic mental health illnesses such as obsessive-compulsive disorder, borderline personality, bipolar or generalised anxiety disorder. But you don't have to be diagnosed with any of these diseases or have their symptoms especially to be neurodivergent. A typical example of this phenomenon would be that well-known character from *The Big Bang Theory*. Creators of the show keep telling us over and over that Sheldon is not autistic, but he sure is neurodivergent! Other signs may include feeling like an alien amongst other humans, needing to overprepare for every interaction, sensitivity to light or sounds, getting frazzled when plans change, being completely drained after interactions with others and social anxiety-related behaviours such as arriving late or leaving early or hiding in the bathroom to avoid an overload of social situations.

Some people don't know they are neurodivergent, but once they realise why they feel and act different from everyone around them, and experience life in a different way, then everything starts to make so much more sense and they can stop blaming themselves for being different, too shy, too introverted, too quirky.

I'd like to stress that neurodivergents are just as worthy individuals as neurotypicals (if you doubted that, given your low self-esteem). Many excel in life and display amazing creativity. I only have to mention Elon Musk, who founded his companies, originally because he was too shy to go to interviews and get a job. As writer Thomas Armstrong notes in his book, *Neurodiversity in the Classroom*, numerous acclaimed neurodiverse individuals stand out in their chosen domain, which could be further capitalised on if some advanced learning strategies were used that are tailored to each neurodiverse student's unique strengths, along with an education system that teaches students about emotional distress and trauma, anxiety, depression and relationships. We need some sort of understanding and acknowledging that we are different, that we may get triggered sooner, that we may interpret things differently to our neurotypical counterparts, that we may be struggling with intrusive thoughts that could wear us out to the extent of being debilitated and our emotional reserves depleted. We may question someone's courteousness and have major trust issues and none of this is our fault. It is out of our control. So please stop pulling us up and blaming us for being too shy to get involved in a conversation, or settle on us as the scapegoat because we are too scared to stand up for ourselves! I also find the societal norm to ask 'how are you?' and not wait for an answer despicable. Worse is that if we respond with anything other than 'fine' or 'how are you?', they get uncomfortable. What the purpose of this farce is, I will never understand. If they want something, they will hint at it with little looks or questions the neurodivergent finds hard to understand. Why can't people just say what they want? Why is it so hard and something like a taboo to be honest? They say that neurodivergents lack an understanding and ignore the other person, but isn't it worse to pretend you care and have social conventions of how to avoid showing the smallest of regard? I'm sorry, but neurotypicals are weird. There are of course many pluses to being neurodivergent. For example, most neurotypicals are trapped by societal expectations that seem absurd and farcical, but neurodivergents see through social constructs.

Thankfully, with the trend to focus on the individual and their particular needs in education, it has become more acceptable that neurodivergents can reach the same levels of study as their neurotypical counterparts if different methods of education are used. Hopefully this trend will seep out into common awareness and it will become less isolating to be neurodivergent. Just the same as neurodivergents need different methods of study, they could also benefit from different approaches to work life because they could achieve the same results as everyone else if they were allowed to function differently to neurotypical rules. If only society would stop using the same capitalist propaganda-based measure on all, much more could be achieved, not just on an individual level, but for the whole of humanity as well. To exemplify this, a lot of scientists, musicians, successful businessmen and other outstanding achievers were and are neurodivergent, such as Sir Anthony Hopkins, Dan Aykroyd, Daryl Hannah, Courtney Love, Susan Boyle, Wentworth Miller, Roseanne Barr, Greta Thunberg, Justin Bieber, Simone Biles, David Blaine, Sir Richard Branson, Ryan Gosling, Woody Harrelson, Paris Hilton, Greg LeMond, Adam Levine, Michael Phelps, Channing Tatum. Hardly surprisingly, many of these people and other neurodivergents have never excelled within or prior to being released from the structured cages of a neurotypical-based education and an extrovert-oriented work culture.

The ordinary person doesn't know how hard it is for neurodivergents just to waddle through an everyday life tailored to a different type of person. In society, we have to repress or mask our natural traits or we'd stick out even more and this not only takes an enormous amount of energy, but causes stress as well. We can just about survive under those conditions, thriving is rarer.

What is even more sad is that many people remain undiagnosed and have to keep battling their invisible obstacles without knowing what they are. It is a hidden disability. So you are heroes, every one of you.

Conditioned to be overachievers from a young age despite these shackles, we, the abused, would very much like to contribute to society and most of all, make the world a better place. Also, because we look at things differently, we can oftentimes come up with a solution and point of view nobody thought of before. Would it be too much to ask to be given a chance by letting us work, study, chip in and function in a way that works better for us?

I'm sick and tired of being told, even by health professionals, that I must be shifty, a liar, or must dislike them because I don't do much eye contact: 'you can't even look me in the eyes' I'm told. Just because eye contact comes naturally to them, it doesn't mean it doesn't terrify us. How could I casually look anyone in the eyes if I feel uncomfortable doing it? One rule does not fit all, yet we're measured by such rules every day.

Another problem many of us with panic and anxiety disorders face and have to put up with regularly is sensory overload.

4 Sensory Overload

Sensory overload happens when one or more of the body's five senses become overwhelmed. In other words, the incoming information exceeds the brain's capacity to process and store it. As an analogy, imagine having many programs open on your computer. What happens is that it will process all the information at a slower pace and sometimes interrupt processing altogether and cause the whole computer to freeze. For a person, sensory overload can happen, for example, in a crowded restaurant, when the radio is too loud or when a passer-by is wearing strongly scented perfume. In these situations, our brains receive too much information to be able to process it properly, with one pathway becoming overloaded enough to cause malfunction in the others. Sensory overload, a sensory integration error, can lead to feelings of anxiety, irritability, being overwhelmed and unable to think of anything else other than the disturbance. It causes agitation, shakes and discomfort that range from mild to intense stress. It can sometimes literally feel like being fried by an electric current or an extreme urge to flee and stop the discomfort in any way possible, which can sometimes be conductive to aggressive behaviour, such as trying to eliminate the source of the pain, switch off the music, rip off clothing tags, shout at people to stop. These uncomfortable situations can lead to a loss of focus, fear and avoidance of experiencing them again, restlessness and in the worst cases, insomnia. Unfortunately, some parents and caregivers label the reactions as bad behaviour, nothing but meltdowns and tantrums, laziness or escapism, making the child appear out of control. But the reactions are completely understandable when we consider the brain struggling to decipher, prioritise and process sensory inputs. An environment we don't understand would then communicate to the body that it is time to escape these sensory inputs for our own safety and survival. It is also no wonder that this message would cause feelings of upset and extreme alarm.

It is worthy to note that sensory overload also includes dealing with stimuli such as hugs and general physical closeness, being in someone's aura, having to look close into their faces, even if via an electronic screen. Especially for a person with childhood abuse or trust issues, touching, embracing or even being close to someone without touching can feel overwhelming and cause panic and enormous anxiety, an urge to get out of the situation immediately. A face too close, a touch on your shoulder, a person standing close by and not showing intentions of moving, believe me, those are the stuff of nightmares! Partially, why sensory overload is so exasperating is owing to the fact that it is so hard to make people who can function well in society understand that I can't stand anyone getting physically close to me. My senses are already overstimulated if there's a repetitive, irritating sound coming from outside, there have been dirty plates left on the table for a second longer than absolutely necessary, the sun shines too brightly, there's something in my shoe, the books haven't been tidied up or someone left the volume of television on too loud. My anxiety levels rocket up instantly and I cannot have a straight thought till I'm out of that position. Now imagine if that person raised their voice and then it's fight or flight all over again!

Everyone experiences sensory overload at some point in their lives. Some children and adults, however, experience its paralysing power regularly and become isolated as a result. For these individuals, everyday situations can be challenging. For them, going to school or an office can lead to sensory overload. The sounds of people talking loudly, fluorescent lighting, strong smells of food, the clanging of dishes, bright or flashing lights, big crowds, sensitivity to types of clothing or fabrics, or other textures on the skin and loud or certain rhythms of music can all trigger feelings of being overwhelmed and uncomfortable. What sensory overload feels like can vary from one person to another. Some people may be more sensitive to sound, for example, while others may have issues with different textures. External sounds are perceived so loud that the individual cannot seem to hear themselves, be able to think, at least rationally. Additional symptoms include depression, needing a clean space around us to feel okay, a changed pain threshold, anger episodes followed by guilt, restlessness, feeling out of control, reduced motor skills, finger flicking or foot tapping, a heightened awareness of people evaluating us negatively. Visual sensitivity can cause someone to lose their spatial awareness, giving them the feeling as if their sight were failing. These heightened emotions then feel unbearable and become hard to regulate. Subsequently, it is easy to see how sensory overload can make day-to-day situations seem like huge challenges, negatively affecting the way we relate to others as well. While most of us will learn to adapt using coping mechanisms and will not show outward distress, the internal struggle and its toll on the psyche remains.

The other choice is avoidance, which can also be detrimental on social and professional lives, even more so if the triggers avoided are related to a disinclination of getting close to people, speaking up or mixing with others. Forcing ourselves into the situation will still likely result in side effects such as a lack of focus that can reduce our ability to conclude work tasks in a meticulous and fitting manner. These situations can lead to high levels of anxiety, additional fear and distress due to being aware of our limitations of performing less than optimally under these circumstances. We also dread being in such situations and we are fearful about spending time in such an unbearable environment. Therefore, we will not enter social spaces unless we have to.

In the case of people who cannot express themselves, such as young children, we need to be on the lookout for outward symptoms indicative of the condition such as covering the ears or the face, fidgeting, not responding to stimuli they normally respond to, stimming motions, like flapping hands, swinging around, rocking back or forth or touching objects, running into things unintentionally, eating inedible things, hyperactivity, avoiding or running away from specific places or situations, and provide these individuals with the means to express their feelings afterwards.

Sensitivity to smell is unique in that it is tied to the limbic system, the paleomammalian cortex, in charge of how we process emotions and memory. Therefore, certain smells can induce sensory overload in the individual because there may be a powerful emotional connection rooted in the past to it.

A related condition is misophonia, selective sound sensitivity syndrome, which is a condition in which particular noises, chewing, breathing, or snoring for example, trigger a pronounced outburst characterised by extreme discomfiture, exasperation, irritability or aggression.

In some cases, such as for those with a sensory processing disorder, there is a biological, neurological basis with brain structure differences for the problem. But stroke survivors, people with PTSD, OCD and generalised anxiety disorder, including those having derived from complex childhood trauma, can also become hypersensitive to their surroundings. The sensory overload occurs either in response to certain triggers that remind the person of the trauma or simply as another factor that raises their anxiety above the acceptable threshold they can cope with. There are many other conditions that can make a person more susceptible to the troubles of sensory overload, for example multiple sclerosis, chronic fatigue syndrome, fibromyalgia and so on.

In my case, I am mostly hypersensitive to moderately loud, continuous noises, dazzling light, strong odours, chaos around me, people's close presence and intense environments or situations, especially if they involve emotions and noise.

In these cases, it might be helpful to write a diary about instances of sensory overload so that we could identify our triggers, signs, the offending stimuli (such as lights, sensations, thoughts, sounds), symptoms, factors (such as dehydration or low mood) and circumstances leading up to the incidents. This is so that after identifying our risk factors, we can plan for them and manage our reactions.

Incidentally, our initial reaction to run away and avoid the situations is on the right track as one of the most effective methods to manage sensory overload and reduce the associated stress without medication. Making changes to the environment to minimise the frequency or intensity of the sensory overload, along with techniques to keep our reactions in check are also useful. These include finding and designating a safe space to escape to when needed, breathing techniques, writing lists to focus on tasks, keeping to routines, wearing noise-cancelling headphones, staying near exits, setting limits for how long to spend in such environments, asking others for their understanding of sensory threats and support in reducing sensory inputs, staying rested, hydrated, well-fed and relaxed.

People with sensory issues are often labelled dramatic, weird or a freak because the disturbance doesn't seem like a big deal to the neurotypicals. Ignorance is not unusual. The onlooker often doesn't understand that there's a lot more going on than there seems and there's hardly any concern given to the fact that this problem might be a result of some old trauma that has been triggered by an unexpected sensory factor and caused painful emotions to rise to the surface, that the sufferer is often in survival or grieving mode and under a lot of stress as a result to the point where they can't control the physical manifestations of their inner world anymore. Be sure, they are trying, and very hard at that. The above should be emphasised for the sufferer as well. Way too often, they feel shame for being triggered. Some people don't even understand why they have so much anxiety and stress, that they have a dysregulated nervous system, they don't know why their world feels poles apart, though they could be living in this torturous state for years. This is why it is so important to study these afflictions, so you can work on yourself to heal your nervous system. This can ultimately guide us to a life with less anxiety and side effects.

The other side of this sensory sensitivity is the ability to enjoy and tell apart textures, sounds, smells and so on beyond the prevailing level. In my case, this advantage is mainly tactile as I can sense the smallest relief difference or change in texture and it has benefited me in two ways: I take pleasure in how surfaces feel on my skin and it has given me the perfect fidgeting aid that I can clandestinely use anytime, anywhere. It's an activity I resort to for comforting myself, especially in moments of stress and social anxiety with quick-moving, repetitive thoughts that are difficult to stop as they seem to happen outside my will, that I will talk about in the coming chapters. Unfortunately, I usually have to focus consciously on not doing it, not touching things and fidgeting, otherwise it is my normal go-to and it can sometimes look strange from the outside.

Hopefully, this short summary gave an overview of how detrimental it can be to struggle with sensory overload, whether or not it stems from childhood abuse. In an ideal world, workspaces and other formal environments could and should make it possible for everyone to function and perform optimally at work. Such environments would value differences and allow for the flexibility required to enhance performance, such as the use of noise-cancelling headphones, adjusting lights, making it possible to adopt a preferred work position, working remotely through video presence or from home, even if it is audio only. More on this in my next book *The Toxic Workplace*.

5 Self-Isolation and (Social) Anxiety

No, I'm not talking about the period of time you have to spend away from people when infected with coronavirus, but the self-imposed isolation and extreme independence of those who did not gain much emotional support from anyone growing up, where, in fact, any attempt to gather such support ultimately ended in some kind of negative experience. It is understandable, then, that as adults, we would prefer to deal with our problems alone as it feels safer that way. What's more, we don't want to end up in a situation where we would be dependent on anyone, which, from our point of view, would be the worst, most vulnerable position to be in. We can't let people in, can't chance disrespect, it is perceived as too dangerous. What people call being shy is most of the time protecting oneself, having intrusive, paralysing thoughts based on shame and embarrassment, a fear of being judged or being the centre of attention, of being humiliated, of hurting someone by accident. So there's a lot of hesitancy and apprehension, giving rise to physical symptoms as well, such as sweating or blushing.

What people everywhere need to understand and be mindful of is that when someone is quiet and keeps to themselves, it has usually nothing to do with trying to ignore or disliking someone. They need to be quiet, they need to retreat so that they are able to cope with life at least to some extent; they need to protect themselves with an invisible wall. Shy is just a word people use when they don't want to think about the truth once again, which is most of the time. Being shy means someone has been hurt too many times to waste energy on people some more.

There is a lot of talk now of independence and the pitfalls of codependency in terms of feminism and women being able to provide for their families on their own. The newer generation is not seeing the traditional family unit as important as previous generations did, and careers are put ahead of children, and more people opt to stay single as opposed to having to live with compromises and having to put up with other people's foibles. We have to do that enough at work, there's no need to have it spill over into our personal lives. Independence is amazing, it gives us a sense of freedom, it is a wonderful feeling being able to take care of ourselves confidently, solve our problems. There is nothing wrong with independence, it is truly hailed as an asset, an achievement, something to be proud of, an essential characteristic in our times – up to a point.

Hyper-independence tends to raise its head, understandably, when leaving an abusive household, relationship or a toxic workplace. But there are situations when we naturally need help, problems we can't solve on our own. We humans, as social creatures, naturally blossom in a nurturing environment and benefit from advice and support from others. In some circumstances, asking for help and accepting a certain level of dependence is the rational and advisable thing to do, something that hyper-independent individuals refuse and then suffer the consequences. It can be detrimental and concerning not to ask for help when we really need it. It can also lead to isolation and loneliness and the exacerbation of mental and physical illnesses the individual refuses help for, and the person will also miss out on experiencing all the goodwill that is out there. As a result, they might never know kindness in this world, after all the hardship, they can't risk letting it in. Anybody can make mistakes, but remember, not everybody is toxic! 'Every time you are tempted to react in the same old way, ask if you want to be prisoner of the past or a pioneer of the future.' – Deepak Chopra[47]. Signs of deep loneliness include oversharing when there is someone to listen, being overly helpful and feeling like no one really knows or sees you.

What is worth acknowledging, even under these circumstances of maybe missing out on positive relationships, is that most of the time, the hyper-independent often feels that they are much stronger on their own. This might indeed be true in the sense that social interaction takes so much energy away from us that could be used for a more important cause. It seems logical that if, as a child, your feelings didn't matter, then you now struggle to get close to people; after being disappointed in people many times, interaction doesn't seem worthwhile. It is also hard to believe that anyone would show kindness without ulterior motives, so generally there's a tendency in us to think we would always have to provide something in return, or feel like we owe them forever, which doesn't bode well with the hyper-independent. I'd rather they didn't offer me anything in kindness so I don't have to feel I am in debt. Every interaction is exhausting because we need to analyse it for signs of danger as it happens, every word, every shift of the mood, which, of course, makes it all the harder to connect with someone.

Asking for favours would mean the same, so I don't ask, not even when I would be due to receive something. Safe people would have to be perfect or they are not worth taking the risk to get hurt again. And nobody is perfect. It is already too scary if they make me in any way uncomfortable. The smallest hiccup and I feel betrayed, unsure if I can trust them anymore. They might be nice, but we would never find that out, we cut them off instead. It's impossible to build trust while overthinking the little things. Spending time with a friend isn't as easy and relaxing as it is for others. A trusted person might still elicit anxiety in the sufferer, perhaps in anticipation for hours before the meeting takes place. Some of us need to persuade ourselves to get dressed and leave the house or that it is safe to be in public, we will be on edge the entire time of the outing and it will exhaust us so much that we will be unable to do anything for the rest of the day, never mind meeting anyone else. The side effects sometimes carry on to the next day.

According to clinical psychologist Emily Victoria Knott, our bodies can perceive 'social contact as dangerous, and prepare us to fight or flee'[36]. Hyper-independent individuals find simply talking to another person stressful and besides, if I can do it alone, I can do anything! It's an extremely empowering feeling.

We treasure being on our own and I find that it is oftentimes imperative for my well-being, especially if I already surpassed my quota for social interactions for the day. While other people can feel comforted by advice and offered assistance, all the negative emotion we are forced to muddle through to get to something positive is not worthwhile the hassle, the constant fear of judgement.

You tell your problem to one person, they want to know more particulars and then another finds out and that simply ends in more stress and a struggle to get rid of all the expectations of others they have projected on us in the form of unsolicited advice. As people-pleasers, we are intensely affected by others' feelings. It's too much to cope with and then I can't concentrate on the original problem, the most important one' I have to concentrate on somebody else, like how my problem is affecting them. 'Some people need to ride out their struggle alone, and the best thing you can do is just let them.' – Stephanie Bennett-Henry, author of *Her View From Home,* who shares her personal experiences through writing and poetry.

Other impacts of mental abuse include not believing compliments, needing and actively looking for lots of reassurance, not trusting one's own thoughts, being overprotective of one's own feelings. The mind habitually jumps to worst case scenarios and we feel out of control if we're not overprepared, based on the assumption that we're not as gifted as others so we need to work harder than everyone else, in fear of being blamed and criticised for making even the smallest mistake.

Having too much social interaction has serious consequences, usually on sleep. We will have trouble shutting down our brains from the stress of conversations, interactions that will endlessly play back in our minds. What could I have said differently, did I do it right? How many embarrassing moments were there, what will be the other consequences? Social anxiety is many things – being too self-conscious about the movements we make or words we say, leading to endless rehearsing of interactions, or feeling like we're not being interesting enough, but it can also be being ashamed of how anxious we are, with its physical manifestations of sweating and shaking, furthering everything down the anxiety spiral. It all makes us unfit and ill-equipped for social interactions, making it feel natural to quit instead of fighting the enormous number of obstacles.

It is hard to not be resentful of those who can function like a normal human being, the people who don't have anxiety holding them back from everything, don't have to struggle to get out of bed or have to put on an act that everything is fine when it's not. They don't struggle to hold friendships and relationships, they don't feel sad for no reason every day. How amazing can it be to be able to hold jobs down and work towards dreams, have self-esteem, feel enthusiastic and safe and see the beauty in oneself?

People-pleasers like us spare too many thoughts on avoiding the discomfort of another person being unhappy with us, even for a moment. It's understandable that if, as a child, nothing you did was ever enough, then you now take on too many responsibilities. Adult children of narcissistic parents fear that they will hurt someone else by choosing to do what's right for them. This applies to babies too. I was unable to let a baby cry. As a result, I crossed every parenting book around. If a child cried, I would not stick to routines, not force a bedtime or a food item they rejected, I would let them sleep with me, breastfeed in bed, I would do anything, give them anything to stop them from crying. I am also no longer able to be cruel or harsh, or shout at or punish a child. I give the world to every one of them, which I did for many years as a childminder, learning to be a better person along the way.

The phenomenon is, however, an understandable trauma response when previous pleas for help ended in negative connotations, such as being overly criticised, unaccepted or abused when vulnerable. The person may fear that if they are perceived as weak, they would be attacked in some way. It is one of the ways anxiety controls the individual.

Another is self-doubt. Some people have trouble with decisions, questioning every thought process. These anxiety attacks involve downward spirals of negative thinking in which they question everything and everybody, the point to life. There is a lot of negative self-talk involved that makes one desperate and unable stop crying. The mindset is hard to snap out of and can last for hours. It only confuses further. We think ourselves unable to advance or keep holding on to what we cherish, and we lose control and therefore self-esteem deep dives again, causing more anxiety, a vicious circle, causing those sleepless nights of worries, exploring worst case scenarios and what-ifs. (I personally find exploring worst case scenarios helpful because when I know I can deal with the worst possible outcome, I know I can deal with anything.) This can cause another vicious circle, one I talk about more in detail later on in this chapter, that of panic in regards to sleep because we now worry about becoming worried and not sleeping, a situation very hard to bring under control. Anxiety can also look like a tendency to cancel plans at the last minute, mood swings lasting hours or days or weeks, being singularly unmotivated to meet people, self-groom or pursue a career, believing people dislike us or hate us behind our backs, believing being a burden to their family and friends, becoming emotionally attached to new friends or relationships to an extreme degree, being emotionally distant or unavailable, keeping to oneself, physically as well as emotionally, having dramatic outbursts over ostensibly small problems, continuously seeking reassurance that others are not angry with us or whether we are still loved, a lot of sleep or very little, comforting oneself with food or not eating at all, frequent meltdowns or frequently changing hobbies, interests or careers.

People with anxiety also have a lot of positive traits, most of them stemming from the fact that they don't want to put other people in situations they themselves would deem uncomfortable or trying to avoid conflict. Therefore, they tend to be empathetic, understanding, diligent, responsible, careful, well-educated, detail-oriented, high-achieving, hard-working, organised and punctual. They are also good problem solvers for having thought about every issue in advance. I often wonder if I'm doing something wrong, if my interactions are strange, as I am not certain my childhood models gave me enough of the right type of interaction to copy.

While, as I have said, this is not a self-help book, even reading it could elicit anxieties in people struggling with repressed trauma, so it would feel wrong not to include some anxiety management strategies that could be put to use right now. With anxiety's connection to the physical body, it may be that your breathing is already quicker or shallow. Bring it under control. Breathe slowly. Continue with some meditations for mindfulness, get outside, into nature if possible. Take a boat across the lake, exercise, go to yoga classes, use uplifting or soothing essential oils. Eat something you enjoy. There's no shame in chocolate. Use your senses deeply, use them to their greatest limits. Take a warm shower or a long, luxurious bath. Eat grapes, eat something healthy, take care of yourself, write something, anything you want, not only your feelings. Let yourself experience something you want. Sleep. Appreciate peace, aloneness and quality time. Find some positive affirmation mantras that suit you and say them out loud every day. Bring it back to your senses, to the moment. Make something, build or achieve something you wanted for a long time, however small, and feel the rewards. Enjoy life, listen to music, pick up a book or an instrument, or watch a movie. Put on your pyjamas. Dance, use your body. Sometimes we need to let go of expectations before we're in a place where we are actually able to go for and get to our goals again. Get support. Sometimes you do need to talk to a professional or be part of a group who went through similar experiences.

Self-care, all this, is crucial because you deserve it and also because you need to be able to calm yourself down when doing the work, bringing up old, traumatic childhood memories and letting yourself feel. Letting in the emotions is important because how can we heal them if we don't let them in. Allow yourself to process the emotions with patience.

Not Wanting to Appear Weak

Another trauma response I am guilty of, that often resulted in overexertion, and making my illnesses worse by not asking for breaks or time off work, is pushing through unnecessary pain. I could have saved myself from it. I would have been ashamed if anyone knew my weaknesses and I thought that asking for help meant that people would think I was not good enough. I am uncomfortable when receiving help and I don't trust anyone to properly do what needs to be done.

Other symptoms of hyper-independence in others could manifest in impulsive decisions, fear of commitment and a feeling of not needing anyone, substance abuse and a feeling of numbness in relationships and of contempt towards those who ask for help. Those displaying some of these traits as children are frequently referred to as 'old souls', so I think specific regard should be taken to check on the welfare of these children.

Not wanting to appear weak is also an intense survival mechanism. We learn to take care of ourselves, relying on ourselves only when we couldn't enlist the help of a single soul because of being intentionally isolated by the narcissist. Asking them for help would indeed have ended up in regretful situations. We could not trust the abuser and it is hard not to transfer this feeling into life after or outside the narcissistic relationship. Add to this the lengthy experience of an entire childhood and it is no wonder we are reluctant to trust anyone.

Further warning signs of someone living in continuous survival mode are being hypersensitive to criticism, needing a lot of time alone or rest to avoid overwhelm, not wanting to disclose personal information, or appearing cold and reserved. Living in survival mode, it is stressful just to try to explain what's going on in your head, never mind anything else. As such, victims of abusive households are more likely to show a stronger reactivity to stress and they also suffer more interpersonal problems as adults.

Living with anxiety, with fears like the above, can also mean a lot of confusion to work through, stuttering, appearing paranoid and having no motivation, as the hardships of achieving something with this burden of anxiety is too much compared to uncertain results. It can manifest as no motivation to study, have conversations, leave the house or the bed, even. It can be really hard to leave our comfort zones, go meet a friend, do a leisure activity, or exercise. For this reason, social anxiety sufferers tend to make plans and then cancel them at the last minute, such as turning down a job or backtracking on a holiday. We sometimes worry so much about the upcoming event during the night that we can't get much sleep and thus end up physically being unable to perform the feared task, leading to insomnia.

Insomnia

During my years at university, late teens, early twenties, I started to develop this insomnia problem. Of course, there were occasions where worrying about what my narc would make me do denied me some hours of sleep and then I'd still have to perform to expectations the next day, but I didn't develop anxiety about the very act of sleeping itself till later.

The term insomnia means ongoing states where individuals feel distressed or are compromised in functioning, social, behavioural, academic and occupational, due to insufficient sleep, regardless of number of hours slept.

At first, it really was just about worrying how I would perform in a test or exam as failure wasn't an option for my mother, then later it panned out into fretting and agonising about social interactions. I started to fall into this pattern where I had to calculate my hours of sleep each night into what I would be able to do on that amount of sleep and then the panic stage came. I would dread going to bed, becoming more and more anxious the closer it got to bedtime. I would panic that I would not be able to sleep and that would make me even less able to perform to expectations. They were full-blown panic attacks, with the heart racing, sweating and dizziness and then I would get scared about them too, first because I wasn't sure what they were and then because I didn't want to experience another one.

The worst part wasn't even the panic attack, it was its aftereffects. I remained tense for days, sometimes unable to engage with others, laugh, smile, and felt fragile about everything, along with all kinds of other random abnormalities in my behaviour.

I developed hypnic jerks and restless leg syndrome, a neurological disorder based on a dysfunction of the dopaminergic system, a very annoying condition where unpleasant sensations in the nerves in your legs prompt you to keep moving them as movement alleviates the symptoms. Hypnic jerks are involuntary muscle twitches of either one part or of the whole body at the moment of trying to fall asleep. I would not sleep one moment as a result of these problems for 24–64 hours. Mostly, I had problems falling asleep, others might have problems staying asleep.

Other common symptoms include impatience, tenseness, feelings of apprehension, gastrointestinal issues, nightmares and night terrors. Post-traumatic stress disorder with its persistent re-experiencing of traumatic moments can create the same reaction. A history of depression also seems to make individuals more liable to experience sleeplessness. Other contributing factors include stress[38], grief[39], poor sleep conditions, the consumption of nicotine, caffeine, alcohol or other stimulants, medications or illegal drugs, uncurbed stimulation before bed, intense excitement, conditions that impair breathing, arthritis or another chronic illness like Parkinson's or kidney disease, heartburn or another gastrointestinal condition, ageing, menopausal symptoms[40], change in environment and an overactive thyroid.

It is pretty logical if you think about it. Being in a stressful situation triggers a fight or flight response, with the release of adrenaline and cortisol into your system. How on earth are you going to fall asleep with those? Additionally, as Professor Kevin Morgan of the University of Loughborough's Clinical Sleep Research Unit pointed out, one 'of the consequences of not being able to go to sleep is that it generates anxiety'. And having developed negative associations with sleep, you're going to be stressed about not being able to sleep. Being tired will also make you more anxious and that understandably creates a vicious circle, sleep anxiety, a type of performance anxiety associated with falling asleep. Sleep becomes almost impossible for all the unrelenting tiredness and whenever sleep is, in fact, achieved, it tends to be unsatisfying, unrefreshing and non-restorative. The disturbing thoughts emerge the moment the person wakes, so falling back to sleep becomes an impossibility. Feelings of vulnerability can intensify overnight for the lack of sleep.

Research based on brain scans from the University of California, Berkeley established that people who didn't sleep enough show less activity in the part of the brain that leads to social interactions and are thus more unapproachable, less inclined to engage in social activities due to finding other people more intimidating. Furthermore, they also discovered that the sleep-deprived look less appealing to others[32]. UC Berkeley researchers also indicated that lack of sleep can activate parts of the brain that trigger undue unease and nervousness[33]. Other common side effects include mood disorders, poor performance, difficulties learning, attention deficit, reduced cognitive reaction times, being at a heightened risk for heart disease, high blood pressure, stroke, diabetes and obesity.

Suggested bedtime routines, relaxation exercises, lifestyle changes, diaphragmatic breathing and turning off electricals I didn't find useful and I would simply roll my eyes at obvious 'solutions' such as making your bedroom comfortable or not drinking coffee close to bedtime. If it were that easy, I wouldn't have been asking! I spent years in this state looking for a solution, till I discovered my mantras; I hope you'll find them beneficial too. It is a way to learn to silence your mind. These are sentences I would say that I could associate with calmness. It is a little bit like counting sheep, but it is these sentences I repeat over and over till I fall asleep. If my mind wanders, I would simply bring it back to the mantras and start over. I have two that I use one after the other, one in Hungarian and one in English and I still find them effective to this day. One is 'no thoughts, no feelings', used when addressing what stops me from falling asleep, and the other is 'calm down, fall asleep', which I find useful in preventing a panic attack. When I'm too tired, the 'no thoughts, no feelings' sometimes turns into 'no sauce, no feelings,' which demonstrates that it really doesn't matter what the mantra is as long as it brings you closer to being calm. The longer the sentence is associated with sleep, the more effective it gets. Sometimes I still have to jump out of bed and write down some of the useful ideas for the next days that are circling around in my head, but at least then they could be out of my mind as I have them written down and they won't be forgotten.

The thought- and behaviour-changing cognitive therapy aiming at rationalising worries of the inner dialogue, and the occasional antidepressant, helps too; whichever solution you need in what dose probably depends on the individual person. Hell, even some of the more simplistic, traditional ideas might help some. And most importantly either way, practice and perseverance is the key! For others, using exercise to quieten pre-bedtime anxiety helps since it lowers the production of stress hormones, but this shouldn't be done right before bedtime[34]. It is also good to know that computers, mobile phones and tablets emit a kind of light that confuses the brain into functioning as if the sun was up and stops melatonin production[35]. Others swear on the usefulness of weighted blankets[37], especially if you suffer from restless leg syndrome because they're known for generating a calming reaction by mimicking the feeling of a hug and help increase serotonin and melatonin production while decreasing cortisol. Some other methods to try are sleep restriction programmes and reconditioning the sufferer into associating the bed with calmness and sleep. Restriction programmes only allow a few hours of sleep at night between given times, while slowly lengthening that time bracket till the individual is back to their usual sleep patterns. An alternate way of getting to sleep is imagining walking down a well-known street and trying to recall every detail. Normally you'd end up asleep before reaching the imaginary destination. Similarly, you can use trying to recall a long-forgotten poem's words or make up your own. The key is distraction.

Regardless of the therapeutic approach, it is vital to temper the anxiety and not only focus on the insomnia with medication, otherwise it can only work on the level of a plaster being applied to a deep wound.

These days I rarely have to use any of the above as I found that my anxiety attacks naturally reduced once I had children and my main focus was on them as opposed to myself. Distraction, right? That was a real cure, along with the sleepless nights I spent tending to babies, the effect of which is being too exhausted to think.

The Department of Psychology of Florida State University did a study on the relation between social anxiety and insomnia amongst others[31] and found that 'social anxiety was correlated with sleep dissatisfaction, sleep-related functional impairment, perception of a sleep problem to others, and distress about sleep problems. Importantly, depressive symptoms mediated the relationship between social anxiety and insomnia, thereby at least partially accounting for insomnia among socially anxious individuals.' So they determined that depression could have a key role in the co-occurrence of social anxiety and insomnia. So it is important to address all three of these psycho-emotional difficulties together and at the same time with their usually common cause.

Nightmares

Perhaps people imagine strong horror-related motives such as monsters and strangulation when they think about nightmares, but I can assure you that anxiety-related nightmares are disturbing enough without those elements. The worst part is that once a person decides to move past an anxiety-causing event, aggressive individual or stressful situation, having consciously resolved it to the best of their ability, the scenario will still appear repeatedly and traumatically in dreams without our conscious control or permission. Frequently remembered dysphoric experiences are referred to as nightmare disorders.

Themes may differ wildly but common anxiety-inducing, narcissistic abuse-related, themes include the sense of failure, being criticised, wrongly accused, caught out unawares, or feeling lost or put on display to be tested. The sufferer will generally find themselves anxious or fretful when forced awake by their nightmare, but they may also experience resentment with the torturing star of their nightmare, sorrow, embarrassment, guilt or dread, potentially lasting for hours after waking. Of course, replaying of the traumatic events themselves is also possible. Sometimes the event itself doesn't replay, but we experience feelings related to it: hopelessness, helplessness, shame. The plot itself can be either directly or symbolically related to the events. Either way, the brain is trying to do something useful by reorganising the elements of these situations, something like a threat rehearsal. Physical manifestation of the anxiety can also couple with the emotions, such as a rushing heartbeat or waking up soaking wet, with the bedding and pyjamas needing to be changed. It is more prevalent in women than men.

Of course, everyone experiences these kinds of dreams from time to time, but as the aftermath of childhood trauma, they are usually triggered by stressful life events, like starting a new job or having a new relationship. They can become persistent, cause distress and interfere with social, occupational or other important areas of everyday functioning in a clinically significant manner. Other triggers can include witnessing a similar situation to our trauma, illnesses, drugs, starting some antidepressants, narcotics, stimulants, pain killers, barbiturates or other sleep aids or withdrawal from them, depression or sleep patterns being frequently interrupted.

Unfortunately, there isn't any foolproof method of treating nightmares apart from trying some of the above as trial and error and addressing the generalised anxiety and other causes, including using stress reduction techniques and lifestyle changes. Therapy should always be holistic, with addressing the whole mental and physical picture because nightmares are a symptom of the larger trauma response. Neurological and some psychological assessments are also recommended to rule out other causative issues, as well as blood tests for liver and thyroid function. With cPTSD-related nightmares, Prazosin may be prescribed.

What I find empowering to do after waking up from such a nightmare is taking a conscious part in what should happen next. Once I redirect the dream's plot and its destination, I find it a lot safer to fall back to sleep again and not experience another nightmare. Sometimes it is also possible to put the anxiety in its place, it being something we already dealt with, consciously telling our subconscious that it is okay.

Another method that can be used simultaneously is associating the bed with comfort as much as possible. You might have a favourite pillow, a favourite position to put everything in, optimum light per individual. This is to make the experience as calming as possible so as not to associate it with anxiety, which should reduce the number of times disturbing dreams occur.

Some react to the disturbance by avoiding sleep as much as possible or they may aid their sleep by drinking, using drugs or abusing prescribed medications. They may not be able to sleep without distracting their minds, such as by listening to a podcast or radio, leading to a different kind of disturbed sleep, again impacting on other sides of life. The daily demands become harder to live up to, which generates more anxiety, leading to a complicated vicious circle. Complex cases can be addressed with specialist help through imagery rehearsal therapy (IRT) and exposure, rescripting and relaxation therapy, relying on different ways to reshape the experience into something much more positive, changing the story's ending and the emotions experienced with it.

When waking up from an unpleasant dream, it can be confusing as to whether we have really fully woken up or not and we risk falling back into the nightmare, but one can condition themselves to temporarily distract from the disturbance using grounding or breathing techniques that would get one to the safety of their bed instead into the nightmare scenario. If the disturbing imagery won't dissipate easy, a handy way to distract from it is thinking of menial tasks such as naming five things on your shelf, the last books you read, the shopping list, a recipe, naming colour shades, anything that can divert attention away from the nightmare without actually making ourselves unable to fall asleep again, like when we'd start to check the news or watch a movie as a distraction. Try to aim for items with the least amount of emotional attachment or charge. A change of scenery like a different room might help too. But I wouldn't discount documenting my dreams either, some of my best plans came from dreams. The upside of this is that the brain is inclined to let go of scenarios and schemes once they are safely tucked away somewhere on a more permanent basis as it doesn't have to keep it in mind.

Something else good to hear is that these anxiety nightmares don't have to be persistent. Some childhood trauma sufferers can get a good rest out of their sleep, not having or not remembering their dreams. It is also important to note that dreams don't actually have any other meaning other than our subconscious mind trying to deal with stressors as best they can. The brain is trying to make sense of these various stimuli and concocts a story based on given experiences. Stressful thoughts for the brain to organise turn into a stressful story, which is why denying giving conscious thought to problems can show up in dreams instead.

Touch Aversion

Unfortunately, aversion to other people's touch is an often misunderstood condition. While it doesn't usually bother me as that is who I am and I don't crave touch, I have noticed that it does bother people I come in contact with, most importantly my husband, and understandably so. People often assume I have an aversion or some sort of problem with them, and getting over this misconception is very hard. A 'normal' person finds the restriction hard to swallow or understand, so for the most part, the touch-aversive individual is pretty much doomed not to have long-standing, successful romantic relationships where instantaneous kisses and intimate hugs would be the norm, which I often try to avoid at all costs. Even if I allow these things to happen, I would often find it difficult to relax throughout and might act stressed out, irritable and annoyed due to the half-unconscious associated anger I feel. You see how this is no good for a friendship, even? Never mind family.

What is touch aversion, then? First of all, it is not to be confused with the autistic's tactile sensitivity or the tactile defensiveness of children with sensory processing problems. I feel rather uncomfortable being touched when not completely in a relaxed state or when I'm not anticipating it and I am not fully prepared, with my heart rate going up and I sense the pores of my skin constricting, especially if it involves skin contact, though I am usually a little less averse to it if I anticipate it. It is probably part of why people's auras and them moving in close proximity to me also bothers me. I can smell you? Way too close! Feeling people's breath has the same effect, that's terrifyingly close! For this reason, I keep certain often-used items in my room or close by so I don't have to interact much with others to get to them, or I simply give up on an activity if it involves conversing with people as being physically close to them could feel really uncomfortable, depending on my overall mental state. I tend not to speak loudly in social situations either, as I prefer not to be noticed, or even worse, judged or criticised. I'm terrified of the situation in the first place and as a result of the intense anxiety, I lose my train of thought and I am more likely to mess up my words, forget my very mission or misjudge my actions. At work, I've been told that I'm too quiet when I give instructions and that I'd have to be louder.

Similarly, I get easily spooked and jumpy by someone turning up close to me. People moving too fast or chaotically around me also fills me with further anxiety because it's unpredictable and my unconscious mind is terrified of closeness, of contact.

I am aware that for some people, this discomfort can reach as far as being scared of being touched, with a select number of individuals developing a full-blown phobia of it, haphephobia. It can be dependent on, or exacerbated by, certain states of mind and there's also a cumulative stress factor that might make it harder on some days to touch. So for some, it can simply be a part of their anxiety disorders when overwhelmed. Depending on my state of mind, I can at times find it physically painful, with the sensation of it going through my synapses or freezing my muscles into rigidity.

There are cases where the victim is unaware of why this aversion happens, and in other instances, the source event(s) is clear, such as a history of sexual abuse. I am pretty certain where mine originates from: while spending most of my younger years in isolation, my main source of touch came from my abuser, and in a pretty disturbing way too. After one of those shouting monologues coloured with terror and frequently some physical abuse, sometimes my mother seemed to have a moment where she didn't like that I would develop negative feelings about her due to the treatment I suffered. My theory is that she needed to know that she was still 'loved', though I doubt she even really knew the meaning of the word. So right after the screaming, she would demand that I hugged her and she declared that it made everything better and that all was fine between us again as I(!) was forgiven. Imagine my abhorrence during this 'touching' hug! As a consequence, I have an aversion not just to touch, but also to hugging, as well as doing similar activities after an argument, such as cuddling or the famed, supposedly marvellous make-up sex. I am also demisexual, but that is a different chapter's topic.

Touch aversion can also involve being rather butterfingered at times and fairly uncoordinated, and finding wild gesticulation distressing. It can also set you back on everyday errands and endeavours, as I can vouch for the fact that I avoid going near another person and have to wait till they vacate the area till I can approach and start on dinner, for example. I can't be close to people so I oftentimes listen out and wait to hear if they are in the vicinity or not as it would be quite awkward to turn around the moment I saw them. This can take quite a long time, during which I remain hungry, for the example's sake, though that exact turn of events did happen to me on several occasions. For the same reasons, standing in queues or enclosed spaces could be difficult. People push ahead as if that would get them to where they want to go sooner. I wish people would understand that not keeping distance could be uncomfortable for the likes of us, never mind claustrophobics, anthropophobics or agoraphobics! Thus, due to other people's ignorance, a simple trip to the shop could become extremely stressful and difficult to do.

All this, of course, can trigger or make anxiety and depression worse. The person might appear pretty unsociable, reclusive or stand-offish, which then can be again mistaken for being diffident and aloof by judgemental, ignorant a-holes. Being touched anyway could make the sufferer want to cry or they may tremble or sweat profusely, which feels embarrassing in itself, so there's one more reason to avoid touch at all costs. And to imagine there are people who are impulsive huggers! Ugh, repulsive! I need to whimper and wail just thinking about it.

Just for curiosity's sake, there's a hormone-related condition where pregnant or breastfeeding women can develop touch aversion, but this is only a temporary condition. People with chronic physical pain might also have it, it can be related to a sensory processing disorder.

Thankfully, the pandemic had the hopefully lasting effect where less people hug or shake hands, especially outside the home and the side cheek kiss-kiss routine has been largely dropped as well. If nothing else, it will benefit public health concerning transmittable diseases. It has always fascinated me why people would let their bodies be touched so carelessly before? You see, my body is mine, not anybody else's, not like when I had to be prepared to be physically punished whenever my mother felt like it. She never bothered with being gentle while fixing my hair either. I can't give that sense of freedom up ever again, and I can't imagine how much harder it must be for those sexually abused as well. Talking about forced social interactions, I would like to urge the unsuspecting parent to stop telling their children they must hug or kiss distant relatives, some of them practically strangers, or even grandparents they don't see very often. 'Can I get a hug?' No, you can't, you creepy, attention-seeking antediluvian, not if you didn't earn it. Affection should never be forced, it feels wrong pretending and it will never substitute the real thing. What's more, it can trigger this affliction, a chain forced on them to carry all their lives!

The downside of the condition is that I also have problems being able to let doctors examine my body. I find them looking, the touching, difficult. I shirk away, I jump and they don't understand why, but in these cases I try to push past the pain for a different goal. Being demisexual or asexual does not necessarily follow, but it is in certain cases linked.

Avoiding Conflict

Not exactly surprisingly, people with social anxiety also tend to avoid conflict. They'd rather never speak to a person again than have to dispute an issue. They put up with other people's faults rather than argue with them, or work diligently to achieve everything a team or group was supposed to do together just so they don't have to call them up for not putting in the effort. In most cases, we don't deem the emotional toll of conflict and disagreement, and the tension and anxiety it comes with, worthwhile to go through. If a person is argumentative, we will avoid them altogether, if possible.

Naturally, this is because of the past experiences of conflict, where with the narcissist we stood no chance and the sheer thought of any type of conflict brings up unpleasant associations and the dread of what it meant to end up in a disagreement with them, including not being able to express our real perspectives, plans or beliefs for fear of retaliation. Reliving such an experience would weigh heavily on our psychological state and the anticipation and pressure of an unavoidable conflict can take away our sleep or peace. Lack of confidence and self-esteem also adds to the avoidance of conflict and we know that, as a shy person with social anxiety, we will not fare well in an argument. Conflict is extremely exhausting, psychologically at first and then the physical symptoms of stress follow, especially if I've been crying, an almost certainty for me during or after an altercation.

Another powerful reason to avoid arguments that scarred people have, is not wanting to hurt the other party. Little things, small inconveniences don't matter, we'd rather get on with it than hurt somebody's feelings. I even avoid people who I see or hear arguing, as I feel there's a hurtful aura around them that almost literally stings, but it certainly gives me PTSD.

So I'm certainly a flighter when it comes to conflict. The term originated from Steve Cohen, author of *Mess Management: Lessons from a Corporate Hitman* (Author House, 2010) and refers to individuals reacting to conflict as if it would be a matter of survival and instinctively choosing the flight answer between fight or flight. One form of this is to submit, but complain about it to everyone bar the other party in the conflict. Not surprisingly, the emotionally abused tend not to stand up for themselves, already intimidated and petrified of further criticism whether it is justifiable with this particular adversary or not, especially if they are an authority figure. Of course, this leads to a strained relationship, suppressed emotions and personal discomfort, possibly worse than if the conflict had been properly addressed.

Because of being purposefully isolated as a child by a narcissist parent, the abused also lacks opportunities to develop their communication skills, which would be further restricted and inhibited by their resultant social anxiety and voluntary isolation.

Needless to say, I am guilty of unhealthy conflict avoidance or delay myself. I do understand that marriages without arguments don't and shouldn't exist because the unresolved issues will raise their heads later in a different, less manageable form, but I still try running away from them, shutting down, or my husband out or trying to solve the problem on my own as a hyper-independent person. It's understandable that if as a child you were put down when you tried to speak up, then it will become harder later to voice an opinion. Certainly, there are issues not worth arguing over, but I do appreciate how annoying this must be for the other person and damaging their emotional health, making them feel like their opinion doesn't matter. The following tension will cause anxiety and feelings of entrapment in both parties and transfer into other domains of the relationship. Partly, this is why it's beneficial to learn to overcome conflict avoidance, along with the opportunities for growth and getting insight into our characters that we are committed to here.

Practising role-playing with friends first could be the answer to increase self-confidence and assertiveness, along with gathering as much reliable information and counterarguments about the situation as possible so that we can become competent and impartial. On this basis, the exposure should feel slightly less terrifying each time, while gaining skill and experience, finding the strength to deal with these issues better and being able to judge more reliably when it is worthwhile to engage and when it's not.

Disclaimer: However, in all this positivity and encouragement, I would like to add a warning here as a little side note that I would feel irresponsible not doing. Confrontations are generally not advisable when the other party is under the influence of drugs or alcohol as generating conflict in these situations can prove very dangerous.

6 (Complex) Post-Traumatic Stress Disorder

As our trauma didn't derive from one single event or some closely connected ones, but over a longer period of time, sometimes our whole childhood and beyond, it is often referred to as complex post-traumatic stress disorder, cPTSD, instead of just PTSD. The chance of developing complex PTSD is more pronounced if the trauma or abuse is recurrent or chronic, is perpetrated by primary caregivers and if it occurs at a developmentally vulnerable age such as early childhood or adolescence, which are critical periods for brain development.

Any sort of threat or danger causes the brain stem to react and activate the fight, flight or freeze response. This causes an increased heart rate, breathing rate and muscle tension. The neocortex becomes less active or shuts down to provide the faster reaction via the amygdala, part of the cerebrum primarily responsible for the processing of emotions. After the danger has passed, the normal response would be for the thinking part of the brain to then rejoin the action in regulating responses, planning, problem solving and allowing arousal levels to return to baseline. But for those who had traumatic childhoods and developed complex PTSD, the amygdala remains oversensitive. As a result, memories do not get fully processed and they remain stuck in the feeling compartment of memory, while the elevated levels of cortisol make learning more difficult as well as they block memories from forming. That being so, traumatic events are re-experienced as opposed to being remembered when the amygdala is activated in a similar manner. It is one of the most torturous and terrifying experiences someone can undergo because it feels like you'd drop dead at that very spot whether you withdraw or fight through it.

It is the aftermath of being subjected to terrifying stress in the long term that we have to deal with. Because timewise it is so far removed from the cause, cPTSD is misdiagnosed devastatingly frequently. I have read the experience of one person who came back from war, and yet their PTSD had nothing to do with that, it was about childhood abuse.

The common, everyday conceptualisation of PTSD in people's minds equates to reliving traumatic moments from your past in the form of flashbacks and memories, detailed but frantic images and associated experience of the trauma, while displaying clearly distressed behaviour. I found it quite surprising when even a high-ranking social care professional referred to my experience of high functioning PTSD as 'invoking unpleasant memories' when that was not what happened at all. Thinking of it as if the traumatic abuse event was happening in the present is also a very narrow-minded interpretation of the syndrome by someone who obviously has no experience of it as it is more than just a memory, it's the reliving of the feeling associated with it, usually a completely helpless terror that is traumatic in itself. The moment isn't usually outwardly noticeable, though the person might get easily startled by some sounds or sudden movement. At this point, stuck in this state, we only have the anxiety, the despair, the flashbacks and the nightmares struggling to unshackle us from that prison the narcissist built for us and that we still live in. The sufferer would like to let go of their past and never think of it again, only the past is not willing to let go of them.

Coming from the point of view that everybody is potentially a possible cause of getting hurt, PTSD frequently involves being in a room and knowing where every single person is, what every person's disposition and energy is, who to stay away from and where all the exits are. This constant state of alert makes it very hard to go anywhere or enjoy doing anything. People feel like this because there 'are some things people should never go through, see, or experience. There are some things that the human spirit just cannot handle or take in. Some things happen to people that are just too much for the soul to process. Those things cause severe trauma. Trauma changes your mind, your body and your spirit. You feel different. Like something took over you and you are no longer you anymore. It feels like a soul rape. You feel permanently shaken. Frozen in time and you don't know how to get out. That is what it is like to experience the kind of severe abuse and trauma people go through at the hands of a sociopath narcissist.' – Maria Consiglio.

Symptoms of both forms of the disorder pan over a wide array of problems and range from physical, psychological and maladaptive coping strategies that include nightmares, intrusive reruns of events accompanied by poor memory in other aspects, panic attacks, states of hyperarousal such as impatience, rage, anxiety and invasive thoughts, hyper-alertness, an amplified startle response, states of hypo-arousal such as feeling paralysed or cut off, feeling flat or empty, emotional dysregulation, negative self-concepts, relationship problems, substance abuse, self-harm or suicidal thoughts, mistrust, insomnia, poor judgement calls, being startled easily, impatience, hypervigilance, mood swings, poor concentration, the feeling of hopelessness over ever being able to feel any less miserable, a disinterest in daily events, a tendency to self-isolate. They may exhibit reckless and risky behaviours to escape their terrifying moments.

Lamentably, memory loss is a problem that is widely overlooked in mental illnesses. Memory problems don't just refer to blocking out traumatic events, but also encompass a person's ability to perform a good job, given that they forget words or their meaning for example, they forget target objectives and other events that would have had a determining factor in their relationships, their own coping strategies and effective communication methods at work, they forget taking their medication or can become confused due to some missing information. They may even possess a fractured identity as a result of having forgotten or repressed life-changing experiences.

Other complex PTSD symptoms include being certain we would never fit in or that no one can understand us, derealisation, intense and rapidly changing emotions, depersonalisation, difficulties with developing and maintaining relationships, avoiding friends and family because of feeling inherently defective or crippled, unexplained pains, headaches, migraines, sleep disturbances, dizziness, eating disorders, problems with concentration and sensory processing, addiction problems, difficulties controlling or expressing emotions. A state of hypervigilance or hypo*-arousal can also occur, characterised by emotional numbness, drowsiness, detachment, an inability to feel pain or to respond and a blank mind with the inability to think right down to temporary loss of consciousness. Some sufferers believe that they are completely different from other people and find it hard to explain it to others, but sometimes their sense of identity is not easy to understand even for themselves.

PTSD sufferers find it difficult to trust others while at the same time experiencing a fear of abandonment. Some experience hallucinations, with self-harming, suicidal thoughts. Self-harm is usually thought about as cutting, but it isn't only that. It's putting oneself in harmful situations such as getting into relationships with abusive people, negative self-talk, neglecting illnesses or personal hygiene, self-isolation, sabotaging relationships and jobs. Empathy without boundaries is also self-destructive.

Not to mention that each reliving of events can be traumatising in itself, which is why some sufferers protect themselves with detachment, which, however, can result in an inability to enjoy life or feel love. They simply operate on autopilot throughout life.

Dealing with these problems is incredibly hard and also takes an immense time away from valuable time others have at their disposal for studying, developing themselves, their relationships and careers. Another cumbersome complication is that past trauma can make it seem like the world around us is never safe. Our reactions to this feeling will then come across as crazy or at least exaggerated to other people with a more normal upbringing because they don't see the same dangers lurking everywhere. The PTSD sufferer might retreat over and over, but given patience, they will employ great effort or energy to try over and over to engage with the world on healthier terms till they are no longer triggered as much by their environment that they have to stay away or hidden. They might take longer to realise that some people are indeed safe, but eventually, they will start feeling safer. You can't just logically decide you're going to feel safe when your body has been bracing against impending danger for many years, so a sense of safety within has to be cultivated first.

Survivors may also re-experience their trauma through images, emotions, memories and in other ways, like the traditionally thought-of flashbacks. As expected, re-experiencing those scarring moments and hours can be immensely upsetting and could also trigger uncomfortable emotions such as dread, exasperation or grief, emotional distress and worrying thoughts and feelings strongly or loosely relating to the trauma or bodily responses, referring to a wide array of physical and mental manifestations from being bad-tempered, easily startled or hostile, to concentration or sleeping problems, shaking, headaches or heart palpitations.

The person might be aware of their location, activity, people or sensation-based triggers, certain noises for example, and be very keen on actively avoiding the harrowing reminders, or they may try to repress the intolerable thoughts and emotions using drugs or alcohol or other addictive, distracting activities, leading to a loss of interest in normal life, isolation and detachment from loved ones in a state of generalised anxiety. To stay away from triggers, they might need to avoid certain places, sounds, tastes or songs that remind them of their abuser or the abuse. They might have severe anxiety even in expectation of having to revisit those events.

A trigger can be anything at all, so it is hard to judge when a PTSD sufferer will react. It is one of the reasons why we should be considerate and avoid negative interactions, you never know what a person went through. PTSD is like being overcome with anxiety and panic because it feels like someone is about to harm us, but we don't know who or where they will come from. The brain is convinced that something terrible is about to happen, so it is looking for a reason, but it can't find it so it just keeps alerting all systems that danger is everywhere.

Typically, they will not want to talk about the trauma to avoid the negative feelings, but at the same time, stuck in their terror and a state of hyperarousal, they are also unable to enjoy positive moments, resulting in further dissatisfaction with life and oneself.

Some may have, in fact, lost the actual memories related to the trauma, but they still feel on edge all the time and react negatively to events and circumstances associated with the trauma. People with PTSD often suffer from other related conditions as well, such as depression, an eating disorder, overthinking, borderline personality disorder, or chronic pain. Physical symptoms can include but are not limited to headaches, light-headedness, tiredness, sweating, shaking, restless leg syndrome, nausea and vomiting.

Things that can make the anxiety worse include the obvious – caffeine, alcohol, lack of sleep, and also dehydration and not setting boundaries, overextending ourselves to please others, a very likely cause with those abused during childhood. This is what the onlooker tends to not understand, that an attack cannot be halted by being told not to worry and explaining why these things we fear won't happen. The anxiety is caused by the things that did happen already, there's no changing that. It is not really about the present or the future, it is about what we remember and what effects it has on us. PTSD can make you feel like you're about to die at any moment. Not that you might but that you will. So those of us with cPTSD are real warriors, even if we don't want to be. What we went through altered our brain and put us into survival mode. Most people wouldn't be able to endure the amount of anxiety and distress we undergo every day. But here we are, living and enjoying life notwithstanding and in defiance.

However, I admit that living in this terror takes much energy and resolve. To facilitate functioning, trauma 'survivors often need as much information about a current situation as possible. This may seem intense to others, but we've lived with so much uncertainty around areas that were out of our control that having facts about areas we can control helps us feel safe.' – Nate Postlethwait.

There are some techniques that can be used to cope with triggered traumatic memories too. One is using grounding exercises akin to meditation, bringing oneself back into the present with the help of getting in touch with the senses, breathing strategies, relaxation, distraction, mindfulness, trigger awareness, sleep hygiene. Understanding anger and the neurobiology of trauma can also be helpful in giving the victim a sense of power. A change of scenery might help too, going outside, breathing fresh air, having a warm bath. Exercise might help with releasing endorphins and self-care always makes me feel better. There are more targeted ways to manage the disorder yet, such as trauma-focused cognitive behavioural therapy, taking medication, psychoanalysis, Gestalt therapy, family systems therapy, transactional analysis therapy, rational emotive therapy and eye movement desensitisation and reprocessing. The latter involves recalling the traumatic event while making rhythmic eye movements similar to the eye movements we make while we sleep and are processing memories. This helps the brain process the traumatic experiences and reduce their emotional content so that rather than reliving the experience, the experience becomes a memory and thus the distressing symptoms associated with the traumatic event are minimised.

If not treated, these anxious states, and the overthinking, can in turn cause physical problems such as an increased heart rate, nausea, high blood pressure, sickness, chest pains resembling heart attacks, stomach pains, shaking, fatigue, headaches and muscle tension, which is unfortunately underemphasised by the medical profession.

There are different types of fatigue as well, such as helper fatigue when we are compelled to pour all our efforts and energies into others and have none left for ourself, depression fatigue from fighting off and carrying the weight of negative intrusive thoughts, future fatigue involving spending so much time working towards a future goal that current needs are neglected, anxiety fatigue from constantly being in fight, flight or freeze mode and never being able to let our guards down, compassion fatigue from being overwhelmed by the emotions of others, with or without additional sensory overload. Anxiety disorders should be taken more seriously for their effect on the body if nothing else. They cause tiredness, for one, all those adrenal crashes. It is exhausting being on edge all the time and doing anything remotely social will cost more energy. People with anxiety are not tired for no reason, they are tired because they have an illness that makes them tired and we all know we can't exactly be our best selves when we're alarmed, exhausted, intoxicated or feeling intimidated. The real self is staying buried somewhere while we're under extreme pressure or stress, which can be most of the time in our case. That real self is worthy of return and liberation.

So if doctors are not understanding, at least we should be more so ourselves when exhausted due to our disorders, for not having the energy or the time to catch up with others.

Having a highly unsympathetic, physically and emotionally abusive, unapproving, controlling, invasive parent can also manifest as negative self-talk, having weak boundaries, rebellious behaviour and self-sabotage: narcissistic abuse syndrome.

7 Narcissistic (Victim) Abuse Syndrome

Thankfully, psychological professions recognise narcissistic (victim) abuse syndrome nowadays. This condition is said to be characterised by a cluster of dysfunctional symptoms such as emotional dysregulation, weight fluctuations, constantly thinking about the abuser, how to appease them and what they have experienced due to the abuser, chronic pain, a low self-esteem and feelings of shame, disgust with oneself and a strong sense of humiliation that compromises their ability to make decisions to the extent of acting inferior or helpless, PTSD, self-harm, panic and anxiety states, depression, sometimes to the point of suicidal thoughts, somatisations and having no confidence, manifesting in not looking people straight in the eyes, being too scared to try new things, addictions, talking or walking fast all the time. Some targets develop Stockholm syndrome and want to support, protect and continue to love the abuser regardless of what they have done.

Either way, those suffering from narcissistic abuse syndrome are ready to blame themselves and take responsibility for happenings not in their control as a learnt behaviour and survival mechanism while living in close quarters with the narcissist. It could all be boiled down to a typical saying of these individuals: 'I'm not good enough'. In their minds, they replicate hurtful, harmful words and sentences alike to those that were spoken to them. This is the result of long-standing abuse. The sense of terror might never stop, not without it being addressed.

While I've already addressed most of these afflictions, somatisations are also worthy of note. The abused individuals often go to the doctor's with a variety of decidedly physical and sometimes severely debilitating symptoms, but their medical investigations tend to lead nowhere, pointing to a psychosomatic illness instead, a result of childhood narcissistic abuse which has never been dealt with. These illnesses often mimic various symptoms of panic states that randomly reoccur when the unconscious is trying to get past repressed trauma and kick itself into appropriate function, raising cortisol and adrenaline levels and exhausting emotional and physical reserves the same way as if we were still experiencing the traumatic events. Oftentimes there are physical symptoms too, clearly the effect of complex trauma like sleeping or eating difficulties, irritability, hypervigilance, flashbacks, hopelessness, avoidant behaviour, loss of interest, detachment, descriptive nightmares, self-harming, thoughts of suicide, and the resulting further emotional strain. Only just having some of these can stop victims reaching their potential in their professional and personal life. It is in this way that their sense of a limited future due to their perceived worthlessness becomes a self-fulfilling prophecy. The reason isn't being lazy, or anything that is the victim's fault. Everyone only has a certain amount of energy and the trauma victim is using all of it just to survive the aftereffects. I hate that question everyone asks at work every Monday: what did you do on the weekend? Well, as opposed to you, who went canoeing, mountaineering and to countless parties, I spent all my energy trying to survive. It is an unseen disability not acknowledged often enough. And that means not just missing out on fun but using the time to achieve something, to advance in life as well.

Some victims can end up with phobias relating to past traumatic moments, such as holidays, celebratory events, going to certain places, avoiding some people, topics – answering the phone, in my case. A common coping mechanism with these problems is thought censoring and avoidance. Personally, I have a mantra, a sentence I replace troubling, invasive thoughts with. It is not a pleasant experience, but it feels better than reliving the trauma. One of the things I avoid is looking at myself in the mirror, pictures, wherever. This is not because I find so much fault with myself or my appearance, but because my appearance reminds me of my own mother due to strong genetic influence. I have no intention of seeing my 'mother' looking back at me. Many people whose abusers were genetically related to them experience this problem.

Not working through childhood trauma can also manifest as trying to fix others, codependency, living on high alert, a need to prove oneself, ignoring our own needs for the sake of pleasing people as a result of always needing external validation and being afraid of rejection. Not to mention that disappointing the abuser proved to be dangerous, so it would (semi)logically follow that making others happy and content at all costs and at all times is the exclusive chance to secure our safety. For the same reasons, the adult narc victim might tolerate continuing abusive behaviour and also attract a narcissistic partner this way.

The Correlation Between Hypersensitivity and Narcissistic Abuse

As previously seen, the plethora of afflictions developed as a result of the chronic stress of narcissistic abuse leads to added difficulties of being able to deal with life's everyday challenges even outside the narcissistic relationship. It can be argued that the abused become more sensitive, less resilient to further trauma given their shredded nervous system and self-belief. Any stress will affect us more, leading to a feeling of not being able to cope with life, thus suicidal thoughts or an anger with oneself for being 'weak'.

And here comes the controversy because at some point, people will accuse you of being too sensitive, overdramatic, of taking a comment too seriously or personally, of reactions not equivalent to the cause. If you're a woman, you will probably be labelled hysterical at some point, due to a cultural bias. If you're a man, don't you dare express emotion for similar institutionalised reasons. Your abuser will most likely accuse you of being too sensitive as well, and by this time, compared to a healthy individual growing up in conditions indicative to thriving, you possibly are.

But calling someone sensitive as they are being disrespected in the first place is one of the highest forms of abuse. Being accused of being too sensitive and touchy hurts as well. What is important to remember here is how you got there. You can't put yourself down for being too sensitive, especially by your abuser, if they put you in that position so they could feel superior. It is all a play to them so your anger with your abuser remains well-founded. We need to also remember that being called out on being too sensitive is also part of gaslighting and a tactic of discrediting, so it is further abuse, a neglect of your feelings, no matter the circumstances. Your abuser has hurt you again, they are blaming you for it again and they are projecting their own delusions on you again, and then they will make fun of you for not being able to take it. It is basically like saying toughen up so I can get away with hurting you more! A mentally abused individual might not only become hypersensitive, but will also have trouble letting others in, might be saying sorry too many times and break down in tears even at the smallest conflicts, and this will only exacerbate their belief that they're not good enough. People don't realise how much the smallest little things they say hurt us. Or they might think we'll forget; they have no idea that the sensitive ones keep these things in their minds forever.

Brain scans prove an intensified measure of amygdala fear response the longer the eye contact in autistics, while it tends to be lower in neurotypicals, so they are actually hardwired to experience eye contact a lot less intensely. Neurotypicals do not get as unsettled by eye contact so they do not have to avoid it like us.

If you did become a highly sensitive empath and your nervous system has been rewired as a result of your complex trauma, then acknowledging and working through your abusive background is all the more important for the chance of recovery. But being sensitive doesn't mean you are a lower class of individual, on the contrary! Forged from trauma, the sensitive people

I have met are the most wonderful, caring and sincere individuals because they don't want to ever harm another, they don't want to see anyone suffer similar to how they've suffered. 'They live with guilt and constant pain over unresolved situations and misunderstandings. They are tortured souls that are not able to live with hatred or being hated. This type of person [...], despite the tragedy of what they have to go through in life, they remain the most compassionate people worth knowing and the ones that often become activists for the broken-hearted, forgotten and the misunderstood. They are angels with broken wings that only fly when loved.' – Shannon L. Alder, *Characteristics of A Highly Sensitive Person*. There are the people who usually get labelled 'too good for this world' or 'not for this world' and it is pretty close to the truth because it feels like being damaged like no one understands, not unless they've been through a similar hell themselves.

But the existence of trauma itself isn't the proof of this fragility. The trauma is the consequence of such unbearable and devastating events that the brain and, therefore, the body has to change to be able to survive the situation. Given its decidedly physical base, it isn't possible to simply change with a positive outlook. Not that we are capable of a positive outlook at this point. The brain and the body have been in a state of imminent danger for decades so it isn't easy just to convince them that it is ultimately safe out there. At the very least, it takes time, spent in a state of a relative sense of safety and security, and then the mind and body will be able to start countermanding the ramifications of continuous childhood abuse.

Sensitive people are highly attuned to the world around them. They are a rare breed of people who go all in. They keep their word. They give it their all. They put themselves last for those they care about. These individuals rarely receive the same compassion and effort in return, yet they continue to give freely. They cry a lot and it doesn't even have to be about themselves. A string of a melody, a movie theme, another crying person, being reminded that someone suffered and the tears flow freely, hard to stop. And I haven't even mentioned the moments when someone said a good word to us and we cry because there's finally proof of goodness in the world. Crying for ourselves is usually done in private, how we learnt to do it in childhood, in bed while you stuff a pillow into your mouth so you can't be heard. There will be no need of deliberate thinking of the event, malicious words will play back over and over in our heads. Indian mystic Osho talks about people whose 'eyes are open to a world that is in need of repair. They literally have an increased ability to feel the emotions of people around them'[46].

The highly sensitive empath cannot stand lies and pretence and is a fairly good judge of character. Their triggers are, amongst other things: inauthenticity, banal chitchat, crowds, mess, being harried, disagreements and loud noises, drama, not having time to process what happened, intrusive or narcissistic behaviour and powerful scents such as perfume or flowers. They feel the injustice done to them deeply, with its justified anger, but being who they are, they would never intentionally harm another so they turn that rage inward. Some other characteristics of the empath are: finding themselves easily overwhelmed, crying or literally sobbing without being able to control it when reading or watching something sad or seeing another person cry or about to cry, quick highs and lows between fluctuating feelings without any real cause, knowing in advance when something is going to happen. Other signs characteristic of an empath are fine-tuned intuition, being sensitive to other people's and their own feelings, disliking big gatherings of people, getting quickly overstimulated, having trouble setting boundaries.

A note of caution here: some empaths coming from a narcissistic household have been brainwashed to think that their needs have to take a backseat to other's needs so they will voluntarily take the blame for another person's unhappiness. Thus, they take on the role of comforter or some knight in shining armour, with the responsibilities that come from these roles, holding themselves back forever from realising their own potential and achieving their own happiness. 'Both narcissists and empaths suffered from early childhood trauma. The empaths took that pain and became more compassionate, not wanting others to suffer the same fate they did. while the narcissists got angry and decided to take their anger out on the world, vowing to put themselves first. Empaths were strong enough not to let the trauma destroy their goodness, while narcissists were weak and let the trauma overcome them.' – Maria Consiglio.

The people-pleasing tendencies of the empath usually initially originate from the need for self-preservation. Trying to avoid the toxic parent's criticisms, judiciousness and their fault-finding at all costs, the child becomes an expert at anticipating their words and needs, an ability that is transferable to use with other people as well. Empathic people hold their morals high and approach everyone with mindfulness and prudence. Ironically, people-pleasing for the sake of being accepted usually leads to the opposite outcome because a sense of belonging only arises when we feel seen and accepted for who we really are.

Unfortunately, the mechanism can then become a vicious circle of over-giving, overachieving and putting too much emphasis at every detail in every situation till it becomes overbearing and too much to handle for one person. They may also try to consciously avoid being like their narcent so they will go out of their way to be accommodating with people even more. They might also excuse the narcissist for their mental health and childhood. Empaths then blame themselves and may attract another narcissist who notices this forgiving trait of theirs.

If the abusive background is not being acknowledged and dealt with, the victim will often end up using self-harm, self-hating, obsessive-compulsive perfectionism, or some form of addiction from alcohol and sex to exercise and risk-taking, as a self-regulator. My escape to my dissociative fantasy life qualifies, I think, as I have wasted so much time hiding in this world, running away from the real one. I do a lot less of that now that I gave myself permission to remember and sort through my past and dare to live in my present.

So if you are one of these sensitive people, don't despair. It is well known that the loveliest humans are those who have known loss and heartache and have come out at the other end, not stronger than ever, but willing to use their light to guide others out of their darkness too. It is beautiful. It means to be aware of all the suffering and extinguish it with your loving heart.

I do not believe the saying 'what doesn't kill you, makes you stronger'. It doesn't. Poet J. Raymond says it beautifully: 'things that didn't kill me, came so close that they're still damaging. They didn't make me better. Some things made me worse. And can't that be okay too? Can't some things just break you? This whole fucking world wants you to believe that admitting defeat makes you weak. For God's sake, bleed. And bleed openly. There can be pride in vulnerability. Honesty is maturity. And really, it's the things that did kill me, that made me.'

And I am thankful for who I am.

8 The Physical Impact of Childhood Trauma on the Body

As we all know, stress on its own has dreadful effects on health. Many complain of being mentally and emotionally weary to start with. However, growing up with a narcissistic parent puts the body in hypervigilance mode for decades, so it is natural that that should have consequences. Bradley Dearman (Dip A.Hyp Psych) has published articles about the physical effects of trauma, amongst which are changes in brain architecture[20], such as shrinkage in the prefrontal cortex, responsible for the planning of complex cognitive behaviour, the expression of our personalities, decision making and moderating social behaviour, and the corpus callosum, essential for physical coordination.

A surge in the stress hormone glucocorticoid destroys cells in the hippocampus that take part in the formation of new memories associated with learning. A major impact, then, on learning! Chronic stress can also wear you down and lead to depression. Long-term stress weakens the immune system, leaving us more vulnerable to infections and inflammations. The nervous system doesn't care if we're overreacting. Stress hormones still tighten blood vessels and cause the liver to release extra glucose into the bloodstream, which over time puts people at risk for type 2 diabetes.

The amygdala, however, playing a central part in the processing of emotions, becomes enlarged and more reactive. This part, deep in the brain, is also behind survival-related threat recognition and attaching emotions to memories. After trauma, the amygdala can get stuck in a process where it considers everything a threat. Traumatic memories in the amygdala generate cytokines, chemical messengers that elevate inflammation in almost every part of the body. If the traumatic memories keep raising the alarm for years, they cause too much inflammation for too long and the body can become desensitised to the controlling effects of cortisol. Recurrent stress can also contribute to inflammation in the circulatory system, notably in the coronary arteries, one way that is thought to connect stress to a heart attack[24]. And because abuse reduces cortisol, severe inflammation of the respiratory tract can also occur. This is how low cortisol links abuse to asthma, as researchers at the Brigham and Women's Hospital in Boston revealed[25]. Such unchecked, cortisol-related inflammation is also the cause of many other diseases: arthritis, diabetes, multiple sclerosis, Crohn's disease, dermatitis, ulcerative colitis, neurodegenerative disorders like dementia and Parkinson's, just to name a few! Either way, chances of happiness through quality of life are limited by this inflammation.

Through this cortisol and inflammation link, chronic stress has also been demonstrated to account for disease outcomes, including of several types of cancers[26]. There is also a correlation with tumour growth, progression and metastasis[27].

Brain inflammation can often be found as a consequence of complex post-traumatic stress disorder. PTSD changes the brain structurally in a way that interferes with nerve impulses, immunity and the vascularisation in the brain.

Some neural oscillations, also known as brainwaves, rhythmic or repetitive patterns of neural activity in the central nervous system, can travel in the wrong part of the brain as a result of trauma, leading to anxiety, an inability to focus, sometimes seizures. Numerous neural pathways would be wired on the basis of faulty, unnatural thought patterns and practices, both conscious and unconscious, that we will need to unlearn[19]. Due to dopamine transmitters and receptors not being properly developed or becoming damaged, the individual will become prone to addiction. Lack of dopamine receptors also decreases motivation and focus and causes tiredness.

Their low serotonin reception causes depression. Prolonged high cortisol and ghrelin (commonly known as the the hunger hormone) levels create pronounced reactivity to stress. The intestines and the kidneys become less able to eliminate toxins. There is long-term damage to cells through shortening telomeres, the caps at the end of each strand of DNA that protect our chromosomes, which prematurely ages and reduces the reproduction of cells and can give rise to cancer. The thyroid gland suffers in particular and there has been blunted endocrine* and cardiovascular reactivity reported in young, healthy women with a history of childhood adversity[22].

A continuous elevation of stress hormones tampers with the body's means to self-regulate. The sympathetic nervous system, typically involved in responses that prepare the body for fight or flight, stays highly activated, which leads to depleted reserves in the body's many components, most markedly in the adrenal glands, which are endocrine glands that produce a variety of hormones.

This makes people alternate between highs and lows. The excess cortisol released curbs functions that would be nonessential or detrimental in a fight or flight situation. It alters immune system responses and suppresses the digestive system, the reproductive system and growth processes. Some other ways the emotional pain of unhealed trauma can show up in the body are, for example, a weak immune system, osteoporosis, fluid retention and digestive issues, high blood pressure, back and neck pain and tightness, bruising easily, high blood sugar, heart failure and fibromyalgia. As we've seen, chronic illness is rife with trauma sufferers, along with the accompanying chronic fatigue. It is another concept that is hard to understand for the average 'normal' person when we're trying to tell someone of our afflictions. They rarely understand chronic illness or tiredness either. They think it can be sorted with coffee or exercise! The sheer impossibility of them understanding is sometimes striking and laughable at the same time. They have no clue, they are unable to comprehend.

Another study by the Ohio State University[23] also demonstrates that the emotional pains endured in childhood can lead to weakened immune systems later in life. 'What happens in childhood really matters when it comes to your immune response in the latter part of your life,' explained Janice Kiecolt-Glaser, professor of psychology and psychiatry. The study showed that for some children living through significant abuse, the long-term consequence might be a life shorter by seven to fifteen years. Shockingly, even some genes turn off in adaptation to the perceived dangerous environment, with an effect that can last for generations!

Another effect that tends to happen as a side effect of abuse, trauma and the resulting depression, is the brain getting accustomed to the intense stimuli experienced during and closely after the abuse and seeking out well-known emotions and situations even when in happier circumstances. This is also a normal reaction. Given that the brain almost exclusively only experienced negative stimuli, it has no precedence on how to respond to good events. We've all been there too. Make no mistake, it's a biological reaction, it is not because you deserve to be punished. So not karma. And that is regardless that I don't believe in unprovable fairytales and theories, so I don't believe in karma either.

Other observed effects of childhood trauma include:

an impaired readiness to learn,
problem-solving difficulties,
language delays,
problems with concentration,
poor academic achievement,
a smaller brain size,
eating disorders,
poor self-regulation,
social withdrawal,
aggression,
poor impulse control,
a tendency for risk-taking,
adolescent pregnancy,
illegal activities,
acting out sexually,
drug and alcohol misuse,
difficulties controlling emotions,

trouble recognising emotions,
a feeling of helplessness,
a lack of self-efficacy,
suicidality,
relationship and attachment disorders,
poor understanding of social interactions,
difficulties forming relationships with peers,
problems in romantic relationships,
intergenerational cycles of abuse,
neglect.

The most disturbing issue, however is that most graduates of the medical profession do not take these findings into consideration. I've never heard of a doctor asking about childhood trauma when taking down medical history and unfortunately even therapists tend to ignore the physical manifestations of abuse. I would very much like to topple down this wall of mindless childhood trauma ignorance. Childhood trauma has such a substantial effect on our continued physical health and the longer these people in charge of our well-being refuse to address it, the worse the effects become on us. Deeper investigations would be necessary to pinpoint and address the undiscovered processes that trigger the physical imbalances, not people being completely dismissed because the physician is unable to see anything wrong, and then discredits the patient. I had been called a hypochondriac for the years leading up to my cancer diagnosis. Healers and psychologists should be admitting to not having much success with trauma survivors, not improving their lives enough. Many survivors fall back to self-harming behaviours and addictions because these professionals don't seem to appreciate the repercussions of childhood emotional abuse properly. Wouldn't it be their responsibility to do everything they can to understand?

Therefore, I am calling out to everyone to educate their care team on this matter and if they are not responsive, then a change of medical team is recommended. Emotional abuse and its consequences have been ignored long enough. The answer is with cognitive therapy, a way to rewire our brains. Even the subconscious mind can be reprogrammed!

To summarise the above, our nervous system is misfiring so we need coping skills, aids and solutions, not judgement!

Shaking

A pretty obvious physical symptom I tend to suffer from is shaking, especially the hands, sometimes worse, sometimes better. It is worse when I'm tired, have had some caffeine or something stressful is going on, and more pronounced in the mornings. While I do drop or spill things as a result, that doesn't bother me as much as people noticing at the most inappropriate times and assuming it is due to drug use. It can be irritating, inconvenient, humiliating and it affects my motor function and handwriting. It is culturally frowned upon.

Trembling knees and shaking of all or any of the body are, however, common symptoms of anxiety disorders[71] such as generalized anxiety, social anxiety, panic disorder and others, with or without being accompanied by other indicative symptoms. It is most likely to affect the hands.

A tremor is when the muscles contract rhythmically and unintentionally. Sometimes the shaking or trembling isn't outwardly noticeable, but the individual feels like their chest, stomach, vocal cords or the entire body is vibrating inside or as if they were on edge for no particular reason. The voice can shake too. The shaking can be accompanied by other physical symptoms such as hyperventilating, heart palpitations[73], chest pains[74], dizziness[75], jelly legs or muscle weakness [76], pins and needles, a burning sensation in the hands, numbness[77], feeling weak[78], asthmatic symptoms[79], excessive yawning[80], derealisation*[81], brain zaps*[82], chronic pains[83] and fatigue[84], body jolts[85], muscle tension[86], lump in throat[87]. Hand shaking can also be exacerbated by genetic predisposition and a plethora of different illnesses and circumstances such as low blood sugar, neurological disorders, hyperventilation, thyroid problems or physical exhaustion.

Some people will then start to worry about these sensations, which can make the symptoms worse.

These symptoms are due to the body being in a constant state of being half-ready for the fight or flight response[72] and it can take a while for the body to recover from such hyperstimulation. The shaking makes it possible for the body to release built-up stress hormones produced during the anxiety attack so it is actually a good sign!

With it being an anxiety-related condition, the cluster of symptoms can be relieved through conscious effort by more sleep and other restful and self-care activities, such as massage, yoga, deep and slow breathing, coordination, visualisation, desensitisation and progressive muscle relaxation exercises, and reducing stress in life in general, dialling back a little, taking a break, using herbal oils, having a healthy diet or taking beta-blockers or valerian. Stretching can get rid of extra adrenaline and as such, make people more relaxed. This is why practising yoga regularly can keep the nerves in check.

Working out coping strategies for every situation can relieve a lot of anxiety. Stay hydrated. Exercise helps burn off excess energy, produces endorphins, relaxes and distracts the sufferer. Sometimes exaggerating the shaking makes it stop quicker. As the song says, shake it out. Herbal teas such as chamomile or wild thyme are also recommended. Targeting to stop one body part from shaking at a time has also been helpful for some. Different methods will work for different people.

Some similar conditions are fidgeting and leg or foot tapping or bouncing, which is usually started by excess epinephrine (adrenalin) and cortisol in the body, meaning rushes of energy, which, added up, can affect people at different times, seemingly unrelated to stressful events. If someone is constantly anxious or stressed out, there will be a lot of those in excess. Some people self-soothe this way as well, which makes perfect sense as it releases the pent-up stress hormones.

Stress can also cause the body to drain its stores of magnesium, water or other vital resources or nutrients, which can cause shaking in itself, or make the condition worse.

But, as usual, unless the underlying sources of the person's general state of anxiety is addressed through cognitive behavioural therapy as a preventive strategy, stress relief targeted methods will only work temporarily.

The sooner the better as we have seen how stress affects health. Long-term stress is likely to cause tremors too. A form of solution that has been tried successfully without getting down to the root cause is exposure therapy.

9 The Problem with Authority (Oppositional Defiant Disorder/ Control Aversion)

As you have seen, I have grown up under the thumb of an overly controlling, authoritarian, repressive mother. As such, I have trouble imagining putting myself voluntarily into a situation where I am subordinated in a similar manner. Starting mainly from my teens, I often refused submission to teachers, officials, arbitrary rules and regulations, superiors, laws, elders, guides. I am not an obedient citizen; I literally get a jolt of happiness hormones when I cross rules and I admit that it is only my good driving skills that have saved me from consequences of my many infractions, especially during my younger years. Until recently, I was practically unable to hold down a job because I could not imagine being controlled by an authority figure and spent most of my working years self-employed because, in that case, you have clients and not bosses.

Part of this reaction comes from a mistrust of people that has been proven and justified over and over by my experiences. In addition to the adults who disappointed me while I was growing up, I have encountered many other authority figures or who had either wronged me or who were obviously wrong about something, such as their methods or morals – lecturers, superiors, civil servants, doctors, who act like gods with their ultimate say-so for example.

After all this, I wonder how anyone puts their trust in authority? It makes no sense to me. My default is to think about any written or unwritten rule I encounter and judge for myself whether it can be reasonably applied to the situation or enhanced in some way. Quite often, rules that suit the majority do not prove applicable to a certain type of person, one the rule-makers did not think of when establishing their rule book. How many times have we seen the subordinate taken advantage of? Blame being shifted to them? The authority figure taking credit or at least monetary gains for their subordinate's work? Authority does not have a good track record in history, there is too much abuse of power, classist bias, religious fanaticism and racial prejudice governing their actions and law-making systems. What is good for them, what makes sense for them, might not be good for me or other strata of the population, which they either purposefully ignore or are ignorant of. If I was to trust an authority figure or any person in particular, they would have had to prove that they were honest, genuine, considerate and therefore worthy of my trust. Even then, I will take it into account that individual decisions can be a result of some mistake on occasion. If no one challenged authority, we would still be living in caves, or the very least have slaves and no rights for women. How do you accept authority in a capitalist system that is built on exploiting you?

Authorities do not like being challenged of course. It is not really surprising then that anti-authoritarians are often diagnosed as mentally ill[21]. Russell Barkley, a mainstream key authority on ADHD, claims that people suffering from the disease have shortfalls in 'rule-governed behaviour' and are less bothered with consequences. Those with oppositional defiant disorder are also said to have those same shortfalls. Therefore, it is pretty typical for young people to have the dual diagnosis of ADHD and ODD. Resistance to authority is added to the files of many patients with various other illnesses as well, from schizophrenia to a more prevalent generalised anxiety disorder. To make matters worse, some professionals would then label the sufferer 'noncompliant with treatment', increasing the seriousness of their diagnosis and the doses of their medications. This in turn would enrage the patient further as an authority figure, a doctor, failed them like they'd expected. If they are not institutionalised, then an anti-authoritarian will be criminalised and certainly marginalised. It is again, a no-win situation, not one I had intentionally put myself in.

There is a hefty positive side of being anti-authoritarian and that is that I don't believe anyone or anything I'm told without double-checking or fact-checking first. Falling into a cult? That's not likely to be me. Government announcement? Not until I see the science behind it. Doctor's wisdom? Should find many similar accounts elsewhere. I'm not taking anything at face value and that is a major component of critical thinking.

10 Grief for a Non-Existent Childhood

Sure, I may have some other memories I have not shared here, but for the most part, what I have written here is pretty much all I remember about my childhood. Most of what I haven't shared are unrelated memories, of school, of friends, of other places and family members. So my recollection of my early years is pretty sketchy to be honest, especially of things that happened before I was eleven or twelve, and I can pretty much say that I am completely missing years between six to about nine or ten. This was the time after my father left and before my brother came back to live with us for a few years after his university studies, so the part where my mother was a single parent with nobody looking in on us, where she could do exactly what she liked with me. Coincidence I'm missing these years? I don't think so. What happened during these years? I was the only one around she could take her anger out on, so I was practically at the bottom of everything that has ever gone wrong in her life. I don't even dare to think of it.

But, to my relief, I have been told that this lack of recollection is often due to repression of unpleasant memories, a way that our brains are protecting us from these detrimental moments to reach our consciousness and cause more havoc in our lives. Sadly, the occurrence is also not unusual for people who grew up in other kinds of toxic, tumultuous or abuse-filled homes or circumstances. This fact nevertheless makes me feel a bit better, lets me know that my lack of memories is normal.

However, not having access to these memories does not protect us from those physical consequences discussed in earlier chapters, or the mental illnesses associated with childhood abuse, such as generalised anxiety or depression.

Tiredness, of course, is a common feature of depression and not surprisingly, because depression means we are fighting with our brains and bodies all the time, trying to make them do all the other things people without depression do. They can also convert into phobias, addictions or violent behaviour that doesn't seem to have an obvious trigger. 'The repression of negative childhood memories contributes to subsequent re-victimisation as one is subconsciously acting out the dynamics they have repressed with the subconscious hope to master the trauma.' – Rev. Sheri Heller, licensed clinical social worker, psychotherapist and certified coach. Some consciously choose to repress feelings, never think about them, use distraction, or even a mantra to substitute them with whenever they occur. Some use outright denial, tell themselves nothing bad happened and force themselves to believe it. Symptoms and behavioural issues still manifest despite this or their wills.

There has been a lot of research into the phenomenon of repression, including that of Jelena Radulovic, professor in bipolar disease in psychiatry and behavioural sciences and pharmacology at the Northwestern University Feinberg School of Medicine, who found that there are a kind of receptors in our brains that identify a stress reaction to an event and then proceed to conceal the particulars of said event and store them somewhere else[28].

The easy way to understand the phenomenon is through phobias. If someone is scared to death of heights or open spaces, dogs or being sick, then it is very likely there could be a repressed memory at play. Personally, I get a fright, not quite a phobia, but a strong reaction nevertheless to people shouting, even in good faith, out on the street or anywhere which I know comes from being terrified of my mother shouting. Now imagine this as an unconscious reaction. A lot of people don't know why they're afraid of certain stimuli. Some find themselves responding anxiously to other sounds, settings, faces, odours, names or surfaces. I can't watch a movie if a character's haircut reminds me of my mother. On the other hand, I love the smell of fresh paint as my father was a painter and decorator in his second job and took me along on some weekends when he worked. So there is a positive connotation to the smell of paint.

Naturally, every symptom previously mentioned can also manifest without the person knowing its cause, from self-hate to reclusiveness. So, as mentioned earlier in the book, abuse victims can suffer from haphephobia, which can be the result of experiencing or witnessing a disturbing event that entailed being touched. Not everyone will remember the event that triggered the phobia, especially if they were very young at the time[29]. A similar situation can occur with fearing showing skin. Unexplained moments of nausea as a result of a certain type of situation indicate repressed trauma as well. Furthermore, as we have seen, actual unexplained illnesses are characteristic of victims of abuse, so finding yourself ill on a regular basis and with a compromised immune system can also be the side effect of repressed traumatic memories.

A pretty big clue is feeling uncomfortable around a specific person or type of person without any reasonable explanation, in which case there is a pretty big chance that that individual or somebody very much like them did something wrong to you as a young child. Having been or felt abandoned can manifest by an expectation that everyone will always leave and you will always have to deal with your problems on your own. Being overly defensive could be an indication that the brain has noticed something familiar about the circumstances and is alerting you to possible danger. According to Priscilla Chin, a culturally-sensitive, psychodynamic and cognitive behavioural therapist, these are "important things to understand and work through in therapy so that what was once painful and traumatising can have less of a hold on you."

Sara Makin, the founder and CEO of Makin Wellness, licensed therapist and humanitarian, a dynamic leader who earned the Empowering Women in Philanthropy Award from *Inspiring Lives* magazine, says that recurrent and frequent self-victimisation is also an indicator of early, repressed memories. 'Being the victim becomes a part of a person's identity, hindering them from moving forward.'

In addition, the act of suppressing traumatising memories can draw on a lot of mental energy that leaves the person lacking the ability to manage the everyday hardships of relationships and work life. Repressed or partially remembered events can then leave the individual wary, disorientated and bewildered by why they act the way they do, which is why it's so important to work through these experiences, to be able to start living a better life and not remain a slave to unconscious instincts.

So however little you remember of this stolen childhood, whatever the remaining symptoms and in spite of the secret it might be and who denies or devalues it, it's important to acknowledge that the trauma is still valid. It doesn't matter that maybe it isn't as bad as some other people's experiences.

And then there's the what could have been. The very notion of not having had a happy childhood hurts as well, that it wasn't given to us. Sure, some of it stems from jealousy, but then again, is having safety and security growing up so much to ask for? It's fair to mourn the non-existent fantasy of having had our needs fulfilled, to have lived a nightmare instead of a dream. It hurts because we can just about glimpse the idea of happiness and the very reason it hurts so much is because we're mourning something that never really existed. The longing to be understood by our parents and family is also normal. But ultimately there's nothing else that can be done but accepting this limitation and working on protecting our peace going forward. There has been way too much paid on the altar of that fantasy already.

The saying is wrong, trauma does not make people stronger; it often doesn't make their skins thick. It still resulted in not having had a happy childhood, not having had a mother to be able to rely on. Mother's Day can be a sad occasion for many who lost their own mothers or a child. To this day, I loathe Mother's Day for personal reasons too, all those messages on social media thanking their mothers for a wonderful start in life. I can't help but feel a little bit jealous, but can you blame me? I will never have a relationship with my mother as these people do, going out together to cafes, shopping, poring over the grandchildren, discussing everyday issues, big and small, my opinion will never matter to her. If I started talking to her more, we would only end up in the same cycles of abuse. I can only hope to be the mother or grandmother in this hypothetical happy scenario, when my own children decide to have some of their own.

It is hard to imagine for some of us, but there are people who don't think about the reasons behind their actions and do not use self-reflection to better themselves, but simply stumble through their lives dependent on what their environment shaped them to be, some due to shock, disbelief and denial, some not. It is still worth looking out for certain symptoms of psychological trauma with these individuals such as confusion, difficulties focusing, having a temper, impatience, mood and anxiety disorders, agitation, undue guilt, delinquency, shame, self-blame, isolation, hopelessness and so on, in order to explain and maybe excuse their actions, even if they themselves do not.

I believe, however, that this toxic shame, having no self-worth, this self-hatred, constantly wondering if something was my fault, also makes some positive changes in the world. For example, when I do something wrong, like accidentally cut someone off on a road, or due to my less-than-usual social experience I think I may have said something in a hurtful way but I can't apologise because the stranger has moved on, then I obsessively try to give back two good random acts, for one 'bad' one, to right the balance, sometimes being caught up in the task all day so that I can complete it. People-pleasers are also very capable and self-sufficient as they had a lot of practice at it!

Of course, everybody reacts differently to trauma and childhood abuse. I have always been proud of how much I know myself, realisations of the reasons behind my characteristics and actions. Going to a more profound level is still an ongoing process and it takes a lot of work. There is a plethora of other symptoms and syndromes not yet discussed here such as anger outbursts, bullying, dissociation, being a workaholic, codependent or a perfectionist, difficulties making decisions, making friends or sitting still, and becoming controlling, in some cases a narcissist, spiralling the generational trauma further. Every wrong reaction is connected to earlier experiences, conditioning any later action. I particularly dislike people being called lazy because, in most cases, they aren't at all. They are incapable of action for one reason or another. In the abused individuals' cases, it's usually due to a lack of energy or the time they've spent dealing with the side effects of trauma. They have no more left to give, not even to themselves. It can also be that they are stopped from acting because of the low self-esteem they've acquired in childhood. So can we please stop calling people lazy? They cannot just change their mindset.

11 Depression and Hopelessness

Contemporary research has probed the association of emotional abuse with subsequent depressive symptoms and hopelessness among patients and found high levels of both. And hopelessness pronouncedly mediated the association of emotional abuse with depressive symptoms[56].

Depression affects the way individuals view themselves, others and the world around them, bringing with it emotional and physical manifestations of the problem. It can make you feel like the day is pointless, whatever you do; it can feel like being empty inside. Some of the most common symptoms and indicators of depression are insomnia, low energy levels, hopelessness, sadness, anxiety, lack of appetite, poor concentration levels, suicidal thoughts or actions. Everything is harder with depression. Picking up the phone and speaking to people requires more effort. Getting the motivation to cook or leave the house is harder, exercising is harder, putting in the effort to look nice seems pointless, you don't find things funny. Everything seems like a big, futile, hollow or inane chore. A depressed person might be sleeping a lot and use sedatives to do so as a way to escape from angst, apprehension and other unpleasant emotions. It would feel safer for them that way, the same way it feels safer for the abused individual to just be alone.

As stated in Abramson's hopelessness theory of depression, when something bad happens, most people will pose the question why and tend to give answers on three, dimensional scales:

internal to external
or generated by a personal trait or something within the environment;
and whether the reason is stable or unstable or has a broad or limited scope.

How much a person will become depressed will then depend on how much they attribute to each factor on each scale, which of course will depend on their experiences in the first place. For example, narcissistic child abuse victims are likely to blame themselves and internalise negative events, attributing the cause to personal characteristics. They are told they are useless, and sooner and later they will believe it. What's more, this happens in an environment they can rarely influence.

The most negative inferential style would indeed attribute reasons to global, stable and internal factors. Unfortunately, as a child's brain begins to form causational links, these negative associations become the baseline. These associations are then very hard to undo.

A depressed person is often exhausted as they tend to suffer from nausea, insomnia and wrestle with suicidal thoughts, the side effects of their medication and flashbacks, body image issues and, unfortunately, very often the judgements of others. They are not lazy or weak, however. Just think about how hard it is to fake a smile, how exhausting to do it all day. Feeling misunderstood only adds to the hopelessness and the burden, feeling unlovable. For example, a doctor's visit is not just a doctor's visit for a trauma survivor. It is having to put ourselves in a vulnerable situation, knowing that we will be judged and will be trapped in circumstances not of our choosing. It can be an issue for anyone, never mind those already prone to lack trust in another human being.

Meeting another person will fill us with anxiety and panic for being outside our comfort zones where we have control of what is happening. It is like preparing for a situation where we are most likely going to suffer in one way or another. The anxiety we feel is a reminder that the body and the mind are still stuck in a state where they function as if whatever trauma that happened in the past is still a close threat to our lives today. This is why anxiety can be exhausting and oftentimes goes hand in hand with depression. The body is actually conserving energy to prepare for whatever threat it believes is on its way.

Add having to always analyse ourselves, regulate emotional responses to appear normal and calm the anxiety, the effort put into avoiding nightmares and flashbacks, having to concentrate on being grounded in the present as it doesn't come natural. Like all the time. We have to rest. Being called lazy is an insult at this point. You're not unmotivated, you're struggling with depression. I wish the average person would understand that we don't avoid them because we hate them but because it is the only way we can manage our triggers and the resultant stress. We aren't disengaged from work or uncaring, we are experiencing dissociation. We're not hypersensitive, situations outside our comfort zones trigger the heightening of our emotions. And when we refuse help, it's because of past humiliation when asking for help and having been brainwashed into habits of self-blame.

A stable, global cause given to a negative event is unlikely to change in the victim's mind. They don't think they can change the situation as they have no life experience that tells them otherwise given that they were always powerless to change the circumstances of the abuse. Whatever they do in life then becomes meaningless. Subsequently, this vast hopelessness is more likely to lead to depression, self-harm and suicide. Some sabotage their own relationships or studies because they don't think they can prevail anyway. Internalised, negative self-talk taken on from narcissistic parents' criticism can further pull outcomes down with the upholding of stable, global and internalised causes given to negative events in the person's mind. This is why some people, victims of narcissistic child abuse here, are more likely to find themselves depressed and suicidal after suffering negative life events or environmental stimuli. While being suicidal has some positive side effects, such as not being too bothered when diagnosed with cancer, we can all agree that in general, it is considered an undesirable state. For me, my children saved my life, I need to live for them, smooth out their way to happiness as much as possible and they also made me understand that it is a hard job being a parent.

How much pleasure one can take from an ordinary life at any one time also depends on their resilience. Unfortunately, unresolved trauma reduces resilience as well. But the good news is that it isn't only good parenting that cultivates resilience, but healing from traumas develops resilience as well.

One way of doing this is coming full circle: combatting a common factor in many of the problems abuse victims suffer from – hopelessness. Hopelessness beliefs are not the same as facts. We can filter out each factor we can control one by one, build on them and eliminate automatic hopelessness expectations systematically and, this way, develop probability thinking.

A first step out of hopelessness is realising that we're still here, we haven't given up. If we haven't given up, then we still have the fight within us to reach happiness so all can't be hopeless, can it? You are learning, you are fighting, you are constantly looking for ways to improve yourself and your thinking. What a great big step!

12 Developmental Delay

As we have seen, chronic stress affects the brain, with detrimental effects in particular on memory processing, selective attention, self-control and the ability to turn off the stress response. So it stands to reason that constantly being in a state of high alert hinders children's ability to concentrate, learn and socialise with others. Missing vital moments in their social or academic development then creates even more gaps they can't build on. Instead, they are perpetually trying to keep up in further states of high alert based on the stress of having fallen behind or not understanding what was asked of them. Eventually, the functioning of neural systems becomes set in this way, eternally faulty. 'Toxic stress during this early period can affect developing brain circuits and hormonal systems in a way that leads to poorly controlled stress-responsive systems that will be overly reactive or slow to shut down when faced with threats throughout the lifespan' – Centre on the Developing Child, 2005. It's easy to see how this then affects the child's developmental path. The more risk factors, the more likely the child will have pronounced developmental delays. The victim also develops a belief system detrimental to learning and success based on their caregivers' attitude to them. They may believe they are not worthy of love or that other people can't be trusted in any circumstances. The result is a further burdensome edge given to the stressful circumstances. The child has ample evidence to believe that the world is a dangerous place and therefore can't ever relax and arrive in a psychological state where learning feels right and occurs in a natural way.

So childhood trauma is costly in the long run. Resilience is not a common development amongst victims either. In a longitudinal study of individuals who had experienced abuse and neglect during childhood, only 22% achieved resiliency based on a comprehensive assessment of healthy adult functioning, by the time they reached young adulthood[57].

Of course, in the case of trophy-child parents, as is often the case with narcissists, developmental delay and not performing well in school is simply not an option. The child will be beaten to death before they are allowed to have any less than perfect academic results, sometimes including sports, so they will have to study and persevere despite the obvious difficulties they might be having. There was hell to pay if I wasn't one of the very best in class. Apart from the punishments, I would never hear the end of it.

Other times, victims use learning as a means to escape and thus they perform well for themselves, hoping that their results will propel them into a situation where they do not have to suffer abuse anymore. Others enjoy learning, as while they are occupied, they do not have to think of the abuse and their circumstances.

Having fallen behind in social development however, victims can sometimes display poor social discrimination skills, leading to questionable choices regarding their social interactions as far ahead as early adulthood and beyond. The process of developing adequate emotional regulation and the ability to take the perspective of others might also suffer. Additionally, interpersonal trauma can influence children's reactivity to stress and other emotional situations. Therefore, people who have experienced childhood trauma might feel emotions like being anxious more intensely at the same time as struggling to control their reactions.

Unfortunately, outside a wider diagnosis entailing learning difficulties, social skills deficits are rarely approached in the same manner as we would handle academic or other learning problems. The person is often simply labelled difficult or weird and is shut out from interactions, due to their own deficiency, or by being dismissed. They may cry easily and the average person may find that uncomfortable to deal with. Granted, any behaviour that differs from the norm can be really perplexing, but this is why victims experiencing the behavioural ramifications of trauma are regularly so deeply misunderstood.

Teaching the neurodivergent how to read social cues would be of enormous benefit, but the average person can't even imagine why we don't understand their body language and facial expression. Alas, anyone having difficulty interpreting these cues might miss them and jump to the conclusion that, for instance, the other person harbours negative emotions for them, a self-fulfilling prophecy once their mistake leads to anger, resentment and maybe even aggression in some cases. Or the person might internalise the conflict and withdraw from others, becoming emotionally numb or depressed. Either way, the outcome is commonly lost chances for learning and strained relationships, resulting in another bygone opportunity to learn about identifying the correct social cues, and staying off course and disorientated in what feels like the storms of social interaction.

These patterns then create consequential difficulties in forming and maintaining healthy relationships or, misinterpreting cues, sufferers engage in relationships with emotionally unavailable or even abusive people, if not engaging in codependent relationships, each detrimental to all areas of life.

Additionally, trying to avoid or experiencing the abuse itself makes focusing on education more demanding, tiring, puzzling, out of place as the victims have more weighty things to worry about in the moment. As a result of these missed learning opportunities, it is not unusual for survivors to continue the pattern of underachievement in their adult lives.

13 Minimisation and Denial of Childhood Trauma as a Defence Mechanism

Although defence mechanisms are understandable reactions to trauma, they are, in general, not very helpful in the long run. Sometimes denial is necessary so the victim can continue on, especially practical as a buffer if they find themselves in circumstances where it is not safe for them to take their time to work out some issue.

One way to do this is by simply distancing the mind and emotions from your traumatic experiences. Out of mind, out of sight and the brain then circumvents the overload of emotions. Other times, denial occurs because the trauma was so significant that the person is in shock and would be unable to deal with it otherwise. Having to accept that your parent doesn't love you like other parents love their children can be a hard pill to swallow and the accompanying journey a savage ride that burdens the spirit.

The victim might experience feeling disconnected from their bodies, emotional numbness, avoidance, watching from a third person's perspective or experience emotional blunting at the same time. This may give the sufferer some semblance of control in a tough situation, strangely signifying the opposite in truth, or they might be able to protect themselves from depression this way, or keep their self-worth. Other times denial might be necessary for a time so that the sufferer can stay loyal to someone hurting them, at least till they can get out of the situation safely.

Denial can also be conscious in cases when the victim is intent on not being labelled as such and avoids any contact with mental health services just so they are not thought of as crazy in any way. A shift in how mental health problems are generally viewed by the public would be helpful in this case.

It is natural not to want to always be reminded of the person we escaped. We want to live freely, but lingering symptoms remain a constant reminder anyway. In the long term, denial means suppressing or bottling up emotions and is associated with decreased psychological functioning and adjustment. The trauma doesn't disappear, but will be carried around till it can be confronted. Pent-up emotions tend to reappear, then, at the most inopportune times, in instinctual reactions the person might not understand themselves and regret later. Somatic symptoms may mislead the victim into incorrectly thinking the symptoms are the source of their problems. It crushes the chances of self-insight and full recovery and healing with it. It can stop one achieving a sense of inner piece or intimate connections with others. The person is also likely to experience mental and physical symptoms despite their denial, such as sleep, mood, concentration and appetite disturbances, a racing heartbeat, feeling exhausted or apathetic, panic attacks, despair, restlessness, anxiety, impatience, a quick temper, negativity, flashbacks, self-harm, distrust, loneliness. Some remain developmentally stuck or regress by not examining their own actions and their reasoning or will have to copy someone else as they didn't develop their own identity. Apart from deceiving themselves and suppressing their own emotions, they may repress desires they're uncomfortable with, like a homophobic homosexual.

Some might genuinely not know of being traumatised because complex trauma is not a single event and this trauma is their normal. They may assume everyone lives that way.

What people fail to understand at first is that it is this denial that gives the past power by letting it unconsciously direct reactions. Freud maintained that repressing emotions creates emotional pain itself. 'Healing from old wounds is not about forgetting what happened. You can't and shouldn't forget what's happened to you – it's a part of your story.' – Paramahansa Yogananda.

Another condition some might also experience is anosognosia, 'a neurological symptom of some health conditions that refers to an impaired ability to understand and identify the health symptoms you live with'[59].

The most obvious sign of someone being in denial is avoiding talking about the subject, sometimes even being scandalised that it was brought up or that someone suggested that their past wasn't exactly how they claim it was. They may immediately change the subject or insist on its unimportance. Internally, they will try to avoid thinking about the trauma by always being busy, overworking or using substances to cloud and distract their minds. In the case of a strong denial mechanism, sometimes they aren't even consciously aware of the traumatic events or have difficulties remembering them and have a need to steer clear altogether whenever people around them get emotional or vulnerable, no matter the subject.

Some will not completely deny, but will minimise their experiences. They may say that it's too far in the past to be bothered with, that forward is the only way to go, that it's way too common of an experience to contemplate, that they've emerged unscathed or that it wasn't traumatic enough, that no good can come out the past, that it wasn't so bad for them after all, that they're over it. Others engage in certain therapies to feel whole, ranging from exercising and meditation to massages and religious experiences, anything but focusing on the source of the difficulties they are having.

Of course, the same type of childhood trauma has different effects on different people. Medication, deep breathing or grounding exercises can all have a place in recovery, whatever works for the individual, but healing can only happen after acknowledging childhood trauma.

Some people, unfamiliar with the concept of narcissism, might not be aware that they were abused and need to act on healing if they wanted to feel better. This is one of the reasons that it is vital to get the word out there about what narcissists are like, their way of being, the type of abuse and the expressions they use. Then, when a victim of their abuse begins looking for answers about why they are the way they are, they will quickly be able to tell that they were abused by a narcissist.

Not wanting to relive the pain is an understandable response too. Not many would want to feel pain if they don't have to. But the past will still affect them and keep many from improving[58]. That being so, the individual might need to consciously break down their own defence mechanism and decide they do want to remember, despite the pain.

While I spent some time in denial, my more pressing problem was that, for a spell, I felt like I had nobody to connect to with these past experiences, partly because other people were in denial. Without guidance and before my psychology degree, I thus felt quite lost, not sure how to address my symptoms and I was suffering from a lower quality of life as a result. Others will turn to addiction to deny themselves of their own experiences.

There are a lot more therapy and support groups these days however, places where one could feel safe starting to explore these old memories in the company of like-minded people who possess the skills and experience necessary to deal with past trauma, cultivate self-exploration and a healthy mindset.

Working through and integrating the trauma will take time as well and it is unique to each person. You are not responsible for the programming you received in childhood, but as an adult, you are responsible for working through it and not letting it affect other people. Additional therapeutic methods that stimulate and boost the mind, body and spirit such as yoga or somatic work are also recommended, depending on individual predilections.

There are other harmful defence mechanisms that arise as a result of denial and not working through trauma. For example, low self-esteem can be compensated by workaholism to the extent of a burnout. As another example, unacknowledged anxiety can turn into psychosomatic illnesses or high blood pressure. Taking the anger out on someone who is not responsible is called displacement or transference and taking it out on ourselves is introjection. Constantly pointing out the faults of others they have themselves is projection. Another related defence mechanism is the fawn response.

14 Fawning

Although this behaviour has already been mentioned, it deserves its own section because of its long-reaching and detrimental effects. Reacting to abuse comes down to four basic types of response: fight, flight, or removing ourselves from the situation as much as possible, freezing, or struggling to choose, and fawning. The fawn response is about solving every problem and conflict by swiftly pleasing the aggressor to the extreme, whatever the issue is. The person will try to follow the abuser's word to the letter to the detriment of their own beliefs, needs, sense of self and feelings and then, because it worked, it saved them from further abuse or allowed them to experience some form of twisted love from the parent. They will extend this behaviour into adulthood and to everyone they meet, causing conflict in every aspect of their existence, both in their personal and professional lives.

As you can imagine, always being on the go to satisfy everyone takes enormous effort and time. Not to mention that it isn't even possible to please everyone because people want different things. All that happens is that the fawner becomes exhausted and unhappy, unable to pursue their own goals and needs. Accordingly, adherents of this maladaptive survival response tend to lose their sense of identity, experience guilt for not succeeding and become angry with themselves if trying to follow their own beliefs. They might feel uncomfortable when having to speak their own minds. If they do something to their own liking, they will try to endlessly explain themselves as if they don't see themselves worthy enough to have wants. Which is why exactly they have to seek external validation as a proof for being accepted instead.

Blending in seems to them like a more walkable path than expressing any individuality. This dysfunctional pattern also de-escalates potential conflict and is seen as a way to make themselves more likeable. But living in survival mode is supposed to be a phase during the abuse that helps save you from hardship, in some instances even your life. It is not intended to be how you live for the rest of the time.

Some sufferers will outright deny their response, as they were conditioned to do very early in life. Being controlled by the brain's autonomic nervous system, they may, in fact, be unaware of why they're having trouble saying no to others even though they already have way too many responsibilities and are overwhelmed. In this perpetually harassed state, every potential conflict seems like more of a threat than it is and danger responses are heightened further.

The most obvious way of identifying a fawn response is by asking the person if their first instinct in a conflict is to please the other or say sorry, regardless of whose fault the issue was. These people have been conditioned in childhood to think that expressing their thoughts or emotions would be out of order. Fawners have low self-esteem, are empathetic, kind and thoughtful towards others and are not only often being taken advantage of based on these characteristics, but also experience unusually strong unanticipated, bitter emotional outbursts because of the amount of suppressed feelings and needs. Then, of course. they feel guilty for it and ashamed that they aren't in control of their responses, all sometimes to the extent of self-harm and depression. It's a stressful life to live. Having long abandoned the concept of standing up for themselves and unable to form healthy relationships, fawners often become codependent, with attachment and depersonalisation issues. After normalising not feeling safe and secure in relationships[60], they are a perfect target for another narcissist or some similarly toxic abuser to come along and instigate a trauma-based codependency and then passing on this model of behaviour to their children.

As seen, this response can be just as harmful as the other trauma responses and should be addressed for the bettering of the individual's quality of life[61]. This automatic response is hard to overcome, but it can be unlearnt little by little by thinking about and analysing our feelings and reactions. Delegating some tasks or writing an own needs list could be a start, and EMDR can help here too.

15 Facial Recognition Problems

Due to fearing eye contact, first with my mother, then distrusting others, I do not have the standard ability for both facial recognition and expression recognition. In essence, it means I am unable to remember if I've seen a person before or not, I mix people up even if I've met them several times and certainly do not ask me what colour eyes they have, as I would not notice or check! Sometimes it is a huge challenge to remember what people look like and I fail to recall where I met them before. And heaven help me if they've changed their hairstyle, fashion sense or if they are in a different setting.

People on the autism spectrum battle with similar problems due to eye avoidance, proven by studies such as Robert M. Joseph, Kelly Ehrman, Rebecca McNally and Brandon Keehn's affective response to eye contact and face recognition ability research that suggests that autonomic reactivity to eye contact may interfere with face identity processing in some children[88].

This issue was accentuated by the fact that up until a teacher's discovery when I was twelve years old, my mother neglected my needs for strong prescription glasses, thus I missed crucial phases in face recognition development. It is not as strong as having full-blown prosopagnosia, but my face blindness frequently causes me problems in relationships, especially in work situations. It makes for pretty embarrassing situations, ones that neurotypicals don't understand, such as being pulled up by my boss to question me on why I don't know who this or that person is.

My father was also an eye-contact avoider for his own childhood trauma reasons, so I am sure that is a contributing factor for me as well where I modelled my behaviour after his. I never learnt to copy the proper example.

I try to purposefully hold eye contact to combat this issue, but due to my natural instinct to avoid it, I don't always catch myself in time. As it has to be a conscious effort on my part, I don't always have the energy or drive to keep at it either. I am tired or nervous, the effort required is bigger while for most people it is automatic and not thought of.

It is also well known that maltreatment affects children's recognition of emotions[89], solidified by studies that have shown that child abuse victims are less accurate than control subjects when performing facial recognition and processing tasks. Moreover, these children display a shorter reaction time for recognition and electrophysiological activation of the amygdala and of the anterior insula to faces with negative emotions, especially anger, showing that abused children have a recognition bias for negative expressions, for the most part for fear and anger, which is a matter of survival for them.

These differences are exhibited both in an abnormal anatomical brain and physiological formations, as well as in psychological and behavioural changes that impact the lives of these individuals. The increased perception of only negative emotions regularly impairs their interpersonal relationships in every part of their lives as they often mistakenly attribute anger to neutral and happy faces too, partly because those were the predominant expressions seen most often in childhood.

Another reason for the deficit in processing other's facial expressions other than anger and fear is hypothesised to be a childhood spent in a relatively emotionally-deprived environment with less exposure to appropriate social and emotional stimuli, which will have entrenched the development of accurate emotion recognition. What's more, we know that abuse affects neurodevelopment, especially the amygdala, with a pivotal role in the emotion regulation neural network[90]. A background of childhood trauma changes the amygdala's response to downcast facial expressions[91] and scared, tense or displeased ones[92]. Hypoactivation of the fusiform gyrus, an area involved in face processing and social communication also plays a part[93], partly due to a reduction in grey matter of this part of the brain in the case of a child abuse history[94].

On that account, professionals in the field should pay attention to the existence of this background as it influences correct identification of emotions, thus having an effect on the person's whole social life in terms of false alarms, which would in turn influence how they feel about themselves as well.

16 Lack of Intimacy, Trust and Sex Drive (Demi- and Asexuality)

Apart from feeling like it is not worth risking the pain of an intimate relationship, giving ourselves and our deepest secrets away in fear of appearing weak, there are a lot more factors at play here.

It is perhaps self-evident how childhood sexual abuse can sometimes lead to being tense or completely intolerant of being touched or having intimate relationships. What a lot of people don't know is that physical and emotional abuse can lead to the same result.

For simplicity's sake, I will regard both demi- and asexuality under the umbrella term inhibited sexual desire. I would also like to stress that not all suffering from the disorder have suffered child abuse and vice versa, not all child abuse victims end up with ISD.

As more and more LGBTQ+ rights emerge in the Western world, more people also come forward to admit that they asexual or demisexual. It is seen as both a sexual orientation, one that a person can feel very comfortable with, and as a disorder that the sufferer would like to address. Some are naturally born that way, but it can also happen to individuals born into a cult or religion preaching an overly inflexible upbringing in regards to sexual acts, negative attitudes of the child's immediate environment toward intercourse or traumatic experiences.

Temporary ISD can arise as a result of depression and certain other illnesses and medication, especially if they can affect hormone levels, or it can be caused by other sexual issues or inhibitions like associating sex with failure or pain.

There are various experiences of ISD, with some people being completely disgusted by the thought of sexual relations, or only some aspects of it, or being neutral about it. Personally, I experience attraction and can enjoy the male or human body or a person's character but I have problems with taking it further once the touching starts, which is why I call myself more demisexual than anything else. Of course, my mother's disdain for sex played a part in it too and how derogatively she talked about anyone partaking in the act for something other than procreation inside a marriage, a more socially influenced standing rather than a religious one on her part, also coming from her father's views and how she was kept obsessively 'pure' for her husband and was not even allowed to kiss a boy. So I think I wasn't necessarily born that way and environmental factors definitely influenced me to a large extent, which, of course, doesn't make my sexuality any less valid. It was not a choice I've made, it is an instinct I have, I am that way out of no fault of my own. Intergenerational trauma played a part.

Asexuality is a valid sexual orientation. If it suits a person and they feel most comfortable that way and they don't harm anyone, then there's no need to treat it. It has been viewed as a stigma and a sexual dysfunction to be remedied long enough. If it does originate from a traumatic event suffered during childhood, however, it is the trauma that should be treated for the general well-being of the patient as opposed to trying to change their sexuality. Let's be clear, nobody should be made to have sex if they don't want to, not even through using brainwashing techniques enforcing them to feel abnormal and agree. That is only going to cause further trauma.

The effects of trauma can of course seep into a person's sexual life in other ways. They can become the opposite, as in overly sexual, they can be addicted to masturbation, certain dirty words, imagination, they can get involved in prostitution because that's what they know, or they can develop paraphilias, fetishes and kinks related to body parts or pain. Mine is whump, not to be confused by sadism. More on that in a different book.

I'd also like to stress once more, that not all asexuality is related to childhood or any kind of trauma. If it is, there might be some telltale signs, the most obvious ones being flashbacks to unpleasant experiences, but there are others more subtle such as out-of-body experiences during sexual acts as a form of dissociating from the event, inexplicable fear, overwhelmed nerves or anger even though the intercourse offered would be consensual otherwise and there are no danger signs. Again, it is important to remember, if finding yourself in this situation, that you don't have to have sex. It might be a longer process for you to get there, or you might not be ready to face these issues for quite a long time. For some, the answer is to repress their trauma. Either way, the best place to address trauma from is a calm, safe state. If that isn't achievable, it is best to leave it for the time being or it will cause further discomfort and harm. You're an ACE (short for asexual) and that's perfectly fine!

A lot of other asexuals still have sex because they feel they owe that to their partner for both their loved one's happiness and for the relationship to work. It is a compromise and as long as it is consensual and you know what you're getting yourself into, it is completely fine to make that choice as well. Some other people will want to have children and will accept the compromise for that reason.

17 The Lingering Financial Costs of Childhood Abuse

No, I'm not talking about the therapy bills. That is the smallest part of this cost. What is costing more is only partly the medication we try to alleviate the symptoms with as well, both for mental or physical problems. As detailed before, the number of ailments arising from childhood abuse is vast, and accounting for all that entails is still just the tip of the iceberg. Turning to alcoholism, drugs or other addictions also adds to the sum.

The number of working days lost due to these illnesses is still just a partial cost. Some will need to leave work or go part time to be able to cope. Those abused rarely reach their potential and if they do, it generally takes them a lot longer than those with happy childhoods. Social anxiety will keep us from making connections that would lead to advancement both in work life and private life. The same goes for education opportunities for some. Affected children might leave school early or choose a profession that keeps them away from people, regardless of wages. Pair that with the incapability to make a phone call to the doctor's or change energy suppliers and you've got major losses, dragging you down at every moment.

Then, once in work, we can't advance the same way for similar reasons, all leading to enormous costs throughout life, and those are only the personal costs, with low self-esteem sufferers self-regulating their progress and thus restricting their own potential and applying for jobs for lesser goals they've set for themselves.

The family is affected, so is the community and health systems, and governments spend billions on treatments, along with losing out on taxes not earned by the affected, of these individuals when all could be avoided if child abuse could be recognised and made less prevalent in the first place. It is an economic burden in every way. Not to mention that when compared to other health actions such as vaccinations or tuberculosis control, interventions for mental disorders are not the most cost-effective or inexpensive treatments available to health professionals. The truth about mental illness is that there are no cheap options to overcome it. 'Mental disorders therefore account for more economic costs than chronic somatic diseases such as cancer or diabetes'[95] and it is pretty objectionable these costs are rarely taken into account when assessing a person's progress.

18 Oversharing

First off, I believe that in an ideal society, there shouldn't be such a thing as oversharing being a problem. In an ideal society, people should be able to be honest with each other, discuss every matter as opposed to sticking to the weather. They should be able to ask for help, not fear the consequences of exposing some secret or, heaven forbid, making someone uncomfortable by having to hear about their problems. What's more, with a lot of mainland European cultures being more open, oversharing is more of an issue in British and American societies. For example, it's completely normal to ask someone how much people earn in much of Eastern and Central Europe, but it is considered rude in England, along with a great many other things that are treated as taboo in the British Isles, something I have made a great many mistakes about since arriving in the United Kingdom. Apparently, death is not much talked about, and neither are periods or religion. Weird people, right? Basically, anything that might be uncomfortable for the conversation partner on the receiving end is a no-no. Anything for their comfort.

On the other hand, as it stands, oversharing can be seen as a sign of a psychological problem, including anxiety disorders, with or without history of childhood trauma, and of borderline personality disorder amongst other things. A number of academics have demonstrated that intense emotions make people want to share more information, with social inhibitions that get in the way reduced under conditions of arousal whether it's anger, pain, joy or the adrenaline high from a workout. Anxiety or ADHD can lead to over-explaining, we may do it to validate our choices and ease guilt, which can happen as a result of a strict upbringing where we always had to justify our choices.

Oversharing is also often fuelled by self-doubt, feeling we have to compensate for other perceived shortfalls. We worry too much about what others think, so we desperately try to make ourselves look good and, losing control of the whole interaction, we end up giving away far more information than originally intended. Over-explaining can conclude with the same effect, with devastating, dehumanising results.

Of course, it's hard to do it in the moment, but one way we might stop ourselves from oversharing is imagining the butterfly effect of the words just about to be tumbling out of our mouths. How would our conversation partner react, both in the short term and in the long term? Will it change our relationship with them and, if so, in what way? Would they tell anyone else? Visualise your significant other, the boss and any other relevant person knowing what you are about to say. Is it still all right to go ahead and share? Usually, this amount of delay and thought is enough to deter one from divulging, and if not, it is then probably okay to do so.

Thankfully, sharing one's private life has become plenty more socially acceptable in the internet era and the revolution of authenticity. Sometimes people overshare because they aim to be more intimate with the other person. Unfortunately, however, a lot of people get uncomfortable or confused while learning someone's secrets or are not inclined to wear their hearts on their sleeves, especially when it concerns trauma-dumping and specifically if it is in the workplace. It may interfere with their tasks or they don't know what to do with the information and whether they are supposed to do anything with it. Some might even take advantage. Some simply don't give a damn. An attempt to make someone understand us can easily turn into a misunderstanding, especially if trust between the conversation partners hasn't been established yet. Some people might think we are sharing to gain sympathy or they won't understand us anyway.

For the relationship's sake, therefore, it is vital to remain cautious and weigh up whether it would be advantageous to release a piece of information in detail or not, especially in regards to who you are sharing it with. Will they be able to understand? Will they merely regard us as attention-seeking or does sharing have a functional purpose? Oversharing wearying events and incidents can push people away. Will we be mortified after having shared? It might come back to haunt us for a long time to come.

It is not a foolproof method of course, we will make mistakes, misjudge the other person's reaction. This process, like everything else, is a learning curve. Some people don't deserve to have a piece of your life, or they don't like getting intimate themselves and some will become resentful when learning your trauma could have an effect on their (work)life, but there's no need to beat ourselves up over it if we err.

As adults, it is also our responsibility not to burden other people who are not ready to hear our plight. Venting is, of course, a part of healing as a way of processing feelings, but there are still plenty of other people out there more appropriate to address if we need help, those we can trust. Professionals, if nothing else, people who are not only mentally able to handle the interaction, but also remain non-judgemental. They can also direct the individual towards more healthy methods of dealing with trauma other than dumping aimed at forcing sympathy, consideration or encouragement. Trauma-dumping isn't conducive to self-reflection, it tends to be repetitive, with no real progress in self-perspective, partly because the people chosen to share with were not the right ones to advance the situation. Habitual trauma-dumpers are also less likely to listen to advice, and be stuck in a rut.

Above all, we have to get past our need for outside emotional validation. If you still feel unheard, write everything down and choose someone you can share it with safely. But remember, everybody is going through something, so it can be beneficial to ask if they're going through something bothersome themselves at the time of the conversation as they might not be in the right headspace for the heart-to-heart.

While it needs to be carefully done and, most advisably, anonymously, venting online on established, specialised platforms is also an option, for those frequenting it will have similar experiences and are more likely to offer valuable advice or present points of view that can challenge and change your own response. Writing the problem down in itself can lead to looking at it from new perspectives, presenting solutions and a sense of empowerment with it.

A similar occurrence to oversharing, over-explaining is a recurrent standard trauma response too for narcissistic childhood trauma and abuse sufferers as they were always used to having to explain themselves in an attempt to reduce the amount of time they were criticised. This can be conscious conflict avoidance or an unconscious response. We are anxious so we over-explain out of habit. We need to remember that not everyone will criticise us and if they do, it is most likely not our fault, but it's to do with the other person's personality or reactions. Besides, living dependent on other people's opinions is no life, it's over-tiring and hopeless. No more fawning! Particularly as we are not in the same abusive situation. It is a matter of self-regulation and, again, rewiring our brains.

We can do this by analysing ourselves, why we had the over-explaining or oversharing response we had. Once done, what was the resulting outcome in ourselves? What were the consequences to the relationship? This is best done in writing as well, as expressing thoughts this way allows for more coherence and comprehensibility. Neurodivergents express themselves in writing anyway.

Then, reflect on how a more positive outcome can be achieved in a different way. One such way might be setting boundaries or self-validating ourselves or our experiences without resorting to another person's validation. Sometimes it's unavoidable to upset or disappoint others and we have to accept that, and sometimes it is necessary to fall short of their expectations for the sake of one's own sanity or well-being, and we need to accept that too. Some worry that not helping others makes them like their abusive parents. But self-love and self-respect has nothing to do with narcissism. Narcissists want everyone to appreciate them as they are perfect in their own eyes. Self-love involves wanting to become better.

Let me stress once more that keeping from oversharing and over-explaining is particularly crucial at work. In professional life it is all the more critical to ask ourselves what would happen if anybody took advantage of or passed our revelations on, both in the short and the long term. I unfortunately learnt this the hard way.

Sometimes other people ask too many questions about our pasts and private lives that would be hard to avoid if we wanted to be truthful. Even when solicited like this, we could reveal too much. It is completely acceptable to communicate a need for boundaries respectfully, making it clear that we have nothing against the other conversation partner and that way people are more likely to accept and respect our privacy. You have the right for privacy at work as well, which is emphasised in law. Practice makes the master here as well and different individuals might need different approaches. It is another way to practise establishing boundaries too, reinforcing the idea in your head that you are allowed them everywhere, including in work life.

19 Missing or Misunderstanding Social Cues (in more detail)

This handicap has caused me a lot of problems over the years. Partly due to my abuse-induced isolation during childhood and again partly because my eyesight deficiencies were not picked up until I was twelve, I was behind in recognising social cues and my anxiety and self-imposed isolation didn't help matters later. Thus, I never learnt to correctly identify and how to react to some social cues. It is like a hive mind situation for neurotypicals, a hive that we missed joining somewhere along the line, and which they don't teach in schools as it comes naturally to those who are part of the hive mind.

One of the groups of people having a lot of problems in the above area are those with avoidant personality disorder. The syndrome is characterised by persistent anxiety, feeling socially inept or inferior, uncurbed preoccupation with being disapproved of or dismissed, a disinclination to become involved with others and an avoidance of social or professional situations that require notable interpersonal interaction.

Social cues are ways of communicating that do not make the use of language and they accompany verbal communication as well. These can be through facial expressions, movements, gestures, stance, the way we position our body parts and behave towards one another, meaning different things at different times depending on who we are talking to, as well as the overall circumstances and context. These social cues are how we express ourselves and our aims, reactions and feelings in addition to language, which altogether should give the other person a comprehensive picture of our meaning.

For instance, body language can reveal a person's true intentions even though their words are saying otherwise and can also give away their emotions, such as somebody unconsciously trying to hide away with their posture, crossing legs and arms, leaning away or positioning themselves partially out of sight, behind a chair for example. This usually means that they are either uninterested or are uncomfortable for some reason, either related or not related to the interaction. They may be too anxious, in pain or simply not into the topic. The opposite is also true. Mirroring someone else's posture, facial expression and movements is a key element of communication as it conveys a connection, a way of letting the other person know we are interested in them or the topic.

Gestures oftentimes underpin the words, making the meaning clearer, and are even utilised by sign language users at times. They are social cues particularly sensitive to culture as is touching, encompassing extreme denotations from establishing rapport to intimidation. This is based on how intimate such an act can be and how it can require consent in most situations, one that can be obtained through other social cues. This whole situation is a minefield for sufferers inclined to miss or misunderstand cues. An even more weighty social cue is how someone responds to touch. Subtle differences in facial expressions are often missed by those accustomed to childhood trauma as they either intentionally avoid eye contact or are too overwhelmed by the experience to be able to process when surprise changes to annoyance, fear, aversion or regret, for example. Missing eye contact clues robs the individual of vital information conveyed by the eyebrows, the pupils and the eyelids, as well as the positive, smiling wrinkles around the eyes. Like eyelid positioning could signify irritation or hesitation.

On the other hand, our neurodivergent behaviour can be misunderstood as well. As discussed, touching itself can be difficult for trauma sufferers, so they might intentionally misunderstand cues and withdraw at this point, creating further confusion in the conversation partner. Similarly, our fidgeting might look socially inappropriate as it is generally seen as being disinterested or disengaged and people misunderstand our looking away as detachment, hostility or disinterestedness. If a neurotypical is really engaged in the conversation, they look at the other person's face consistently, but for others, the length of eye contact could be a problem as well. What's too much, too little, too uncomfortable, strange? People who it doesn't come natural to will often misjudge this period of time.

Another area to keep the attention on is the mouth. Stiff or pursed lips could mean that the individual is irritated, scared or doesn't trust the other. A wrinkled nose usually signifies a negative reaction. Being tense or impatient may show up by someone licking or chewing on their lips a lot. Of course, there are so many more subtle cues that go unnoticed if we aren't watching the person's face. There are so many social cues neurotypicals give and receive without consciously thinking about them and without having to be explicitly taught. For example, it is hard for some people to tell when a conversation partner is ready to move on from a conversation. But there are social cues for telling. When someone doesn't want to talk about something anymore, they will start glancing away, longer and longer, respond less and less, till they may not be verbally responding at all, but perhaps they are still smiling with a closed mouth. Some neurodivergents are not responsive to this.

Then there's the tone of the voice, volume, accentuation and cadence, all meant to aid clarity, not just to what we are saying, but in regards to how we feel about it as well. Not much change in intonation is likely to signify that the person is losing interest.

Trauma survivors often have trouble with the distance another person is standing at while interacting as well, preferring a larger space than those described in the proxemics by anthropologist Edward Hall, eighteen inches or less between close family members or romantic partners, one and a half feet between close friends, four to twelve feet between friends and colleagues and more between strangers, though these unwritten rules also differ a lot between cultures.

Clothing norms also qualify as social cues. Maybe there's no need to spend lots of time worrying about looks for certain types of neurodivergents, but others will assume you do and they will make an impression on that basis. A person may be expected to appear wearing a specific type of clothing in some settings and not wearing them will single them out. This doesn't just apply to workplaces and fine dining, but casual appearances also. If someone is clearly the odd one out in terms of how they dress, then they will have difficulties with acceptance. People tend to be socially influenced in designing their outward appearance. Their clothing, hairstyle and the way they spend their free time reflect trends and a bias for affiliations, from small groups to belonging to bigger classes and classifications. So people will infer that our clothing choices were made to show allegiance to some group and heaven help you if you don't conform to the rules. I would like to state here this is not something I agree with as I prefer individuality, it's just how it is.

As with everything else in this book, it would be useful if more people would be aware of and mindful of the fact that childhood trauma can change the way in which some of us recognise social cues and could modify their interactions accordingly to one more honest and transparent so that we can't miss their meaning. This would largely help to enhance social connectedness. A background of childhood trauma can also affect the way we perceive power, relationships and belonging so childhood trauma survivors may need additional help and support in this area as well. People should in general be aware that those who make very little or no eye contact do so because of a handicap and not because of sinister reasons as I keep hearing. Unfortunately, it wasn't just once I heard an everyday man say they don't trust someone who can't look them in the eyes. So I'll say it once again, it has nothing to do with trust. It's quite the opposite, the trauma survivor will not look others in the eyes because they are the ones not trusting, not because they are untrustworthy. For example, people with social anxiety judge others with happy facial expressions even as less friendly than those not having the disorder.

Similar handicaps entail not having mastered presenting facial expressions, movements and gestures that match what is being said, and having a tone of voice in contrast with the usual ways of speaking in the given circumstances, especially if it concerns subtle nuances in communication. This deviation can irritate or anger others and they will instinctually come to dislike the person out of no fault or intention of the speaker. Misunderstandings can ensue and behavioural issues can emerge as an upshot of more anxiety and the resulting frustration, some leading to criminal behaviour. All because of an inability to read or conform to social situations, because not everybody is on the same page as a result of a malfunctioning part of one participant's neurological system.

Subsequently, it might be worthwhile for the trauma sufferer to put some intentional work into studying social cues. One method is looking at facial expressions of people with someone who is a trusted neurotypical and understanding how and why they interpret them the way they do. There could be subtle nuances we have never learnt to identify or notice, such as what their way of dressing tells of that person or how they might feel based on the fact they haven't put make-up on that day. Practice is the key, the more the better, as we are behind with this, again, through no fault of our own. However, as an adult, it is our responsibility to try to fix these shortcomings as much as possible, for everyone's sake and foremost for one's own sake. Nothing is lost. New relationships can be formed with newly learnt social cue skills, and old relationships mended.

Even with these steps, sometimes it's still hard to figure out what others are thinking or if our relationship with them is still on track, but there shouldn't be any harm in asking the other person if there is something wrong. More often than not, whatever they are upset about will have nothing to do with us.

Craving honesty after growing up with a two-faced parent, narcissistic abuse survivors tend to be extra guarded when it comes to dishonest social cues such as wisecracks, lies, banter, jokes and clichés. I cannot stand fake laughter. For example, I have to switch to another radio channel immediately if I hear it. I also do not understand them and try to avoid having to abide by the accepting reaction to these hollow-appearing social cues that people are expected to have. People seem to establish connections with these interactions while I become disgusted by the insincere undertones. It is unquestionably a big turn off for me. Others would most likely perceive it as me not playing along, not following the social script. It's like everyone's an actor bar me. I'd like it better if people and their reactions were authentic, off the cuff and not textbook or playing a role.

On other occasions, I have recognised social cues sent in my direction, but refused to react to them because I did not psychologically feel up to being social. That is a handicap too, energies wasted by anxiety. Other times I did not react in a way that was suitable or proper in the circumstances because I felt aggrieved about what the social cue was trying to elicit, perhaps on occasion inclined to see disingenuity where there was none.

Regrettably, though, I have to admit that this behaviour is not sustainable if one wants to advance in life. We have to play along, no matter how uncomfortable it is and how fake and superficial the interaction feels. People who grew up emotionally abused or abandoned know things about the human condition that many never get around to noticing or handling. Partly, this is why childhood trauma survivors have little patience for small talk, hypocrisy or phoney people. Old souls don't happen by accident.

Due to these differences, another skill we might have to practise is how our communicating looks to others. Use a mirror if necessary and note how you talk to others. How does it come across? Does your anxiety level change how you come across? Feedback from a trusted person might also be helpful, and then practising a potentially better way to appear open and friendly if necessary.

It is also good to know that most people will agree with you if they like you and disagree if they do not. It is usually not about actual opinions. They will say they like something even if it is just that they don't hate it, but they say yes because they want to be friendly, they want the relationship to evolve. But the neurodivergent often conned during childhood wants the truth and often says the truth, not empty platitudes.

Another social convention that happens that I don't like is the custom that it is considered impolite to interrupt someone talking. It is harder for neurodivergents to understand and abide by this social understanding because other things tend to be more worthwhile for us than social connections. For example, I think if something is more important at that moment, we should be able to interrupt. There's no reason why the initial conversation cannot continue after. We are different and it's frustrating to live within the confines of the neurotypical majority.

20 Mr and Ms Perfectionist

Perfectionism is a behavioural pattern rooted in a persistent need to obtain validation, the endorsement and positive regard of others that at the same time makes the perfectionist scared to show their authentic selves, their faults and vulnerabilities. They are often convinced that other people's feedback shapes their worth and thus affects their self-esteem and importance, through which it becomes a self-destructive pattern designed to curtail painful feelings of embarrassment, intolerance and criticisms.

I'm not saying of course not to try to finish a job right, but falling short doesn't need to wane our self-worth. We are only flawed humans, so stop beating yourself up about it, especially as any success found was despite living in a world not built for neurodivergents. That makes us strong, resilient, unbreakable!

The perfectionist, however, goes through many unnecessary cycles of worry and effort. They agonise over every little detail of life, hopelessly trying to desperately control consequences, themselves, everything. Not thinking about and organising every detail may as well be failing as it commonly leads to more anxiety. The perfectionist keeps trying, pushing, second to none, up to a point. Nobody can live like that, give a hundred percent at everything, so sooner or later, the pressure becomes too much and the individual will have to admit defeat, often in the form of being burnt out, becoming ill, too exhausted not to quit or they will use delaying tactics so that they don't have to admit defeat, not yet. A perfectionist might physically remove themselves from the situation, change cities, professions, disappear to start anew rather than show up with nothing. They either do something well or not at all. Either finish something or not start it at all. Such behaviour often ends in self-sabotaging, self-doubt, anxiety and with it, unnecessary pressure. Other signs of perfectionism are disassociation, being on edge all the time, mistrust in our own self or abilities and being committed to the outcome rather than watchful of the process. Perfectionists seek validation and guidance from others rather than trusting the self, struggle with addictions, depression, hopelessness, suicidal thoughts and might give up on a task too soon.

To be able to stop this impractical pattern, we need to understand where our ingrained reactions are coming from as we did with the rest of the effects of childhood trauma, which should undo some of the conditioning. Furthermore, perfectionism can then be reaffirmed by the way of society as it chases the ideal body, reinforcing the consumerist need to possess objects and chase status to demonstrate success, perpetuated through social media, the education department, damaging relationship dynamics thrust upon us by our families, doctrine or workplace.

In childhood, we had no choice. A toxic caretaker and we had to keep on trying no matter what, perform as superlatively as possible to their expectations and then maybe we could obtain love and acceptance for a moment. The target however had a tendency to move, still does. Perfection is not obtainable and the more we try to reach this impossible goal, the more hopelessness gets a place instead. We failed because we chose something that wasn't possible.

What's more, we forget we have the power to set our own rules, we forget that we have a choice. We are not abused children anymore with only the one option of being perfect or suffering the consequences. In most cases, there are no consequences, apart from those emotions felt by the perfectionist. Feel them and let go. Shame and embarrassment for not being faultless has no place in a relationship with oneself. Besides, perfectionism is an elusive concept. Who determines what's perfect? Which outsider has the authority?

When children grow up feeling like they have to demonstrate their value for love, they will generally try harder to become a model specimen. It is a form of a false identity[97], a persona we put on that we assume people will like. This false self however, with a life of its own, literally, is exhausting and hard to maintain, leading to further helplessness[98].

On top of that, unfortunately, the effects of the coalescing of capitalism and the values of respectability coming from the puritan work ethic are now in full swing in modern society and as such, being relentless and exceedingly ambitious is valued to an extreme, regardless of the cost to our health or relationships. It leads to burnout that can at times look like having little to no motivation, increased levels of anxiety resulting in insomnia and fatigue, which then goes hand in hand with being easily triggered and emotionally overwhelmed.

There is a fine line here. There is our drive to become accomplished and there's putting the unnecessary pressure of perfectionism on ourselves that may very well stop that very accomplishment. Easier said than done, given our almost Pavlovian conditioning, which is why we need to understand case by case what pushes us into overdrive. Working on our self-worth and confidence will also help.

So let's reiterate: perfectionism is learnt behaviour and it emerges as a result of trauma, its most common form being childhood trauma. Let's admit, some of our parents did try their best, even if that best wasn't exactly conducive to the child becoming a healthy human being. You don't have to have a narcissistic or even toxic parent for this syndrome to arise, it is much more commonplace. It was enough that our caregivers had their shortcomings in our formative years, vulnerabilities, ineptitudes, struggles. Maybe they were overachievers themselves, go-getters or excessively power-hungry or maybe they were only particularly disapproving when having a low mood themselves, it doesn't matter. It is normal that as children we wanted to please our caregivers, our sense of security and emotional safety depended on it at the very least.

Unfortunately, some parents want to live out the dreams they never achieved through their children and therefore push their offspring to their limits, overtaking their entire study and extracurricular activities plans, barely allowing them to take a break, dismissing their feelings and needs. They scare them with worst case scenarios of what happens if they don't perform to expectations and only reward them for the success they expect. They are belittled or punished for not being the perfect offspring. Simply being repeatedly told by a parent that they were disappointed in the child can lead to tendencies for perfectionism. Another common phrase parents tend to use in these cases is 'what would people say?'. People would probably say nothing, to be honest, as they either don't care or don't think it's a big deal, but the result is the same. The child will feel humiliated and be weary of other people's expectations, leading to perfectionism and a feeling of disappointment in oneself if the plan for whatever achievement, big or small, doesn't go as expected. It doesn't even matter at this point that literally no one sees it or gives any consideration to whether the kitchen is clean, for example, but we know. We know we didn't do it perfectly and at this point it becomes a self-stressor. In extreme cases, it can give rise to further feelings of jitteriness, trepidation, anxiety and mortification, further perpetuating another cycle of perfectionism, aimed to reduce these unwanted feelings. But if we wanted to be perfect, it will never be enough because there will always be something more to finish or execute so that we could feel recognised and approved of by ourselves as the perfect human specimen.

To be fair, perfectionism is not always down to bad parenting. Bullying by peers or teachers can have the same effect, especially if happening during the early teenage years as it creates the same feeling of being not enough. Another root of perfectionism is having experiences traumatic events or unexpected changes experienced in the course of childhood[100], events that shook our world in our formative years that proved to be overwhelming. If a child cannot control their circumstances, they will try to control themselves and perfectionism is only round the corner as a final attempt to try to control ourselves and institute some safety where there was none.

To summarise, perfectionism is a coping mechanism that helped us endure and negotiate our way through life when we were children, mainly having the function of appeasing our caretaker. As adults, however, we should acknowledge that it is an outgrown tool and that it is impairing us more than it is aiding us. The objective should now be to change our negative self-talk and disposition. 'It's not good enough', 'I am useless', 'I will never earn enough to sustain my dreams', going hand in hand with hopelessness, these kinds of thoughts seem to be automatic as they appear, but they do come from somewhere. Let's internalise that, know that they are the result of trauma, not reality. Cognitive therapy comes in handy at this point, and a truthful and profound conversation with ourselves where we can hopefully arrive to a more Vulcan answer. So ask yourself in every pressing, disturbing situation: what happens if I am not perfect? What happens if this task isn't completed perfectly? What is the worst that can happen? Logically, the answer is mostly reassuring, once we go down that road. It might be easier to start with practicalities at first, but be sure to arrive at the bigger questions later on as well, such as, why is the situation hopeless? Is it really hopeless? What makes me less than others? Even if your answer might have some negative connotations at first, it will pinpoint where the unconscious statements come from, which is most likely to be an outside, childhood, invalid source. And the moment you realise where they come from, you will become aware that they are not your truth and most certainly they are not facts.

21 Crying Easily

While in some situations, male or female, crying is considered beneficially cathartic, there comes a point where the sheer amount of it becomes conducive to anxiety in itself. Additionally, it is one thing crying in the privacy of your own room in the middle of the night but another being unable to control yourself and breaking down when it's least convenient, especially at work where it can impede professional relationships. Often, the person on the receiving end doesn't know how to handle a crying co-worker and/or will consider them weak for getting emotional.

Unfortunately, the old saying of 'what doesn't kill you makes you stronger' has been proven wrong once again as for example, women who experienced traumatic childhoods commonly shed tears more than what is considered a normal reaction ' because their sympathetic nervous system experiences trauma or anxiety in the same somatic responsive way, regardless of the scale of how traumatic the event actually is' – Dr Kate Cummins, PsyD. In other words, we can become highly sensitive people as a trauma response, it is now part of our brain's anatomy. As described in earlier chapters, we can also be more sensitive to external stimuli and highly responsive to slight changes in our environment. Feeling everything so much more intensely on top of the problems of everyday life becomes overtaxing pretty damn quick. Other people may have the impression our extreme reactions are unnecessary and our behaviour might seem puzzling. In all actuality, it is a completely justified response to so much environmental stimuli that we process.

Feeling easily overwhelmed is a common anxiety symptom. Some of the other effects of childhood trauma, such as PTSD, anxiety or depression, is of course an additional factor making someone more likely to cry or being unable to stop themselves from crying. The more someone suffers from anxiety, the more difficult it becomes to handle some accompanying psychological responses. This downward spiral puts the body under immense stress while at the same time it takes energy and other internal reserves to lessen that anxiety. Anxiety can be so powerful that the accompanying stress essentially continuously hammers the body with a never-ending stream of somatic and mental manifestations. While these don't inevitably trigger additional emotions, they do grind away at inner resources and diminish the potential to be able to manage an event or incident. Anxiety might not automatically result in extended periods of depression at this point, though the stress on the brain and the accompanying feelings of persistent trepidation and fatigue frequently lead to temporary low moods and, consequently, crying.

It is not unusual, either, to feel like crying leading up to, throughout and following an anxiety or panic attack. Many experience the feeling of impending doom like they were about to die. They respond by crying since it is a natural reaction to that feeling, besides the physiological responses that arise with a panic attack. In the wake of the anxiety attack, some might still experience extreme feelings, usually in regards to the inability to protect themselves or act effectively during the attack. These anxiety attacks can be so powerful that when they're finished, the need to cry is natural and anticipated. Not everyone cries following an anxiety attack, nevertheless the exhausting quality of them makes it natural to feel like crying.

Lacking an appropriate amount of self-esteem, another side effect of childhood trauma, can make people extremely fragile both mentally and emotionally, with very taxing impacts on one's mind, making it hard to go through any scary, stressful or argumentative moment without ending up crying. As we have also seen, emotional dysregulation is also more prevalent in those with a past of childhood trauma, so yes, so many factors it is certainly no wonder we often find ourselves crying! Disappointment with someone, ourselves or our situation can often bring crying with it, similarly to anger when our expectations are not met. It is also possible that we may find ourselves in a situation that reminds us of the past where we were helpless to stop the abuse. Maybe someone uses the same words that a past abuser used or forces us to do something that feels the same way. Either consciously or unconsciously, this might catapult the individual's mind into their childhood and expose their wounds. They break into tears because their mind or body perceives the moment as if they were in the past.

Personally, it's mainly confrontation moments that make me cry, which of course quickly ends in disaster because after a very short time, all my efforts are taken up by trying to stop crying as opposed to resolving any problem at hand. Understandably, the other situation that makes me cry is where I feel unfairly treated. If I see someone upset, I cry as well, and movies, books, any emotional score, I cry at the drop of a hat.

Usually when not alone, I try very hard not to be seen crying. The best way would be if I could take myself out of the upsetting situation, but unfortunately, this usually isn't an option. As an alternative, hijacking the conversation might work, though typically not in formal situations. I sometimes have to use everything I can think of, from digging my nails into my palm to intentionally dissociating, but most of the time I can only delay the silent tears, not completely avoid them. Other strategies include focusing on breathing, avoiding blinking, drawing lines with my tongue inside my mouth, making a slack face, squeezing my teeth together, freezing all movements or trying to move my nose. Drinking something or tilting the head to deter the tears from falling might also work for a while. Tensing up muscles can trick the body and the mind into feeling more composed, in control[102].

Apart from these immediate measures, we can reduce the number of times crying occurs by reducing the number of things we commit to so we don't overstretch ourselves, given our background and excitable nervous systems. Contemplate which ventures, chores or events can be cut out to help reduce overall stress levels.

Our communication difficulties based on missed social cues, possible developmental delay in interpersonal skills and the resulting misunderstandings can be conducive to exasperation, bitterness or resentment, situations that often open the floodgates, which is why it is so important to try to catch up on these skills intentionally, and familiarise oneself with ways to communicate while staying calm. If necessary, count to ten again and again.

The exercise also helps control breathing, thus getting you more oxygen and calming you down. Despite the issue being the urge to cry and not have a panic attack, counting can take the edge off overpowering emotion.

Another strategy that can be used at the same time is taking a conscious, direct note of everything around us. Refocus the energy away from the upsetting affair and experience everything else instead. Ignore the hell out of that person making you agitated and upset. Appreciate the colours, feel where currents of air originate from in the office, enjoy the smooth leather under your fingertips, hear the music filtering out a faraway room, use all your senses to ascertain what else is going on in the place. This breakaway from the trouble in hand can reframe our outlook, put us into a more logical, factual state of mind rather than one based on intense emotion.

It also helps to remind ourselves why the urge to cry appeared. Usually, it has not much to do with the situation at hand, it is only that we are too tired, too overwhelmed, to deal with the problem. The truth is that we are overwhelmed because our rattled nervous systems can't handle any more abuse. This state of mind will put the current problem into perspective.

Some people have props ready to use as distractions, a stress ball, a glinting light display on the window, a logo jumping about on the screen, family photos on a screensaver. I sometimes scribble to distract myself, if possible, pretend I'm writing something important down that my boss has said, showing them I'm listening while in fact I am fighting tooth and nail not to break down crying.

The next port of call to try is relaxation techniques such as breathing exercises, stretching, evoking a pleasant place or scene and repeating a mantra to calm the body and mind. Since tiredness is a factor in eliciting crying, make sure you get sufficient rest. The need for professional treatment might be the answer, however, especially if depression is also present.

There are some things that can be done in advance as well, if we know we're going to enter a situation where we might cry. According to Lauren Bylsma, assistant professor of psychiatry and psychology at the University of Pittsburgh, 'allow yourself to cry it out beforehand. You'll be more likely to keep your composure if you've already done that.' If we rehearse situations beforehand, if possible, we can also circumvent emotional escalation by practising adhering to certainties only, without hypotheticals that can unbalance us[103].

22 Being Judgemental, Inflexible and Opinionated

After yet more fruitless interactions with my brother, I have decided to add this chapter about a further consequence of a traumatic childhood amidst toxic parents. You see, it has got to the point that it is virtually impossible to talk to him about any topic because no matter the subject matter, he will always try to force me to agree with him. Agreeing to disagree is not a possibility with my brother. Everything that he says has to be right and accepted as such and boy, does he have opinions about all subjects!

Unfortunately, it is also not a possibility to have him acknowledge that this rigid behaviour is the result of childhood trauma in his upbringing, that he has built this world for himself where everything is dead sure and cannot be compromised so that he could feel safe and secure. Any threat of anything being false in this made-up world of his would also mean the crumbling of the rest of his world, so no chinks can be possible in this armour. Sadly, this means relationships with others not willing to mollycoddle and agree with everything he says will crumble. It is also hard to keep a relationship amicable when all you hear from the person is how they judge you for not following their 'perfect' one for all, regardless of the circumstances model. Their tolerance level for others being different is low as well, so they often end up being racist or homophobic. This can sometimes present in categorical verbal condemnation, disapproval and hostility towards others or some passive-aggressive behaviours. Some people even go so far as to believe and maintain that they've suffered a personal attack by those who hold different opinions. These people often grew up being overly criticised at home themselves. It is a learnt behaviour as much as it is a way to deal with having been disparaged and scorned while growing up. The resulting judgmentalism develops partly as a defence mechanism that benefits them in the short term by tricking them into feeling worthier and self-righteous.

Without being enlightened about their own personality and willing to explore their trauma, they continue this behaviour, doomed to experience hostility and arguments for the rest of their lives.

Characteristics of such people include always dominating conversations. They tend to choose the topics and rarely run out of things to say, consisting of their views presented in a preaching manner, models to be followed. Clearly, this indicates a lack of listening skills. They rarely change their minds, not even when presented with new information. The information is simply discarded as a matter of non-interest and their perspective is the one and only truth that lamentably often also includes on how everybody should live, think, look and act. If somebody doesn't perform to their expectations, they will see that as a deficiency or weakness and pester them harshly and consistently about it. They will also put the other person down about it in conversation with others. That is how horrible it gets. If asked about the incident, they will say that they were simply trying to help and were widening the circle of helpers by letting them know what was happening. That they hoped that the next person they talked to would be able to do the convincing instead. Almost like a flying monkey situation. They will not back down and will repeat the issue over and over in the hopes of breaking the other person down and making them believe they should follow their instructions.

Do not be tempted by giving in! Once humoured, they will always find a new issue to criticise to make themselves feel better. They brag about their lifestyle choices, achievements or holidays. My brother's favourite is pushing dietary choices and attributing my physical ailments to not eating just like him. He also believes in miracle drugs or cures of the season, trying to force them onto me, not even acknowledging that his miracle drug of choice periodically changes itself.

Judgmentalists cannot fully grasp the concept that others are independent, autonomous agents who aren't exactly like them, that other people's circumstances determine their capabilities, tendencies, morals, tastes and choices. Therefore, they end up with unrealistic expectations of people that don't match their circumstances or abilities, nor the respective people's own choices. They decide for them instead and keep to it in a stubborn manner, personality and personal dispositions be damned. They don't tolerate it when someone points out to them what they're doing and where it may come from. They also tend to be controlling, their rigid viewpoints serving as a crutch that alleviates their fears, of illnesses, of dying, of facing their past and dealing with it in healthier ways. Ironic, really, as just like a lot of other coping mechanisms, its existence is really what keeps the person from growing and getting over their developmental trauma.

Such rigid viewpoints are hard to deal with, so below are some tips on how to approach such a person if we have to or would like to keep up a relationship with them without sacrificing our own peace of mind, a situation pretty likely to occur in our families as we are all affected by similar trauma and might have family members dealing with it in this way.

As every person and situation is different, not all approaches will work, but it is worth trying them out to de-escalate a conflict. Then later it might become clearer which method is best for dealing with a particular person.

As the individual in question is unwilling to accept a straight no as a way of setting boundaries and changing the subject, one might say, 'this isn't the right time for me to discuss the issue' or 'I have to concentrate on work' or any other area you are particularly focusing on. The person you are facing is unlikely to change their minds so explaining to them the reasons behind our choices is pretty pointless and may have us regress into our trauma-induced over-explaining mode. Simply tell them firmly that 'it is my choice.' An alternative to not having to explain anything is thanking them for the advice without having any intention of following it through. A straighter, but still diplomatic version could be: 'it is fine for me the way it is now, but thank you, I'll think about your advice.' In this case, they can't push the issue further as they have to be satisfied with our thinking about it and we have not lied either.

A quick change of subject could be a lifesaver as well. They keep talking about one thing, we ask them about another, over and over till they drop the hurtful subject. You probably know the person well, so you can ask about a different topic they also like talking about but isn't so bothersome. I like this method as it gives the difficult family member's topic that they are obsessed with zero importance. We simply fly over it, no damn given, putting it into the place it deserves.

Unfortunately, there will be some instances where none of these methods will work and all we are left with is cutting contact like we would with other toxic relatives, especially as those under narcissistic influence might well grow up to be narcissists too. It is only the self who can take care of the self the best and if it hurts too deeply, too many times, it's just not worth keeping the relationship up.

Then we will have to deal with the mourning and letting go of the relationship we hoped to have, an admittedly painful period, which will, however, lead to peace in the long term.

If the person reading this recognises themselves in the judgemental role and is willing to change their behaviour seeing how people turn away from them, they can start by putting themselves in the shoes of the person they're about to give advice to. Imagine their circumstances, calculate in everything they've said about themselves. Does the advice still apply? In most cases the answer will be no. Doing this exercise on a regular basis should at least shake the foundations of judgements and lead to a more open mind.

PART 3: ROAD TO RECOVERY

First Steps Out of Trauma

Nothing can describe the horror of childhood trauma well enough to make those who haven't experienced it understand it fully. It feels is as if you've lost a part of yourself before you ever had time to find it in yourself, having to cope with being an adult, feeling like part of you is unaccounted for, stolen, missing. A huge part. Having to venture out in life incomplete, without the tools to manage in society. It is a terror that no one should have to experience.

Unfortunately, again, the naive outsider often thinks that overcoming childhood abuse is simply a matter of forgiving and forgetting unpleasant memories when it's nothing like that at all. Forgiving might help some, if they can do so, but mostly it is the aftereffects of abuse we struggle with, so forgiving has nothing to do with overcoming it. It might be hard to relate to that unless you are a survivor of emotional abuse, but the way it presents is as if we were still automatically fighting daily battles in our heads with a person we might not even have any contact with anymore. The effects of trauma return as a reaction, not a memory. For a while, at least, during the healing journey, we might have to disengage from people who don't understand this in order to protect ourselves from trying to analyse why they don't get us. No need to waste any more time analysing their system of psychological defences as we know why they don't understand us. The primary goal is to understand oneself so that we can function better.

Based on personal experiences, it is clearly hard to shed the chains of trauma, it's hard to move on. Thus, it is quite common to be stuck in a mindset, in a pattern of behaviour, experiencing a certain negative emotion over and over again. Most sufferers would understand how it is commonplace to be angry, or, in fact, numb, and it's also normal to keep our anxiety and fears in adult life. The most common misconception, however, is that you have to forgive. Well, sometimes the abuse is too much to be forgiven and even if it's not, there's no reason why you'd have to forgive the abuser to be able to work on mental health. In fact, oftentimes the only way to go forward is not to forgive, to keep a healthy distance from the abuser and acknowledge the wrongs for what they were. Only after this distancing is it possible to see the big picture, a different perspective and realise that what you have to do is to continue getting better.

One of the first phases of healing for a survivor of emotional abuse is sorting through and deprogramming all the deception of the narcissist, sociopath or psychopath carer. This is because the harm we suffered will not disappear by itself regardless of how much we try to disregard it, forget it, forgive it.

Healing, unfortunately, is complicated, the same as with learning to love oneself. It's more about going back to the times we stopped doing so and rescuing that little individual by remembering why we stopped treating them right ourselves. It is usually because from our childhood, we don't know, we didn't learn, what a healthy relationship encompasses, what genuineness, dependability, equality, mutuality is, how validation is meant to feel. Intimacy feels false because we don't trust anyone. Since we were not allowed to respond appropriately to the injustices we've suffered, we have no idea how to express them or cope with them. We do not know either how to respond appropriately to traumatic events, leading to more confusion, dissociation, pain and turning inwards for help, fearing anyone else.

We need to learn all these things as adults, starting way behind our counterparts, taking a big chunk of our energies before we can concentrate on anything else. Accomplishing these goals shouldn't mean the same thing for everyone. It should take into account individualised obstacles and handicaps. Some of us are so damaged that simply getting out of the bed is an accomplishment and if so, we should be proud of those moments too.

Regrettably, men are less likely to employ the help of a professional because of the way society views males, who are supposed to be tough, rather than resort to crying or admit any sort of weakness. Disclosing sexual abuse is also harder for them. Similarly, adults over the age of fifty find it far less natural than younger people to disclose having experienced childhood trauma of any kind and ask for help, says Michael Barnes, clinical program manager at the Centre for Dependency, Addiction and Rehabilitation at the University of Colorado Hospital in Aurora.

Unfortunately, the longer people wait, the more detrimental it tends to be for their mental health. They are generally unhappy, hypervigilant and distrustful as they could not rely on their primary carer not to hurt them, with a destructive effect on their marriages and other relationships later in life. According to an Australian abuse support group, men with the history of childhood abuse are four to five times more likely to commit suicide. Due to their low self-esteem, they repeat the abuse cycles with partners in adult life, leading to feelings of extreme despair and detachment.

Other abuse survivors react with a need to control everything in their lives to feel safe. Self-employment or un(der)employment is common amongst childhood abuse survivors as it is hard to make everyone happy at a place of work, a compulsion a lot of sufferers feel they need to accomplish, and a workplace also gives a lot of control over to someone else.

The other angle to acknowledge is that dealing with childhood trauma and reaching the stage where we are leading a more contented and fulfilling life as a result is a long-term process and involves relearning responses and behaviours to triggers, rewiring pathways in your brain. Given childhood trauma's effect on physical health, it is very important to keep an eye on health issues and take care of ourselves, give and allow ourselves happy moments doing what we like to do. The Blue Knot Foundation advocates for learning distress tolerance, comforting oneself in a healthy manner and taming anxiety and anger in addition. Mindful meditation[67] is another great way to help with coping in the meantime. Learnt optimism, dialectical behaviour therapy (DBT) techniques and cognitive behavioural therapy are being used to make strides overcoming old trauma-based habits[68], all meant to target negative feelings as they happen and rewire our brains with the help of lots of practice and support.

Till then, we have hope, and, perhaps, a book or two like this. Take care of yourself and stay away from toxic people! There's nobody else who can love you as much as you can love yourself.

Returning to or Relating to the Narcissist Parent as an Adult Child

However bizarre, given all this abuse and its consequences, it is understandable if, after all this, in an ideal world, you'd still want an emotional attachment to your parents. It feels like it is our right to have a mother like everyone else and sometimes it is hard to accept not having one, even though they are alive. In other cases, we can't stay away because that would mean stopping contact with the other parent as well, or another family member. When someone is trauma-bonded to a narcissist, they experience a strong compulsion to remain connected, indulge the narcissist, notwithstanding how much the adult children are being hurt themselves. Some may feel they still need to look after their parents in their old age despite the abuse.

Certainly, you can't expect any parent to be perfect. They are human after all. Everyone is allowed to make mistakes, take time out if they need it for their own mental health, and we can't blame them for that. However, I advocate, at least initially, a no-contact policy with sick, narcissistic individuals and I have previously explained why. And no contact means no contact. That is, no phone calls, emails, short meetups, group participation together, no text messages, no accepting gifts. 'Victims are in such a trance and state of confusion that they don't know the extent of the abuse till they are away from their abuser. When you are not walking on eggshells, when you are not in a constant state of hypervigilance and fear, then you are able to relax a minute, and see more of what is really going on. When you start educating yourself you see a clearer picture of how you were manipulated and abused. There is so much damage to a victim's mental health and overall well-being. All in an effort to gain dominance and control over them.' – Maria Consiglio. So now you have escaped the worst relationship you are ever likely to have and you survived because you are strong. The trauma bond will eventually fade and you can thank your chosen deities you got away.

Asking a narcissistic parent not to do something that hurts you as an adult remains like talking to a wall, along with explaining the whys and wherefores of this request, because it is absolutely certain that they will still not alter their behaviour, the only difference will be that they might try to be shrewder about it. It is okay to cut off other family members too, other than the main abuser. You may need distance from people who bring out memories of the trauma or relate to you as a person you don't want to be anymore. No apologies needed as it is so that you can survive. No one should have to apologise for how they've learnt to survive, for how they're not able to love unconditionally as a result.

Going back to the narcissist parent too early can result in them being able to suck the victim back in by using the triggers they themselves installed in childhood. They do know their target very well, after all, their wants and fears and their intensities so you need to be sure you know how to handle them, which knowledge oftentimes only comes after a considerable period of no contact.

In the initial stages of renewed contact, they might appear changed, they might go out of their way to fulfil some needs the adult child might have, they could even offer some 'fauxpologies', small apologies which seem to communicate repentance, but do not in effect admit to any wrongdoing. As archetypal that may sound, this is actually the same person who has repeatedly and intentionally hurt the victim and they still won't take any blame, not even after the sufferer expressed how much they've been hurt. Make no mistake, they are the same person who punished you for the smallest mistake without empathy and often, just because they wanted to, and in the absence of an actual, objective mistake. And that, again, is either evil or there is something candidly wrong with their mental health and beliefs and there is something non compos mentis about their state of mind. Nothing the narcissist says is ever what they truly mean. Language is simply a tool they use for deception, manipulation and storytelling. Everything they do is for show or only meant in the moment as narcissists are morally corrupt. They don't know what morals are, they don't understand the concept as it isn't self-serving. Narcissism is a personality disorder, a deep-rooted pattern of behaviour that varies distinctly from standard, accepted behaviour, in other words, not something that can be changed, not just because that is who they are, but also because that is what they want to stay like. With their stunted, stuck, emotional growth, they act clearly and utterly insane, with unstable moods and screwed morals. This utmost emotional immaturity can be seen in their temper tantrums, outbursts and cyclic thought processes, especially if the toy they were concentrating on is taken away from them. I would like to stress that they can't communicate effectively and equivocally, they are unwilling to accept help that would bring about change and they can never heal. Sad and almost pitiful really, if looked at objectively, while I disregard what was done to me by one of these individuals. 'They may have good careers and appear highly functional, but they are extremely emotionally immature and stunted individuals.' – Maria Consiglio. They are incredibly superficial. Not understanding real love, they aim to impress a stranger more than they would offer a real apology in the chances of being forgiven and truly loved.

The good news is that dealing with the narcissist as an adult and not being dependent on them can become easier over time with the use of some techniques.

One would be disengaging. This means opting for not giving them the power to elicit an emotional response, including not letting them lower our self-esteem again.

Another technique that can be used at the same time is letting them know that you've recognised their tactic and that it won't work, quickly followed by changing the subject or taking ourselves out of the situation so we don't have to listen to the usual useless word salad. Letting them talk at this point would be counterproductive as we know how impossible it is to tell a narcissist how we feel in a way they would take into account. They will be aggrieved every time because they think of our feelings as an attack directed at them and have no empathy for the other party. Anything negative contradicts their belief that they are magnificent, supreme entities. The issue cannot be resolved, so it has to be left alone. There's always going to be negative energy there. Some people are just despicable and we need to stop searching for something that isn't ever going to be there. It is too often that we make the mistake of letting people stay longer than they deserve despite the very little benefits we might still get out of the relationship. If that means being alone, then so be it. It is better being alone than being abused.

It is also relevant to note that abusers will not behave the same way every day, so it might not be evident what they are. Especially as they will also have good days and bad days, times where they feel happier and less likely to take their anger out on the child and might give the appearance of being the most agreeable person in the world. It is also a good screen, it confuses people, including the victims. 'The key is to remember that it is just an abuser having a good day. But still an abuser based on all the other days.' – Shannon Thomas, author of *Healing from Hidden Abuse*. Another obstacle in identifying them is that the majority of them 'abuse only their own families. Putting on appearances is what narcissists do best. Don't be fooled. Even serial killers are said to have been the nicest people in the world. Narcissists hide in plain sight. Believe survivors.' – Maria Consiglio.

Normally, taking up relations with a narcissist parent leads to further confusion. Just because we grew up, it doesn't automatically mean we are immune to being hurt by them. So be vigilant and aware of their calamitous gaslighting strategies aimed to confuse: holding back particulars to manipulate the truth, faking not being aware of the situation, lying, changing the subject and underplaying the importance of another person's views, so-called feelings and concerns presented in the form of ridicule.

Any more time in their sphere and we start to question our sanity again. However, we now know that the problem doesn't originate from us. The narcissist's lies, gaslighting and mind games are to blame and if you let it, it will soon start to seriously cloud the brain again, and compromise your overall well-being. I don't know when society will start punishing these people, make these practices prohibited for use with children, but it starts with us. With pinpointing the behaviour, outing these people to the world, we can maybe save a future generation, change the general attitude that walking away from a parent is seen as cruel, regardless of circumstances. 'Walking away has nothing to do with weakness and everything to do with strength. We walk away not because we want others to realise our worth and value, but because we finally realise our own.' – Robert Tew, author of *Homeland Enemy*. Everybody would run a mile if they knew who and what these abusers were. The urge to break no contact is only habitual addictive wiring, leave that be, you know better.

But if you are really intent on continuing relations with the toxic party, you are dancing with fire and darkness and should look out for the red flags and signs of abusive behaviour. You should set boundaries and have plans of escape, should they be crossed. Analyse and double-check what the narcissist says to spot lies. If it seems that they have changed in a way that is a too-good-to-be-true kind of way, it certainly is too good to be true.

Another thing I noticed is that at and after reconnection, the narcissist tends to ask a lot of questions as if they cared. However, this is for collecting information to store and use later, should an opportunity for criticism arise, since they aren't allowed to do it right away anymore. They will still manage it in covert ways. Often, I only have an *a-ha* moment after I disconnect the phone call, when I realise why certain things were said.

Narcissist abuse survivors hate lies especially and the fakeness people put on as a societal norm. They are second-guessing every thought and observation because of the mixed messages given. There was enough of that in our childhood already and we have suffered enough as a result.

Adult children children reconnecting with the abuser should look out for common signs of entitlement the person exhibits as well. These can manifest in self-absorption, interrupting others speaking because they cannot suffer somebody else, their competition, taking all the attention, and seeking special treatment because they are considering their own needs a prime concern, just to name a few.

I'd also like to talk about the narcissist's reaction to no contact. Obviously, there will be a fallout. At first, they will be scandalised at the allegations of being labelled what they are. I call it evil, others can call it toxic. Their pretend amnesia is toxic also. They claim not to remember acting out, cruel behaviour, verbal abuse, breaches of trust they've engaged in. It's part of their gaslighting strategy and is designed to make you feel like you're irrational or mentally unstable, creating doubt in your mind, enhancing symptoms of cognitive dissonance. They will now be affronted that their victim is no longer submitting to the abuse, that they aren't bowing down to their supreme godliness and are not welcoming the nitpicking they call advice, the blaming games, the put-downs, the causticity or the disrespect and the brutality they deliver it all with.

They will be revolted that their opinions are not taken as written in stone. And most certainly, they will be horrified to be revealed to the world for who they are and deny all the dirty laundry to be theirs, to have to admit that they need their narcissistic supply more than we need them. Without that, they hold no power, they never had any as they had to take it away from us to build themselves up. But that supply of love and empathy is cut off now. They never gave you any and the realisation leads to the conclusion that it is better to be without them.

With no contact, we don't have to hear about it, but our family members and friends will experience the narcissist's anger. The narcissist will see themselves as the victim of unfair treatment and will present themselves accordingly. They will think of the boundaries set by us as some wrongdoing and will never see that they were needed exactly because of their harmful tactics. Not willingly submitting to their manipulation, bullying, mockery, callousness and domination makes them furious, aggrieved and indignant. It had seemed to have been their right all our lives before, after all. Don't expect accountability, not even after years of no contact. The narcissist doesn't change, only their disruptive tactics, on occasion. They think asking for accountability is an attack on their person. They will not acknowledge that their behaviour harms others.

Of course, the no contact approach isn't for the purposes of taking revenge on the abuser. It is solely part of self-care and becoming conscious of our values. We don't exist to be abused at the convenience of the narcissist parent. There's no such thing as a simple conversation with the narc anyway. They don't do dialogue, being either unable or unwilling to understand someone else. Every talk with the narc is like a contest in verbal fighting. Their aim is to win, no compromises, even when nobody else sees any competition. Every exchange with them is a weapon that they can use to influence and mystify the opposition. A conversation between the narc and their target typically goes like this:

> One: I would like to see the dictionary definition.
> Narc: Oh, because you don't believe me? Are you saying I'm stupid?
> One: That's not what I said.
> Narc: So you're calling me a liar too now?
> One: We're having a little misunderstanding.
> Narc: So I misunderstood because I'm stupid?
> One: I didn't say or imply that.
> Narc: Why is it always so complicated with you?
> One: Can we have a polite conversation without shouting?
> Narc: It was you who called me stupid first.

Impossible, right? Round and round it goes. They twist everything to their advantage. At this point, the only option the adult child has is to shrug and opt out. You don't ever have to feel condemnable for withdrawing from what's toxic in your life. Sane people don't talk like this.

The only other kind of conversations I've ever seen with a narc are of the envious and jealous type, where they smear another person only because they have something they covet. You didn't deserve this so cut them out. Besides, your happiness doesn't have to make sense to anyone else. Narcissists are well-known meddlers. The less you tell them about your life or problems, the better off you'll be. They stir the pot to create drama and confusion for others, set people up against each other deliberately, have a need to control and have the last say in every situation, even when the topic has nothing to do with them.

A period of no contact is also recommended because there were instances where the abused child, usually very isolated and brainwashed into thinking he/she had to obey, wasn't aware of the extent of the abuse till they talked to someone and it was pointed out to them how much their experiences deviate from the normal childhood.

Another strategy is detached contact where you imagine yourself talking to a wall, trying to avoid it eliciting feelings. You might think that not challenging them over a lie or allegation is counterproductive, but a blank face and no acknowledgement could be better because it proves they had no effect on you, which means they're not getting their cherished narcissistic supply. While no contact is still the best method, you can disengage with narcissistic and other kinds of manipulative people by being brief, matter-of-fact, without revealing much about your private life, appearing dispassionate, without emotion and not feeding into their drama. This is called the grey rock method, becoming as unstimulating, dull and unresponsive as possible without diminishing oneself. Say 'mmm eh, I don't know about that', 'I don't care', 'whatever'.

I'd like to point out that whether you choose to have a relationship with your narcissist parent or not, you are in the position of power and you hold all the cards for once, owing to the fact that they can't trick you anymore, you know exactly who they are and what to expect. One of the greatest awakenings comes when you become cognisant of the fact that not everybody changes. Some people never reach a level of emotional intelligence to be able to do so. True transformation is painful. Often, a feeling of pity comes at this point as you look at this defeated, ghastly shell of a human being who once used to be able to intimidate you, have power over you. Because all their desperate tactics, all the bossy, bullying and immature, abusive behaviours led them nowhere. Generally old and alone, they have no choice now but to accept the boundaries set up and have no chance to abuse, hurt or mock us. Some might try to fix them at this point, show them how real relationships work. This is impossible to achieve so we shouldn't give them the control over us in this way either. It is not our journey, it is theirs. But, if the interplay makes you feel inadequate in any way, if it endangers your dignity or leaves you feeling less attractive, sharp or appealing, then that should stand as a warning that the interaction was most likely harmful and the relationship is falling back into old patterns. We can't forget that narcissists are not fully functioning human beings. They only see others, even their own children, as sources to feed off, supply. Any relationship with them can only be superficial, yet toxic enough to crush the soul of and drain the victim in every way. Therefore, caution is advised at all times. Usually, people can't just turn love off, but a narcissist can turn it off as simply as they have turned it on because for them, showing love is merely an instrument they employ to be able to influence others. 'The moment you feel like you have to prove your worth to someone is the moment to absolutely and utterly walk away.' Alysia Harris.

When they ask for further relations, remember that these narcs do not have the psychological and mental capacity to grasp how their behaviour affected us. We have to accept that this is the kind of person they are and that engaging in confidential conversations with them will take us nowhere useful as they mainly only say things to alter the discussion to their own benefit. There is no need to waste time with people like that. The good news is that you have all the power now. You can stop at any moment, leave your abuser behind, return to your inner peace unencumbered.

The narcissist's biggest weakness is greatly overestimating their abilities and underestimating other people's. You know your worth and nobody can bring that down without your permission. Your rise was amazing. There were times you felt you couldn't go on, but you still got out of bed regardless for another day of trials and that took enormous strength. Life is so different once you escape the living hell of being under the control of a narcissist, it can almost feel like a culture shock. It is a startling experience, not having to walk on eggshells and wondering when the next emotional, verbal and psychological attack against you will be. You are no longer sleeping with one eye open. It's like finally being released from prison.

When you tell the narcissist that they are a narcissist and that you know all of their manipulative methods, they will just reject it. Idealising and missing a relationship that has previously emotionally destroyed you is a sign of a trauma bond, not love. Most narcissists are not self-aware and therefore will just reject what you have to say. When you tell them of all the bad things they have done, they will deny it and they will truly believe that they have done nothing wrong. What then happens is you providing them with some propellant, like any time you are talking to or physically interacting with the narcissist and you threaten their control. While you are attempting to make them accountable, you are still giving them the fuel and they will then attempt to reassert control over the adult child.

I can't state enough that the narcissistic parent tries to pulverise their children's self-worth, their convictions. It is not necessarily what they want and what they plan out to do, they simply need to hold themselves in a higher reward to others because otherwise it is their world that is crushed. But regardless of the explanation for their behaviour, you can maybe forgive them, but you cannot get acceptance from them. It is futile trying and it is only going to anger you. No more parent-pleasing! Don't fall for the derogatory comments. Either walk away or respond dismissively, but without displaying any strong emotion.

Another way to disarm the narcissist is simply agreeing dismissively, but not meaning it. We avoided the conflict and we did not engage, we did not allow our narc to make us angry again, we did not waste energy. Toxic people need our reactions, our attention and low self-esteem to survive, while they dread us becoming our own person, our silence and impassiveness the most. Once a victim of narcissistic abuse finds out that there is a name for what they have been going through, once they find the actual words and definitions of the abuse tactics they have been subjected to, then everything changes. Once the victim recognises the signs, they can no longer erase the memory of it. This is the game changer for standing up and not taking it any longer. To summarise, the sign of such a toxic parent is doing something, denying it and declaring you crazy for thinking so.

Of course, it is so much easier as an adult, when we can say things like 'I am not overly sensitive. This is a valid response to outrageous behaviour,' 'I don't have to defend my discomfort,' or 'I am not interested in having a conversation where you invalidate me' and we don't have to listen to the fallout. It is still possible to do this with kindness and not stooping to the narcissist's level. Nobody is a disgraceful individual for wanting to go no contact with the parent, but they are indeed a bad parent for making that something an offspring would ever want.

Narcissists cannot stand people who tell the truth as it endangers the views they hold, mainly of themselves. This is why so often the truth-tellers in the family end up being ostracised and persecuted by the narc or their enablers as the scapegoat or the black sheep. That also means that some of us will break generational cycles nobody in the family could do. Have you ever noticed how people who don't condone lies, mockery and duplicity tend to be regarded as complicated, always labelled difficult, unstable or bitter? The same reason I hate the everyday lie 'I'm fine' like so many other neurodivergents. But guess what? We can decide to end any family's transgenerational trauma here and now and that is amazing.

We also need to stop giving any weight to how the narcents see their children, because it is a false perception, the same way as they have a false perception about everyone else! On the contrary, it is narcissists who shouldn't underestimate their children as they grow up knowing what their parents are.

People-pleasing is never a sound idea, but there are also others in the world, who can and will offer love and support because it is what they want for you from a non-self-centred perspective! Remember the song 'You Raise Me Up' by Secret Garden with its many, many covers? That is how love should be, not that warped idea the narc taught us. People who love you do not want to cause you intended suffering. It is sometimes an unintentional side effect of what they have done, but it is nowhere near the same level as the narcissist's complete disregard for the other's emotional needs, as they do not need to make other people inferior so that they can feel good in their own skins. There is a huge contrast between someone who damages another by making a mistake and then learns from it and does not do it again, and another who is simply sustaining the pattern without looking at the consequences. It is possible to excuse the omission with the first person, but the latter needs to be avoided. Use those skills honed by abuse and never underestimate the enemy. Never entertain the idea that they have changed, either. Those who destroyed you the first time will do it a second, third time, given the opportunity.

As people who have already suffered abuse, we need to also take into account that in every relationship we are shaped into someone more susceptible to narcissistic abuse. Characteristics of easy targets include being an empath, a lack of boundaries, a tendency to people-pleasing, low self-esteem and so on.

We survivors are strong, as every day we have to fight with so many anxieties and symptoms just to get out the door or every time we lift the phone. But that strength did not come from the abuse. No matter what, we had to survive, despite all these hardships, so the strength was already there. It is in each and every one of us warriors, superstars, courageous champions. I will not grant my abuser that privilege to get the glory for my strength. She did not give me strength, she gave me misery and pain. Rising out of that took all that I had, but I had it, despite all the disappointment I felt in the world that let me down.

So let's carry this torch and educate others so that they can recognise narcissistic patterns easier, lighten the load put on the child by taking them out of these situations earlier and ultimately understand our own patterns of behaviour, where they come from and how to change them. There needs to be more procedures in place to recognise these types of parents, compulsory psychiatric evaluations to prove their narcissistic personalities, laws that support the child or their emancipation in these cases, courts that acknowledge this kind of damage. Can such parents come with warning labels, please? Because let's be clear, narcissistic abuse is lethal. Of course, there are cases of domestic violence when it literally ends up deadly, and other cases where the child eventually commits suicide either as an adult or a teenager, but I'm not talking about those. Growing up with a typical narc as a parent has grave consequences, affecting both the victim's physical and mental health. 'It changes who they are, and minimises their potential. Extreme trauma can even cause brain damage and various other physical and mental abnormalities. This is not a joke and it is far more dangerous than people acknowledge. Some people develop extensive chronic physical ailments, and/or mental processing issues. It also negatively impacts a person's day-to-day functioning. It's not just wrong, it's a damn crime, what people go through. If you are a victim, I am talking to you. Go no contact and save your life.' – Maria Consiglio. Your closure, your rules. Realising that the narc was simply some crazed lunatic is a form of closure.

Exposing toxic individuals is important as well as it can help avoid further transgressions and bring justice to victims. As Daniell Koepke, author of *Daring to Take Up Space* says, it 'doesn't matter whether someone is a relative, romantic interest, employer, childhood friend or a new acquaintance, you don't have to make room for people who cause you pain or make you feel small. It's one thing if a person owns up to their behaviour and makes an effort to change. But if a person disregards your feelings, ignores your boundaries, does not appreciate you for who you are and "continues" to treat you in a harmful way, they need to go.' They are a waste of space, a waste of time. You already know that narcissists treat people like rubbish because they seek to level the playing field by belittling and rejecting others only so they can feel less insecure. This can show up in common gaslighting remarks I've mentioned, along the lines of 'you're crazy', 'you need professional help', 'you're blowing things out of proportion', 'I didn't mean that', 'you did it wrong, not me', 'you have mental issues', 'you should develop a thicker skin', 'you're too sensitive', 'it's always the drama with you', 'you're overreacting', 'you're only imagining it', 'it was just a joke', 'amazing the things you can imagine', 'you're taking rubbish', 'I didn't abuse or hurt you at all', 'that is your problem', 'I didn't do anything, it's all in your head'.

A normal person doesn't need to hoard together fans and servants and people who bow down to their brilliance or dominance like a narcissist does with their harem. We can start living for impressing ourselves based on what is important for us. When you 'start doing that, life starts to shine brighter in front of you, it's all about loving yourself and knowing the reality of who you are.' – Sangeeta Rana.

On Not Believing Victims

I would like to touch on this issue again more in detail, since I have briefly broached the subject on previous occasions. This is because, unfortunately, I keep bumping into the problem, with people not understanding the magnitude of the effects of such abuse, not even after detailed explanations. The other unfortunate situation of concern I keep encountering is people insisting it can all be solved easily and the victims shouldn't as much as think about their pasts, this, also, after our extensive explanations otherwise. But we can't let anyone negate or minimise how we feel, that would be like going back to step one, right into the abusive situation itself! Whatever we feel, it is real to us, it's our internal battle with reality. Nobody has the right to say otherwise. They didn't walk in our shoes, they should not judge. They have no idea how hard it was. For them it is easier to believe that the alleged abuser couldn't possibly do what they are being accused of than to get into the nitty-gritty with the survivor and figure out the truth. Until this behaviour changes, abuse and violence will not cease either. So,

Dear Doubter, Invalidator of Feelings, Invalidator of Personalities, Downplayer – you are the problem! This is certainly part of why the victim rarely gets the support they need to actually be able to move on as planned, given that, as it happens, we don't actually want to stay in the past. It is the past that keeps forcing itself into our awareness in one way or another, usually through spontaneous anxious states or other difficulties that, on the surface, have nothing to do with abuse. We don't hash it up and open up the past for the sake of it or because we want to. As much as one might try to bury it on purpose, it still comes up in unconscious decisions and instincts and so we need to learn to live with it, to understand it, to rise above it by making sense of it. And then, maybe then we can shine and we can thrive. Parallel to that, the last step of psychological healing is always helping others who go through what we went through.

As a person who has extensively studied, lived and discussed narcissistic abuse with others in similar positions and has worked with children for several years, I probably notice more reliably when signs of a toxic parent emerges. But would I have been able, to the same extent, had I not been through it myself? I would like to think so, but realistically, probably to a lesser degree. This is where the Doubter comes in. Not to mention that some people are largely uninterested to learn about such phenomena. So I give Dear Doubter the benefit of the doubt, however damaging and hurtful their actions are. I'm not going to have delusions about being able to set the world on fire at once, but the harmful effect is why we need to at least cause a shift in awareness and understanding. Dear Doubter needs to know that talking about our experiences does not make us weaker, nor is it about letting out the darkness at large, and they need to believe it because the witness of their own psyche says so about themselves. Sharing experiences like this is like worldwide group therapy, we help each other. The world 'needs your light, your warmth and raging courage.' – Alex Elle, author, certified breathwork coach and Writing to Heal facilitator.

Some will throw toxic positivity at us, demanding something that is impossible to achieve. Something like 'don't think about it so much, just be positive', or 'you have to stop being negative', 'positive vibes only', but instead, the first step to supporting a survivor of any abuse or mental illness is believing them.

Moreover, people also talk about healing from childhood trauma as if it were simple, painless, idiot-proof and without much effort while in truth it usually requires more strength than going through the trauma itself. Additionally, it might be more painful and exhausting. It should not be a secret that it is dark and messy and it breaks people, but on the other side, there is healing, so it will be worth it. There are a lot of people who wrestle with trauma, depression and addiction on their own, without help and that doesn't make their experience any less painful or less justifiable. Unseen suffering should be taken into consideration, it counts, it adds up. Feelings, pain, their influences coming from past experiences, all left a mark and everyone should be given the benefit of the doubt. Just because they don't shout it out to the world, it doesn't mean they don't suffer. Childhood trauma could also be based on a lying parent, not being appreciated or heard, having a parent who lives vicariously through their child, being warned not to display or experience certain emotions, having a parent who overcompensates for what they felt was missing in their childhood, having a parent obsessed with looks or who cannot regulate their emotions.

Nature versus nurture: it seems like everybody has had to write an essay on that topic at some time in their lives. So our experiences shouldn't be minimised, there should be no partial blaming, shaming or criticising the victim as they will shut down from further hurt and this will impede progress. The same goes with rushing them, urging them into action. Arguing with them only extends the duration of the healing process.

Learning about their abuse is a good place to start, for someone not used to the phenomenon. If someone really wants to help, they should launch into further, academic study of it as well, understand the pulling mechanisms and fundamentally rethink how adults relate to children. Paying attention and learning – that shows genuine interest.

First, the victim needs a listening ear, working through their emotions, and only then, when they are ready, is when they can move on. Of course, they want to heal! They would have achieved that already if they could. Recovery is neither quick, nor is it linear. There will be unforeseen stagnant parts and even falling back sometimes if triggers occur, such as further criticism from someone who is claiming they want to help. There will be parts when they will want to stop, regroup, take a breather, deal with all the released emotion. This is all normal. Everybody takes a different path, shorter or longer. Get informed, educate yourself on their condition to better understand them, and do not make unfounded assumptions. Listen empathically without judgement, let the sufferer share as much or as little they want. Let them know you're there for them and encourage them to accept help if they need it. Offer to go with them to the doctor's or counsellor's but do not force it if they are not ready. Help by reminding them to take their medication. Be patient. Ask if they'd want help in creating a crisis or emergency plan for some issue they might find themselves panicking about. Don't be scared to ask questions, but be accepting if the sufferer doesn't want to answer or talk about it there and then. They might choose to on their own, later, now that they know they can rely on you. There will be lots of setbacks and improvements so remember to check in on them and let them know you care.

If it is a child who discloses abuse, the main thing is to start by believing the child. Remain calm and allow children to tell their own story while showing interest and concern and offering reassurance. Taking action and reporting the incident can save a child's life. Overreacting or promising things we can't control can be counterproductive, however, as it may further lower the child's confidence in helpful adults they can turn to.

Unfortunately, I have seen therapists or self-help groups reject the concept of healing being a long process as well. They will conform to modern society's push for a quick fix, coping strategies and Band-Aids, not explore the avenue to real healing. They are not interested in anything else but putting out quick, temporary or surface level results. These can of course be useful in some circumstances and I use several such strategies myself, but will never give up on the deeper meaning of healing.

Setting Boundaries

As I have explained previously, the abused child often falls into the typical behaviour patterns of a people-pleaser, limiting their own time, potential and happiness with it. It is why someone abused by a narcissist can fall into another narcissist's spell again and again when they either try to fix them or attempt to make them happy, a situation made worse by the chronic fear about what others think. They find leaving the narcissist hard partly for that reason too, because what would people think if they found out they had chosen the wrong person and now they have to admit it?

Therefore, setting boundaries with another individual sometimes needs to be done consciously and a conscious effort is also needed to see the plan through, especially as, typically, those abused tend to attract people who don't respect boundaries. I'll explain how in a little while. Some of the maladjusted abused also tend to overshare details about their lives in their social awkwardness very similar to those on the spectrum, continuing a cycle of letting themselves be exposed and exploited, an act that can keep them feeling like a victim.

Not Our Job to Fix Others

Thinking we need to fix others and make them feel good comes from the false concept imposed upon us by our narcissist as well, especially when it happens to the extent of ignoring our own needs. Some of us unfortunately might need a lesson in real love before we can understand it and aim to reciprocate it, one in healthy acceptance, empathy and commitment. I am saying healthy because it is all dependent on measures. Acceptance doesn't entail accepting a loved one's behaviour when it harms us or takes advantage of us, empathy doesn't mean sacrificing our mental health and the remains of our energy in the process, and commitment should be comparative too. In other words, we need to be there for them, but not to the extent of sacrificing our own selves or fixing them. It is not possible anyway. You can switch on the light for someone, but you can't make them see the light.

We do not need to fix others to love them and we do not need to feel guilty if we don't, and, most importantly, we do not need to fix them so that we can be loved or happy. Trying to fix them might even upset them. That's not how healthy relationships work! If they have asked for that, then it is their approach to love that is not healthy.

I am aware that some victims of narcissistic child abuse end up codependent. I am not going to claim to have first person knowledge of this condition. Those relationships are on the other end of the scale to hyper-independence, with all the attention being on the partner to the detriment of all other relationships and activities, often so that they can fix the other. It pertains to an unhealthy situation where one of the partners tends to keep quiet to avoid disagreements, gives up disproportionately on their own desires and needs to please, while the other partner behaves recklessly on a regular basis and seldom returns the help offered[51]. In many cases the dynamic validates the other partner's destructive behaviour, such as helping to hide drug abuse, criminal or otherwise dangerous ventures. Clearly, that situation would lead to losing our own selves in the process and is similarly not advisable.

It is often said that we need to learn to love ourselves before we can love and be kind to another. The point is, I think, clearly proven here. There is so much that is wrong with the concept of love that we learn from a narcissistic mother that we need to work through at least some of the resulting issues before being able to care for someone else the right way, and that oftentimes includes a child.

A lot of victims of childhood abuse swear that they will never cause similar harm to the child as their parents did, but a simple statement of such intent is not enough. The predilection is there, undoubtedly, after having suffered such abuse, but the less personal growth and understanding of the reasons hiding behind our behaviours, the more mistakes we will make.

The victim of childhood abuse often grapples with the concept of being kind at all costs as well, not wanting to cause trauma in anyone's life. I like to think of kindness as part of my identity too. Being heartless would be easier, more beneficial, but that's not who I am.

While it is a commendable idea to be kind, caution is needed. Offering too much help, too much kindness, too much of our time might eventually wear us down, endanger our own mental health and make us fall into the old habits of people-pleasing and self-sacrificing. I'm not saying anyone should cause harm with intent, but considering every decision from every person's angle will only ultimately exhaust anyone and limit them from reaching their potential. Again, that is not what kindness is.

It is Okay to Say No

If we say no to a person and they respond negatively, it does not mean we should have said yes. I have grappled with this concept for many years; feeling like saying no means letting people down. Sometimes agreeing to something took all of my energy, all my peace of mind, all my money, all my time and I still thought I had to say yes just because somebody asked. I couldn't let them down, could I? I could not be that person. I could not look myself in the eye if I did that. I had to have impeccable morals so that I could feel as far removed from my mother as I could imagine. Additionally, I still had that instinct to please. I could not imagine people having negative thoughts about me, I could not bear their (perceived) disparaging look. If I wanted to advance in my professional life, I had to say yes to pretty much anything, right? It was such a compulsion, saying yes. I thought I wasn't a good enough person if I didn't say yes, I thought I could not improve.

I had particular qualms about changing my decision to a no if I had already said yes and I had to go back on it because circumstances had changed. I felt like I was cheating, oftentimes choosing between which person to disappoint, obsessed about what valid reasons I had for going back on my word, never thinking that my needs could come first, in fact, and I didn't need to say yes to anything, if it didn't suit. It was a time of my life when I had many friends, always at the ready for other people, no wonder I was malleable to their needs.

Others might not want to say no just so they appear easy to get along with, so they don't upset people. They want to be liked and they don't want to feel guilty for not helping. Wrongly, of course. Let's change the tone. There's no need to respond to anything void of love. We can reset the tone of our whole lives by only being receptive to love and responding in kind. When a request is made from a place of love, the requester will also understand if we need to cancel, choose ourselves. There's nothing to feel guilty for, that feeling was an aftereffect of growing up in a narcissistic home.

Some like to keep busy so they can avoid disturbing thoughts or because they want to avoid a confrontation. Sometimes, it's peer pressure, not wanting to hurt someone's feelings or appear self-serving or tactless and sometimes we want to feel superhuman and be available so that we can feel good about ourselves. It should be obvious how detrimental and debilitating this behaviour becomes over time. Sooner or later, it will undoubtedly lead to burnout and a reduction in not just mental but physical health as well. It can feel like prison in the open air. Research from the University of California in San Francisco [49] shows that the harder it is for someone to say no, the more likely it is they will undergo stress, feelings of burnout and depression. The effect is detrimental to what we wanted to achieve in the first place as well because when you get 'stressed and anxious, you're viewed as a patsy.' – Susan Newman, social psychologist and author of *The Book of No*[50]. So our social lives suffer as well. It is a life of being despondent and unfulfilled.

These negative relationships are to be walked away from, not cherished. How much you tolerate is always how much you're teaching people to treat you.

Everybody needs to choose their battles because contrary to how the narc-parent forces their offspring to be active and excel at everything, achieving so much is not possible for any person on earth. We need breaks and a lot of them and we need not to be exploited by anyone, especially not our own selves, and not even by our work superiors who might put huge pressure on us. But being given the space to breathe and concentrate on ourselves is part of our human right to thrive, even at work. The work itself could suffer otherwise. There's no need to add to this pressure, to forget that it is acceptable to say no, and overwhelm ourselves with over-giving, is there? Don't we deserve joy as well, doing what we want? Our worth does not depend on how hard we work. Someone's lack of reciprocation is not a cue for a challenge to convince anyone of our worth. The issue gets even more complicated given that neurodivergent children are being forced from a young age to mask and change to survive within society, while neurotypical ones are cheered on to be themselves. It isn't fair, we shouldn't have to give in.

Over-explaining our decisions when we are daring to take what we need is also a response to being gaslit. As our narc-parent tended to react badly to such a perceived atrocity, we expect a bad reaction from everyone else too. Not to mention that bending over backwards to satisfy people rarely works. There is an element of acceptance there that we need to get past, we need to accept that we cannot control them and their reactions to us, nor should we want to, for the obvious reasons of not wanting to follow in our parents' footsteps if nothing else. People will always come up with more demands, more issues to raise, more criticism to impart. People who are too agreeable are often taken advantage of. It really depends on the others what they think of us, not us.

It is especially important to say no to emotionally draining people, you all know the type. Eventually, we come to dread interacting with them and need to unwind after just talking to them. They are intense and exhausting, always wrapped up in some sort of hyped-up drama that the average person does not care about, yet it's hard to get free of their influence. Heaven forbid if this is your boss. You recognise the kind by how we need to complain to others after a short time spent in this person's company. The empath will ignore their existence as much as possible as they can't cope with the intensity of their superficial plights and would feel too weary, sick, sad and anxious after each interaction. Stop making excuses for such a person. Just like the narcissist, they don't deserve your yes.

Some connected concepts to do with boundaries is realising that we don't have to anticipate the needs of others and it's not our job to take responsibility for them. Other signs of people-pleasing behaviour is feeling irked when others aren't as thoughtful or in tune with our needs as we are with theirs, struggling to answer questions like 'how are you?' or 'what do you want?', not trusting oneself, responding to emails and messages right away out of a sense of duty, rather being unhappy at an event than risking disappointing someone by not going, dismissing one's thoughts or feelings and assuming that others have more authority, feeling like others don't respect our opinions, and people taking advantage of our time.

People-pleasing is certainly a hard problem to overcome for the victim of narcissistic abuse, but this is exactly why we need to get past it. Haven't we ruined enough of our lives with people's expectations already? We can't let it ruin the rest of our lives as it is impossible to keep everyone happy. It is hard to be successful in life if our energies are spent on trying to achieve other people's acceptance. Destiny awaits!

One way of striving to free ourselves of the self-imposed constraint of people-pleasing is writing down our priorities in life, both professionally and morally, as it can serve as a basis for deciding when saying no is in our best interest, at least till we get the hang of it. It can also convince us that we can say no in a relaxed manner. After all, what we initially thought to say yes to is not so important in the end. Cognitive therapy has great methods of helping with this internal conflict, convincing our own minds what is reasonable and what is not in valuing and respecting ourselves, our freedom and our beliefs. Here are a few other tips on how to say no without any explanations: I don't know if I can yet; I am honoured to be asked, but I can't commit right now; I can't say yes just now, but that might change later; I can do something else for you instead, why don't we do that; I can't tell you the answer at this moment; I would say yes another time, but it is not convenient for now.

Certainly, it is perfectly acceptable that people like us still value being a good person, self-improvement, warm-heartedness, empathy and courtesy as part of our life philosophy. Please don't ever get fed up with being a good person with a big heart. It sucks, being taken advantage of and sometimes it feels like it's better to be cold-hearted. But people like you are what give this world hope. What about self-insight? Authenticity? The trick is to master the balance between these values that are important to us and relinquishing our self-worth in the interest of our overall wellness. Taking care of ourselves isn't selfish and it makes people start respecting us and our boundaries as well. Mindful cognitive therapy, maybe with the help of a therapist, if nothing else, should help with this too, making it quantitatively and qualitatively clear in each case what our decision should be.

We Have the Right to Express Our Real Needs

While it is easier for us to speak up for another person, it is hard for a lot of us to speak up for ourselves. The act of speaking up brings up a lot of anxiety, a fear of conflict and a feeling that our needs don't matter enough to be voiced, especially if they inconvenience others. Contrary to this, in fact, we have many more needs than the standard neurotypical – more room to think, more time, more distance, more profundity. These are rarely convenient or understandable to the extrovert, so, to some extent, we have had to learn not to ask for them. We'll isolate ourselves into our fantasy worlds instead and learn to rely on ourselves because there is no other choice. The majority of the world doesn't understand us, leaving us feeling like the weird one, the odd one out, lonely, exasperated, world-weary, resentful and inadequate.

This is why it is so important for me to speak up now, present our collective needs, give a little insight into our world and make people understand our way of life at least a little bit. We need to understand ourselves, actualise these words in our heads. When we are dismissed, we try harder to please. But we need to remember that it was the narcissist who has conditioned us to do this. We need to stop doing that and not just with our narcissist. Take the power back.

We also cannot make our healing dependent on the wish that the abusers are going to one day feel remorse about what they did. They might pretend they don't remember, they might truly not remember, or they might not think they did anything wrong at all. Yet it isn't all in our heads. It is in our other cells too, in our nervous systems, shaking hands and irregular heart rhythms, our chests that propel themselves into panic every time we try to exercise and the feeling is too similar to anxiety for comfort. Every one of our organs went through the same trauma so it should be addressed in a holistic manner.

Putting our needs forward shouldn't be this difficult, though, and it is also deeply embedded in this compulsion we have of feeling responsible for others' emotions and responses. But are our needs really damaging for them? In most cases the answer would be no and there should therefore not be a problem in purposefully asking for our needs to be fulfilled when in a respectful, courteous manner. As, more often than not, I find telephone or face-to-face interactions stressful and upsetting, I usually use some form of writing for this – a card, a text, or email. Modern technology provides and it's no big surprise that these forms of communication were mostly created by introverts. A large number of introverts communicates much more successfully and constructively in writing[52].

It's just how I communicate and people, even those close to me, had to get used to it over time. It's that or nothing and I (mostly) stopped feeling guilty about it a long time ago. It is one of my essential needs for having peace of mind, something I am entitled to. Written communication is also there to be referred to later, nobody can say I didn't ask or twist the turn of events.

Sure, it takes practice, like everything, but it's more powerful in every way. A way to be proud of ourselves as well for having stood up for ourselves, big steps of courage for us people with little self-esteem.

A Few Words on Trauma Bonding

It might be surprising that, on some level, I love my mother and I appreciate what she has done for me, apart from messing me up for life. I have, however, left that relationship largely behind, unlike some, who persevere with these kinds of unhealthy relationships due to trauma bonding.

Trauma bonding is one of the forms of emotional reactions a person can display to abuse. A well-known example of such a relationship dynamic is Stockholm syndrome where the abused individuals start to feel kinship or compassion for the abuser. These positive emotions don't just develop in those kept in captivity by their abductors, they can occur in any sort of abusive relationship. The abused will try to make sense of their situation, find justification for the horrors committed by the abuser and attribute positive reasoning to their actions because it would be hard to imagine it, suffer it, otherwise. Add situations of dependence where the abused is helpless to choose differently and an affinity for loyalty, and conditions for a trauma bond are complete. Of course, this form of harmful attachment doesn't always follow an abusive situation, but it is worth examining our relationship with the abuser to see if it applies.

Trauma bonds have a tendency to form more often when the abused think themselves isolated and unable to ask for help. A relationship with a parent is always problematic in this way because they are also the ones who should furnish us with everything we should need at a young age and when these positive interactions occur, they will get mingled in with the bad. We become conditioned to the abuse and threats, equating it or seeing it as a side of love. This is why many end up in similar abusive relationships over and over again.

Moreover, often in real danger, our very lives depend on being able to relate in a positive manner to those holding the power. So much so, that sometimes people don't even realise they are being abused. On the contrary, they will believe the abuser telling them that the abuse happened because the child caused it with their behaviour or way of being. The abuser will then 'forgive' them, which underprops the child's perceived belief that the parent was nice to them, with this cycle often going on for years. Religious cults tend to work this way.

Another form of trauma bonding is when the abuse is recognised as such but the perpetrator vows to change, maybe even behaving in an improved manner for a while. With this idealistic goal in mind, the abused will close their eyes to further abuse in hopes of a better day.

Typically for a trauma bond, the abused will try to deny or cover up the abuse and, with a sense of loyalty and idolisation, is resistant to severing the connection. They will excuse to the abuser's behaviour and are generally convinced that their abuser loves them. This is partially why fully closing the lid on the relationship might be difficult and take several tries. But once again, the adult child needs to remember that the narcissistic parent doesn't change and other toxic personality types rarely do either. Let's not lose sight of the implications that the narc-parent's behaviour continuously has on us and our end goals of living freely on our own terms. Let's not forget the love bombing technique of the narcissist either. They might feel like the ultimate way of dealing with problems at times, offering solutions up on a silver platter but let's remember that this is only a tool in their arsenal to assure their much-needed narcissistic supply before they revert back to their harmful selves.

It is also normal to experience distress, loss or sadness after breaking out from such a relationship, feeling like there is a hole where our relationship with the respective parent used to be. These do not mean that we have made a mistake severing a harmful bond, though, or that we need to go back on our decision. You deserve better.

It might take time to feel like you are completely free of their influence, but it's good to be clear on the dynamics of trauma bonding so that we recognise the pattern and do not make excuses for the narc-parent again, or believe that any of it was our fault.

On Being Enough

It is not altogether strange that everything reflects back to the same thing, that we feel responsible for other people's responses and emotions because that was how we were trained, conditioned, focusing on the caregiver's emotions to avert further disasters. That we had to, was the view we got from our narc parent. If we didn't comply, they got angry. It is easy then to make the next jump in thought, that we need to try harder, give more to make a person more favourable towards us, to make them happy. Not having the toxic parent happy equalled us not being good enough.

But for mentally healthy individuals, it isn't so. Everybody should take responsibility for their own responses, actions and emotions and not take them out on a small child. Therefore, as hard a concept it sometimes is to replant into adult life, *you are enough* as you are, without having to bend over backwards to please someone. You always are. Not dumb, not disgusting, not unlovable, not ugly, not a failure. There's nothing faulty with you if you can't make people be pleased with you, happy with you, love you; that will depend on them and their characteristics. Regardless of those, *you are enough*. Your worth isn't dependent on how they see you. No two people speak the same language, our values are all different. Any good intention can be interpreted differently, and to be sure, it will be. There will be a load off your mind if you start to think this way.

An even more liberating, adjacent concept is that your happiness, mood, responses and emotions aren't dependent on this other person either, certainly not in adult life. You can choose to leave them, ignore them, be with them as and when you please, if you please. Happiness is a personal choice, a journey we take within ourselves by exploring our unconscious mechanisms and a way to guide them more to our own benefits. So it is you who shouldn't tell yourself that you're half-witted, revolting, unlovable, ugly or a fuck-up. Nobody has to agree with us and we don't have to accept the reproval, the move for dominance, or the animosity others may want to propel our way. We are responsible for our own inner happiness. It is an individual responsibility. This is what a narcissist will never understand. They will keep blaming others for their unhappiness, in a perpetual cycle of bitterness and self-pity. So if we have no other goal than being better than a narcissist, let's do this, understand that our happiness depends only on us. The reason for our unhappy lives and everyday struggles is our childhood abuse, but we can move past it, we have an opportunity for growth here, to restore the unloved places within ourselves to health.

Once on this path, it becomes a boulder impossible to stop rolling down a hill. Knowing how to fix ourselves gives us more self-esteem, that in turn allows us to ask for our needs to be fulfilled, which again, bolsters self-esteem. It can take a while, but the sky's the limit. As far as Carl Gustav Jung's daemon goes[53], he will tell you the same thing. Remember, it was the narcissistic abuse that makes you feel like you are unlovable, unworthy of time and attention like there was something innately wrong with you, like you are not pleasing enough, like you are going crazy, off course altogether and in two minds about everything. It was the abuse that created the endless sorrow. It was the abuse that makes you feel filled with guilt and inadequacy, overcome and out of control like your heart has been ripped from you. It is the abuse that makes you feel disrespected in every way, ignored, insignificant, dejected, weak and unhinged like a damaged character. You'd also often feel like you're on your own in view of the fact that decidedly not many souls are knowledgeable enough on the topic of narcissistic abuse.

Of course, I'm not going to lie and say that happiness is easy to achieve, not to us. Effort needs putting in every day. Various parts of the brain take part in all this effort, all previously influenced by abuse, including the frontal lobes that are crucial in the compiling of the behaviours that ultimately conclude in us being happy. It being an emotion, a state of the mind, the zones of the brain that are involved the most are those in the limbic system. According to neuroscientists, the part of the prefrontal cortex on the left side is mostly correlated with the emotions of happiness and joyfulness. A group of scientists at the Emory Univeristy School of Medicine in Atlanta pinpointed a bundle of the cingulum, a notable white matter zone that interconnects frontal, parietal and medial temporal sites[54], found under the cortex and curved around the midbrain. In its upper frontal part is where this zone of happiness in the brain has been detected. This area also has many connections that connect parts of the brain associated with complex emotions and mood regulation in social interactions[55] Depression or discontent on the other hand, is nothing else than the absence or a low level of one of the four chemical elements within our brain that make us feel happy: endorphins, serotonin, oxytocin or dopamine.

Endorphins are chains of proteins with a chemical composition and pain inhibiting performance akin to opium derivatives such as heroin or morphine, hormones produced by the body meant to stimulate parts of the brain related to pleasure and attention. Further demonstrating mental health's connection with physical health, they also stimulate the immune system. A way to improve happiness in this case is performing activities that enhance production of these hormones, identified as sleeping, lovemaking, exercising, eating spicy food, singing, laughing and, strangely, watching sad movies. You know those when you cry uncontrollably throughout half the movie, with such a cathartic experience that it feels good?

The hormone serotonin is synthesised by the body through the amino acid tryptophan and serves as a modulator of the functioning of other neurotransmitters. It's possible to increase its production, a sort of fooling our brains, through pursuing activities such as having relaxing massages and regular sleep cycles, remembering happy times, sunbathing or eating dark chocolate or omega-3-rich food.

Some activities block its production so those should be avoided, such as smoking, stress, alcohol, energy drinks and taking antihistamines.

Dopamine is produced by eating antioxidant-rich food and having sufficient rest.

The levels of the hormone oxytocin increase by hugging or breastfeeding, for example. This substance is vital in our journey as it facilitates an internal balance and accommodates emotions that help us connect with ourselves.

Should you check back with your narcissist? At this point, yes, sure, and you'll be sad how pitiful they will seem now and proud of yourself for how much progress you have made.

We Have a Right to Our Own Feelings – a First Step to Healing

What is rarely mentioned is how living life after trauma can feel even lousier than during the trauma itself because the body and the brain keep reliving what happened, and how difficult changing this pattern is. As a trauma survivor, all you wish for is to be able to feel safe but it feels like that will never happen. We are tense all the time, habitually on the lookout for danger, continuously feeling like we are in danger from other people. Repressing these emotions is not healthy either and it poses the danger of it all overflowing and adding anxiety into the mix. Some people try to avoid sorrow by not thinking about them, by refusing to bring up unpleasant memories. They may fear it can only bring them more heartbreak or do not see the reason to look backwards as opposed to forward. It may work for a time or it may work for certain individuals, but giving ourselves the permission to feel can be liberating.

Perhaps there have been things we've been ignoring, putting aside, not being able to solve. Maybe some would have been afraid to display emotion in front of someone, to lose control, so they force a lie to themselves instead, to keep in control. But you are entitled to feel whatever your experience dictates. This isn't about blaming others or even the abuser, it is about taking a big breath and acknowledging that yes, it happened, and now I can start working against the after-effects. We can't work on things we don't acknowledge. Listen to the memory of the experience. What is that associated emotion saying to you? That moment, that admission and acceptance allows for future progress, it opens the door for discovery and understanding connections that will lift us out from the pitfalls of our own minds. And then it isn't the emotion that is in control, it's you. You are free to feel, to love yourself. You are free to be nothing but human, get a respite from the cacophony of repressed emotions by feeling them one by one. Healing is hard, but living in pain, lost forever, is harder.

Recovery from narcissistic child abuse should start with that. Then the learning about how the mechanisms of narcissistic abuse affected us can follow. Different people go through more stages than others. For some, everything starts to make sense once they learn about what narcissistic parents are. For others, comes a stage of denial when they search for other alternatives, anything that justifies their parents' behaviour that would put them in a more favourable light. It could be good to make a list of all the bad things the abuser did at this point, it makes it pretty clear. Intermittent rollercoaster periods of anger, heavy sadness and grief can follow, alternating with acceptance from which there is only one reasonable way to take, and that is building a life that is increasingly free from the influence of narcissist abuse.

Narcissistic parents tend to be so self-absorbed that they arm their children with very few or no life skills or emotional coping skills, common sense or interpersonal relationship skills, simply because they don't have much of those themselves. By modelling or otherwise, they teach their children that you either control others or you are being controlled and that how things look is much more relevant than the truth.

It is also not unusual for us not to know who we are after decades of narcissistic abuse for we could have no real needs, ideas, experiences and emotions as these were all repealed and disallowed and were replaced with the demands of the narcissist parent. Trauma involves some kind of loss, of peace, of a loving parent, of agency, of security. The natural emotional response to loss is grief, but we were not allowed to acknowledge that at the time, so anger fills in instead. And when that isn't allowed either, the only way left for the body to respond is with anxiety, detachment, being frozen, or a shutdown. Through this mechanism, our very identities were being abused, changed and not much else could emerge either as we have in effect been erased. Maybe we can't recover all of ourselves that is lost, but what we certainly have is knowledge of what narcissistic abuse is! The rest of the healing can come from deliberately refusing to be what we were shaped to be through detachment and reconnecting with ourselves. If you're a true giver, that doesn't need to change, just remember boundaries. Keep the positives, don't let this cold world change who you are.

There are many things we need to unlearn too, such as maybe the tendency of making our handwriting smaller to appear insignificant, retreating into ourselves at the smallest threat, downplaying ourselves, so as not to outshine another, refusing help of support networks, abandonment fears, seeking external validation, not allowing ourselves to rest or express emotions, saying yes, tolerating abusive behaviour, anticipation anxiety, apologising for things that aren't our fault, extreme independence, living on high alert, overlooking obvious lies, bending over backwards to please someone, doubting oneself, overworking to feel useful, giving up on things important to oneself to avoid conflict. This behaviour pushes away others, which makes us feel unseen and misunderstood, throwing us straight back to the time of the trauma. This then reinforces our belief that we're not worthy and we blame ourselves, which worry makes us wake up drained and thus fractious and having low energy all day, conductive to negative thinking and other unhealthy coping methods, leading to further pushing away loved ones in a repetitive, vicious circle caused by unresolved trauma, spiralling lower and lower.

Victims of narcissistic abuse often seem unsure, always looking for clarification that they haven't made a mistake or misinterpreted something, which can quickly become tiresome in work situations for someone not functioning by the rules of the same inner mechanism.

For some, procrastination becomes a way to delay the supposed inevitable failure. Every small step in defeating these handicaps is a step forward. Some people are wary of healing because their whole identity rests on the trauma they've endured. To heal from the damage the narcissist parent caused, we must admit that a lot of our thinking is wrong, but without shame, as it isn't our fault. That desperate, fearful, unbalanced version of you was nothing to be ashamed of. It was merely a tenderhearted person's way of reacting to truly malicious treatment. It is the narcissist's fault, they should feel the shame.

Out of the above, I probably find taking a break when I need to the hardest to unlearn, as I still have that mentality that if I'm not contributing, then I'm worthless. I need to prove myself. Not as much to others, for myself, but still, it is a compulsion making me unable to relax for more than a few hours at any one time. Even in my free time I have to create, write, make computer graphics, contribute to a community in some way.

Another important step in averting falling back into old patterns is being able to identify toxic people. They are controlling and the most deceptive of liars. They have to have everything the way they've imagined. The only agenda they care about is their own. They are draining, making people feel exhausted and overwhelmed every time they have to spend time together. They are two-faced so if it looks like they were helping, it will come at a cost, larger than it is worth. They don't have a strong moral code and always sell out to the highest bidder. They dismiss other people's ideas and perspectives without giving them a second thought as if they would be inherently invalid, crazy, unhelpful or banal just because they are someone else's. They play with people's lives and look for hurtful things to say or do to them by harvesting information they can later use against them. They blame and shame and constantly criticise. They love getting compliments and their delusional egos stroked and cultivate a perfect public image that most people who don't know them enough would agree with.

However, we should make a distinction here between an evil person and a broken person. A broken person can be fixed and is willing to try to better themselves, an evil person will not. What the broken person is unwilling to do is deliberately hurt others because they know how it feels to be on the other side of that divide.

More on Refusing to Heal

In the clinical field, therapists often encounter patients who are stuck in one place and are not willing to move on to the next level regardless of how much encouragement or different options and advice they are getting. 'People have a hard time letting go of their suffering. Out of fear of the unknown, they prefer suffering that is familiar.' – Thich Nhat Hanh, Buddhist teacher and peace activist.

Apart from being in denial, there are many reasons for this, one being fearing who they would become if they changed. Even though they are hurting, they know how to live with that, while they may fear the pain the next stage of healing would cause. Other times people get used to chaos and danger so much that they experience stability as unusual and thus they find it uncomfortable. They might still be afraid of retaliation if they stood up for themselves. If they had been put down often enough and were threatened by caretakers, they might still be scared of disclosing their feelings, views, goals and ideas, regardless of whether the feared individual was still around or not. They may feel discouraged from trying anything new because everything was too hard to achieve or battle with previously. Setbacks are also common and pretty normal.

One major obstacle that can occur during therapy and healing is when the individual is refusing to acknowledge their feelings because they are so used to shoving them down as a result of not being allowed to express them, admit to them or deal with them outwardly in any way as children. They might not trust any therapist to help them because their personal experience told them that no one can fix their problems anyway. Targets are inclined to detach from their emotions, body or environment. Dissociation is an automatic coping mechanism against the enormous stress of living in such a war zone. Why leave this comforting imaginary environment if it helped us cope before? Symptoms resulting from trauma can involve psychological numbing and even amnesia about the abuse, sometimes even very shortly after it happened. This extreme brain fog can feel like you have dementia. You know what happened, but you cannot remember the details.

People can also be in denial about their reality, about having depression, or they may not be aware of having it because the general view of depression is something different to what depression actually is. The world tells us depression entails sadness and crying, staying in bed, and while those are certainly possible signs of depression, it can also mean numbness to emotions, especially numbness to lives where every moment is really just a complication we need to get through, where we need to pretend we are actors and appear fine, when in fact we feel we are going mad inside.

Yet the only way to take control of emotions is to accept their existence. Not being able to do this is a red flag in itself, pointing to a defining narc in the person's background. Unhealed trauma can also cause one to condone, be oblivious to, or consider some maltreatment insignificant because they've lived through worse.

Not having a lot of practice at it, some might even need to learn how to recognise their real emotions, tell one from another. Why do you have obsessive-compulsive tendencies for example? Is it to try to obtain some form of control or achieve numbness and avoidance of the real issues? The difficulties come about based on our emotions because we weren't allowed to express them and continue to suppress the unpleasant ones as coping mechanism. But avoiding triggers isn't healing. Healing can't take place while we are still busy trying to survive, they are opposites because survival mode is based on insecurity and detachment, while the other has attachment, attunement and self-empowerment at its foundation, which are mutually exclusive concepts. It is only when the right conditions for healing emerge that we can start healing.

Real healing only takes place when you're triggered and able to move through the pain and the old patterns and arrive at a different destination, recognising your worth and raising your standards of how you should be treated as you understand you are worth it. This might involve making firm, deliberate choices and having to frequently remind the reason you are on this path. The effects of unhealed trauma worsen over time without treatment so please don't wait. Time does not heal in this case (nor does it ever, but that's a different issue), it sets anchor and doesn't let you advance.

It may feel like desperation is just around the corner at this point, but identifying emotions relies on acknowledging them and the only possible way to do that is by being honest with yourself. These emotions were valid responses to abuse, so no need to feel shame about them or beat yourself up about them. You see, this in itself is a mental handicap the narc has forced you into. It keeps their lying manoeuvres going, but you are not dumb or disgusting or inadequate or weak and definitely not a burden, no matter how many times you were told this. You are not deranged or a fluke and there is a way out if you can accept that your worth doesn't depend on your narc's estimation. It doesn't depend on anybody else's estimation either. Offer yourself compassion. 'Don't let anyone invalidate or minimise how you feel. If you feel something, you feel it, and it's real to you. Nothing anyone says has the power to invalidate that, ever. No one else lives in your body. No one else sees life through your eyes. No one else has lived through your experiences. And so no one else has the right to dictate or judge how you feel. Give yourself permission to feel, it is liberating! Your feelings are important, and you deserve to be heard. They are inherently valid, and they matter. Don't let anyone make you believe otherwise.' – Daniell Koepke. People find themselves in different stages of healing and sometimes it takes a long while till they can tackle reality and their demons. Allowing us to feel for ourselves is a turning point and the motivation to heal will appear soon after.

Spending the rest of your life trying to impress everyone, most of whom don't even care, is not a life I wish on anyone. But once we see through where these impulses come from, it is a lot easier to rid ourselves of them.

Unfortunately, a lot of people never psychoanalyse themselves. They are quite simply mechanical products of their environment, robots going through the motions, preoccupied with food, working, entertainment and sleeping. They don't know why they are doing what they are doing and they never realise that taking control of themselves is a key to happiness.

My answer to all the cruelty, negativity and pain in the world is to obsess about love, fight pain with love, try to contribute so the same thing that happened to me does not happen as often to other people. I still think that reacting this way is something to be proud of! I will not regret treating people right. Especially as it takes enormous strength to overcome our problems, insecurities and hang-ups while we interact with others. Not being validated should not divert you. Few know what you've been through, fewer would understand. They didn't feel these things themselves.

Something else that household abuse sufferers tend to forget is that home life isn't supposed to feel like hell and so they tend to accept another situation where they end up being the abused. Trauma survivors have a lot of insecurities so they often need as much information about any upcoming event as possible. This may seem way too intense for others, but it helps us get back as much control as we can after situations where we had next to none. Which is why, again, we need to make their journey as informative as possible, as I'm doing with my details. We might need to dig into every moment, while the average person may think we should simply move on. Some don't even believe that narcissistic abuse exists because the abuser appears stable and the victim seems crazy, dramatic, unstable and unsure of themselves. Neurodivergent, different. Sometimes overwhelmingly angry and depressed, they sometimes lash out at the abuser as a last resort.

Or the problem is that whoever the abused is trying to convince of the wrongdoings may require endless explaining without any sign that they actually got it. This once again exemplifies how hard it is to endure in a world unschooled on the aftermath and ramifications of childhood trauma. So remember, you are blameless, you tried your best. It is your parent who was incapable of raising you right. You are not crazy, it is that our reality is different. For example, many people who were raised in tense, charged circles associate a shift in energy in the room with the potential for abuse and become immediately withdrawn, hide. But we can learn not to overreact, not to allow these triggers to ruin our peace.

We also need to acknowledge that healing is a process and it involves sadness and grieving for what could have been. Sometimes the right decision, like getting onto a road to healing, can still make you sad. But to achieve that better existence that you deserve, the journey needs to happen. Think about it. I have explained the physiological changes in the body. An unhealed memory will cause the same devastating effect in the body, through chemical reactions, as it did the first time. The journey needs to happen so you can start rebuilding your new life, establish real friendships, become stronger and wiser, and then, you can let go.

Signs of emotional healing and psychological growth include knowing when to take a break, being able to admit when we are wrong, no or low contact with narcissistic people, listening more to our intuitions about people and less to their opinions, being able to set, keep to and not feeling guilty about having healthy boundaries, not saying yes when we want to say no, taking responsibility for our own actions and our own actions only, not feeling the need to explain or overextend ourselves all the time or bad about staying honest to oneself, validating one's own pain and researching how to solve our problems, giving ourselves the respect we deserve and most importantly, being able to see a mistakes not as self-limiting but as opportunities for growth.

This freedom, then, will take you to the next level and will allow your psyche to thrive and you will find your true self. 'The first step in healing from narcissistic abuse is realising that you have been abused. You have to accept that they were putting on an act. You were dealing with a very disordered individual. They function in life and in their relationships by way of manipulation and corruption. They don't know any other way. This is who they are. They are wired differently and they see people as puppets for their own entertainment and use. You have to accept that this was not your fault, and that this is the way they relate to everyone.' – Maria Consiglio.

Another reason some might not want to change is that healing takes work. There is a mindfulness technique that can bring up unacknowledged emotions and helps you work with them.

The first step is to find a relaxation technique you feel most comfortable with, one that is the most effective for you. Relaxed like that, ground your body, connect it to the energy of the universe. Once comfortable in this relaxed state, think of an upsetting experience from the past and pay deep attention to the bodily sensations and emotions arising. Think about each one, make sure you know about their existence, that you are able to identify them and know where they come from. Learning about how to recognise these manifestations of childhood abuse is one of the foundation stones of our healing. 'There is no self-development without self-awareness. You can read as many books as you like, but if you're unable to read yourself you'll never learn a thing.' – Steven Bartlett.

The next step brings us to being able to accept these feelings, that they are normal human reactions to atrocities we've suffered, not something to be shoved down and never dealt with. They are a good sign as they're giving us the chance to grow as people. Observe them a little bit more, let them influence your present from the safety of a relaxed, calm place filled with self-compassion.

Your anger is the part of you that needs the most love. Anger is telling you when you feel powerless, it is suggestive of unmet needs, the ones we most try to silence. So anger is very important, it's where the answers lie. Anger is useful. What we went through justified anger. It can be telling of what is missing from your life. It is also helpful to focus on anger to know what triggers you, to be able to learn how to handle emotions in a healthy manner, otherwise people usually can end up causing more hurt to the people around them by suppressing or overreacting to anger. So if you feel anger, it means you should explore your needs. When you feel guilty, apply self-compassion.

When you're overwhelmed, slow down and breathe.

When you're sad, seek support.

When you're anxious, concentrate on the present. Anxiety is just as useful and important of an indicator. It conveys that something in our lives is off balance, apathy shows we're overextended, fear indicates what we care about and mind losing, and so on. When we're drained or upset, we need to pause and recharge, when we're angry, we need to find a healthy outlet, when we're sad, we need to be loving to ourselves, if we feel broken, self-compassion is necessary. Sometimes a good cry or smashing something is the best option to deal with the emotions. You're alone, you're not harming anyone.

Don't let anyone invalidate or minimise how you feel. If you feel something, that means it is real to you. Nothing anyone says has the power to invalidate that, ever. No one else lives in your body. No one else sees life through your eyes. No one else has lived through what you've lived through. Therefore, no one else has the right to walk all over you or judge how you feel. Your feelings are important and deserve to be taken into account. They are inherently valid and they matter.

Exploring each feeling like this without belittling them should make you able to understand more fully where negative thoughts and feelings come from and that they are a mere consequence of the past, not absolute truths. If it isn't clear in some cases, talk to someone from your small circle of trusted individuals, let someone help follow the logic. Once talked about enough, it is easier to feel like it's finally out of our system and understand what needs we have now. We know why the narcissist does things, we now know it wasn't about us, not really. It would also be a chance to show vulnerability, that weakness as we perceive it, the one that we find hard to expose.

Writing about trauma like this feels cathartic and I have reached a number of conclusions to do with my own trauma and abuser as a result, a lot of my negative self-talk turned into more positive. Every one of our stories can be helpful for someone!

The last mindfulness step in this exercise is indeed letting it go. Visualising or ritualising this moment can make the action more effective, like gathering the tension from the body into one place, then symbolically throwing it away. Going further, there are other methods for withstanding cognitive dissonance on the run such as keeping in mind its effects. Memory gaps, not being sure of what happened and whose account is true is a telltale sign that we might have been misled. Once the pattern of how we respond to negative thoughts and emotions changes consistently, it is very hard to relapse. If you still experience some remaining anxiety, denial, lack of focus, sleep problems or passive-aggressive anger issues, those can be addressed directly with their appropriate symptomatic relief methods.

And then, finally, that forgiveness we never thought capable of for the abuser is close down the line. Welcome to the other side!

Healing can also happen through channelling the hurt into any type of creative work.

Working With Trust Issues

Coming from a background where you're not able to trust your caregivers, especially if experiencing trauma before the age of ten, is unlikely not to influence someone. First, there were the abusers, then all those who enabled the abuse, those who didn't believe you or never bothered looking. There was literally nobody to trust, to have our best interests at heart. As a cumulative impact, people with trust issues frequently think the worst about others, stemming from their continuous operating on self-preservation that had forced them to always be on their guard in the past. They believe something will go wrong if they don't do everything themselves. Given that all they've known was self-reliance, they refuse to ask for, or find it hard to seek help due to the imbalance of give and take in their lives.

People with trust issues find receiving compliments, compassion, goodwill, flattery or charity hard to accept and will look for a covert rationale behind kind gestures as their brain has become wired to react in alarm and wariness when reminded of a traumatic situation in any way. This suspicion can also lead to them getting into bitter squabbles over seemingly insignificant matters. To avoid this situation, people with trust issues commonly distance themselves as it feels safer that way. They despise teamwork and often end up doing the majority of tasks just so they don't have to deal with others.

Many will only put themselves into situations where they don't have to rely on anyone else and do not in general stay in relationships for very long, while in work environments, the situation between colleagues becomes dysfunctional, leading to underperformance on all levels. Whoever is in this relationship certainly has their work cut out for them for a long time!

First, there's a need for it to be formally acknowledged that the trust issues are based on the person's past and a general disbelief in everyone's words and actions without justifiable grounds, not their current relationship in particular. For such an untrusting person, distrust should only be based on facts, proof and logic, for safety's sake, not conjectures and imagination.

It is also often that those who have experienced abuse during childhood do not trust others to finish or perform a task or job right. At this point, it seems easier to do everything oneself to make sure everything is as it should. After a while, when the partner learns of this, they might eventually stop doing the housework and fulfil other joint responsibilities because they know the other prefers their own course of action. Eventually this will lead to resentment in the untrusting partner because they feel taken advantage of. The other partner tends to get confused in the meantime because even though they are, in general, aware of their partner's abusive background, they need a lot of time to fully grasp how it affects the relationship and the behaviour of the abused partner. One of the hardest factors in this is trying to separate how responsible they are for the negative reactions that can come up from the once abused partner's predilection to think the worst of any person based on their past experience, for apparently relatively small issues. They have to learn to believe that they are not directly to blame, or they are not the direct target of the abused partner's frustration and anger at times. This is particularly difficult. Although they may not always be the cause of the abused partner's frustration, there are times that they are and trying to differentiate is particularly difficult.

How can this situation be solved? The more the partners understand of each other's conduct and their reasoning, the better, especially in relation to practical and quantifiable tasks, with a growing awareness that the other person has a point. But that takes some experience and consideration, to learn to differentiate between one-time situations and the more emotional, less tangible issues that arise in the background that follow a pattern.

If the other partner is finding the abused partner's behaviour hard to understand, that leads to strong negative responses. Over time, the other partner will gain an understanding of the abused partner's needs and will learn to respond appropriately. Together they can come up with a strategy for dealing with the issue.

To make both people as content as possible, a compromise is usually necessary. In this case, there's no other choice but to understand that some of the control needs to be relinquished. If done first with small tasks, they can maybe be extended later.

People who have been abused take it harder when they have been let down or lied to. Having a shaky trust breached makes a relationship feel completely unviable for us. It has an effect on future relationships as well, each and every one bringing less and less trust with it, till there is none left. This is exactly why it is doubly important to work out trust issues with a partner as it can create a base for other relationships.

If facts had actually proven that trust has been broken, the other party might still have a valid reason to have broken this trust, a reason that once found out, might justify the act. Looking at the person's character as a whole might also be beneficial. Did they proceed out of malice or was it simply a mistake or an accident? A good way of thinking about this is reversal: can you imagine any circumstances where you could justify yourself acting the same way?

If these measures don't work effectively enough, that means the issues are buried further down and the hopelessness, low self-esteem and accompanying negative thinking needs to be addressed. Overcoming trust issues then becomes about facing fears and decidedly and willingly taking calculated risks, hopefully leading to one or two meaningful relationships, that will give people the confidence to take more risks, extra benefits if one of these is with someone who went through similar experiences as they would not only understand the conundrum, but might be able to offer advice and support as well, and challenge you on accepting advice too.

Alongside therapy, online support groups can also work wonders in your journey to overcome trust issues. These often consist of people who have been through similar experiences, share common ground and offer emotional support to one another. Soon, you'll learn to trust which situation or person is worth doing this with.

Further Steps to Healing

Acceptance, of course, is just one of the first steps to achieve healing. But once acceptance is firmly decided upon, it is all a lot easier to steer clear of identified toxic people who would obstruct or lengthen the healing process.

Along with this, a calm environment akin to those created for relaxation and mindfulness exercises might be necessary, therefore it might be worthwhile, at least temporarily, for one to remove sources of stress and drama from life as much as necessary or possible. It may feel like something that goes against our people-pleasing nature, but it is vital to be mastered by every survivor that they are allowed to say no to every situation that puts them in an uncomfortable or potentially abusive situation, and without apology! It is perfectly fine to say no to something if you don't want to do it for whatever reason. You might need the time to recharge, do something fun, something some others wouldn't understand. In the meantime, let's keep in mind that feeling when you're coming out of a really dark place that you never saw yourself leaving and suddenly there's some light and we remember 'ah, that's what being happy is like!' That feeling will come again.

Undoing the effects of our pasts requires some tolerance already, and that's where the self-regulating techniques such as mindfulness and breathing exercises come in. These should never be seen as the cure, however, but will aid refocusing on a possible solution. Deciding to deal with childhood trauma is admittedly stressful and energy-sapping in itself and therefore special consideration should be given to healthy living to counter some of those inflammatory reactions described earlier, but also because how we feel in everyday life influences the way we deal with any additional situation. Pamper yourself with good things as a part of self-care. It gives the soul the message that it desperately needs, that you are worthy of love, putting yourself in a more comfortable position to be ready for healing work. Everything should be safe now and ready for change. The situation is so far removed from what it was during childhood and it was not your fault. 'Many trauma survivors hold their breath and their bodies tightly, bracing themselves for whatever is coming next. Staying alert for years takes a toll. Create spaces where you can take your armour off.' – Dr Thema Bryant-Davis, licensed psychologist, pedagogue, artist and change agent, writer of *Thriving in the Wake of Trauma* and *Tweets for the Soul*.

Now comes the real work and you are allowed to struggle with it, find it hard, it's completely normal. Don't let the entire journey overwhelm you, just focus on one step at a time.

For example, defensiveness can be dealt with in the following manner. When starting to recognise feeling defensive during difficult conversations or new situations, try to remove yourself from the situation, take a break. Even tell your conversation partner that is what you're doing, if the subject matter is sensitive or hard to talk about. Or say, 'please explain what you just said so I know for sure what you mean', or 'could I have some time to think?'

If you feel like you're out of control, you can focus on the things you can control, of which there are many, such as who you ask for help, when you ask for help, when you take a break, how you act, how much effort you put into something, asking for what you need, how you respond to something, your boundaries, how much exercise you take and what you eat, when and if you want to forgive others, if you smile, owing up to your own mistakes, when you show empathy, how you take care of and treat yourself, whether you choose to help someone, your attitude, your goals and focus, whether you choose to look at the positives or negatives. 'Beneath every behaviour is a feeling. And when we meet that need rather than focus on the behaviour, we begin to deal with the cause and not the symptom.' – Ashleigh Warner, holistic family psychologist. We all experience emotions at a different range and intensity. Our emotions act as guides to what we need. Anger can be healthy and indicated, but when we hold in our emotions, they will come out in other, harmful ways. Sharing primary core emotions helps bring other people closer to us. Secondary reactive emotions push people away.

At times, we also tend to forget that our current situation does not have to stay like this forever. When feeling stuck, please remember that this stage is temporary. You have so much to look forward to. There is still room for change, room for you to be happy. We tend to underestimate how strong we are, too. The trauma a parent or caregiver dealt out to you might not have made you tougher and they are unworthy of the reason for your strength being attributed to them, it is *you* who have made you stronger through your trauma work.

Remembering to rest is vital at this point. We often don't know how to switch off and relax without feeling guilty. Some days can be no days and some days low days. Some days will test you more than others. Sometimes you'll be able to rise to the challenge, other times you will need to step down to preserve your strength. Both are courageous choices, they are what is best for you at that point.

There's something we call trauma drive. Living in constant fight, flight, freeze, fawn mode, you learn to use trauma drive to get you to the next point you need to be at, especially at work. It can feel like a superpower, being able to trudge on. But it can become a hindrance on the healing journey, especially as it stops you from taking proper care of yourself. As you start to heal, your trauma drive decreases since your body recognises it's no longer in danger and doesn't need to operate in survival mode. So you will start to feel less motivated to do everything, even enjoyable things. That is perfectly fine. Give yourself permission to rest, recharge and you will move on when you're ready. Nothing needs to be finished on the spot, nothing needs to be perfect. It's okay to do things at your own pace. Celebrate small wins and remember that there's so much more to life than productivity!

Another necessary step is allowing ourselves to grieve for things we could not achieve early in life, the pain and heartbreak we have experienced, the loss of the person we could have been, the plans and dreams we might have missed out on, the friendships we have had to let go of.

Some days will be harder than others and sometimes we need to take a break. That's okay. A little anxiety tip: the brain can't be grateful and anxious at the same time.

When anxiety tries to take over, look for gratitude. Many of us don't rest properly though. 'If you're resting, but you're shaming yourself for not being productive the whole time, that's not actually rest. If you find that you're chronically tired this could be why' – Iris McAlpin.

All you have to keep doing for now is breathe. It is okay not to be okay, to have a bad day, a week or a month. It can, in fact, stop a burnout, the one that happens when we try to avoid letting ourselves be human. Healing doesn't depend on being able to pretend to be all right, you are not fundamentally defective. All your feelings are valid and you are allowed to ask for help with them even if you're not sure what exactly you need. You have the right to be listened to and believed. Stay realistic. We're meant to take it slowly, everything can't be changed at once. Modest changes can already improve the quality of life and setbacks can be learning opportunities. Celebrate each step! Give yourself credit for how much you've grown and how far you've come. Say, 'I'm really, really proud of myself'! Do it right now. Stop thinking you're worthless. Stop thinking that no one cares. Stop thinking everyone would be better off without you. Stop thinking that you can't do it. Stop thinking that you're not good enough. Stop thinking that you're undeserving. Stop thinking that you're a burden. Stop thinking that there's no way out because it is not true. You'll get there. 'Never underestimate the power of a person who is healing their trauma. This person has been through the darkest places that the world has to offer and is still standing before you, committed to seeing the light.' – Dr Mariel Buqué, psychologist.

With our low self-esteem, we might not even recognise for a while that we are already healing. Here are some clues: a greater self-acceptance, being able to talk about feelings, being able to identify triggers, using healthy ways to show love, knowing your value is not defined by others, the fact that you are more comfortable setting boundaries and expressing your needs, you feel whole, safe or lovable. You heal trauma bonds, for example, by learning to self-protect and self-soothe and by lowering tolerance for chaos in relationships, bonding over shared values, spending time getting to know yourself, your own needs and limitations before getting into a relationship, developing an awareness of your inherited beliefs around relationships and moving slowly in relationships.

At this point, let's have a little fun! Here are some self-care exercises, ones that show and aid the progress you're making in healing. Choose something to do for yourself, without thinking or caring if it pleases anyone. Anything, play something, create something, read, sing or dance, whatever you like. Then as a contrast, dare to say no to something you usually agree to out of habit or not wanting to upset somebody else's routines. Tell the truth, even if not everyone will like it. Give yourself permission to do absolutely nothing all day, how about that! It could be taking a well-earned rest, or a date with yourself, meaning taking yourself out to see a movie, take a trip, or to your favourite restaurant or ice cream parlour all by yourself. Isn't that just the best date ever?

As always, we should be careful with triggers as they come in many unexpected forms and can quickly overpower our nervous systems. They can be in the form of certain sounds, people, thoughts, smells, situations, media reports, feelings, places. Smells are strongly tied to our memories. The place or area where the trauma took place can be a powerful trigger, as well as comparable places that remind us of our pasts. Any film or television show can present analogous themes to our trauma. Feeling down or rejected can prompt us to recall the feeling of being in a trauma situation. In these cases, it is fundamental that we remind ourselves how the bad association occurred and not give it any importance it doesn't deserve. If not for the trigger, we would be able to get on with our lives.

This intermediate learning period will pass too, with an informative and transformative journey. If necessary, by going through each of our actions one by one and pinpointing the coping mechanisms and false thought patterns arising from childhood trauma in an honest and deep manner. What are they trying to tell you and are they true? Controlling behaviours, hyper-independence, self-harming behaviours, they all have a solution through perseverance and practice, with, of course, setbacks and missteps on the way. Patience! Rushing it will only mess it up. Obviously, this will take time and you may find yourself working on them years to come, but righting every one of them and letting them go will improve life bit by bit, making you this brand new, wonderful person who – guess what? Doesn't need permission to live, but deserves to be loved, healed, to feel better and to be treated well, to stand up for what we believe in. I see you, I feel you, I am you.

As abused children, we have learnt to have to predict and act upon the needs of those around us, becoming helpers, givers, caretakers. Asking for help for ourselves was dangerous and at the very least carried the risk of being called stupid and shouted at. Perceived weakness still seems terrifying as an adult. For example, I never dared to admit if I didn't feel well because, as a child, I would immediately be blamed for it, told that I did something unwise to make myself ill. So I understand why this is hard. Please also know that because of these inhibitions, asking for help is the most courageous thing you can do for yourself. Please realise that you are not weak for needing support and you deserve to be supported. I believe that when looking for help, the best minds in mental health aren't medical practitioners (excuse the exceptions). They're the trauma survivors who have had to figure out how to keep it together and grow after the bottomless stress of suffering child abuse. So listen to them.

There are some red flags to consider in yourself that might suggest you have fallen back into the faulty habits of old survival mechanism, such as calculating our worth on people's validation or say-so, justifying other people's harmful actions, criticising or deprecating yourself or others all the time, not speaking up to circumvent ostracism or discord, the failure to say no, or extensively over-explaining yourself. It is when you finally let yourself be you in an unapologetic manner, without over-explaining or being desperate for someone else's validation, because you've become cognisant that it really is only you who needs to accept yourself with love, that you are properly honouring yourself.

However, healing doesn't mean getting over trauma. It means we have learnt to cope better. 'One of the best signs of your growth is seeing yourself no longer worried, bothered, or hurt by the things that once used to drain you. You're getting better and it feels so good.' – Idil Ahmed.

Signs of inner growth include being less judgemental, knowing yourself better, prioritising your own health and self-care, being more conscious of how you use your time, avoiding toxic people and situations, trusting yourself and intuition, living according to your own values, befriending your pain until it decides to leave by itself. If you're in the middle of your trauma work and can't manage as much as before you started, then I would like you to make it known, shout it out to the world and acknowledge how demanding that work is. It is so frustrating wanting to do more, but not being able to because all your strength is being used to heal. It is good to remind ourselves that it will not be this way forever. There is life on the other side of the healing process.

After the grief of what was lost was acknowledged, we can stop fantasising and forget the idea that things could have gone differently. If the task of overcoming childhood trauma seems too much, focus on one little thing at a time. Focus on something easy at first, something you're most likely to be able to do with the energy and abilities you have. A little bit is always better than nothing. 'Little wins pave the way for bigger wins. 1% beats 0%.' – Dr Glenn Doyle.

To recap, the way to manage our emotions arising from childhood trauma, is to identify and accept them first. Not to let it overwhelm us, so that we can ask what triggered us and understand ourselves. Be open to the outcome of your emotions and what unfolds, it can either be a big clue or a big step ahead. What's more, when working on altering our negative behavioural patterns, detrimental thoughts and emotions, we are in fact making the world a better place, little by little. People close to us benefit first, and then their more positive functioning can influence others as well. The beautiful thing about life is that you can always change, grow and flourish. It's going to be okay. Of course, healing doesn't imply we'll never feel pain resulting from the trauma again, it means we'll have a better understanding of what our feelings are telling us so that we can make more informed choices and not be merely thrust around in the wind by them. When we avoid certain feelings, we make fear-based decisions without ever really knowing what that fear was about and what it meant for us. When we know what these fears are based on, then we can learn how to manage them, with more suitable strategies. This is why it is impossible to give concordant advice. The solution needs to be suited to the individual and their circumstances. Stay true to yourself and there will come a time when you have a negative experience with someone and instead of it triggering your trauma, it triggers your healing mechanisms and you are reminded of the work you've done to rebuild yourself. The opposite of a trigger is a glimmer. These are precious, little moments of inner peace and happiness, times when we feel elated, comfortable, understood, at ease with the world. Glimmers can be looked out for the same way as triggers, but instead of avoiding them, we can search for these moments, learn how and when we're able to get them.

As I have admitted, my journey is not complete yet and I don't know if it will ever be. Even at this point (at any point, to tell the truth), it really is okay to feel sad or to feel absolutely everything, just feel not okay, cry over little things and face many, many setbacks. Take as much time as you need. As I have said, there shouldn't be overcoming trauma books because there is no such thing as getting completely over it. There, I've said it again. The best we can do is learn how to live with it and not let it affect our lives and of those around us too much with the methods mentioned above. We have to accept this loss as well.

But if I know one thing for sure, is that I have severed the chains of generational trauma. Judging by the compassion and affectionate nature of my children, along with their awareness of these issues, I know that when the time comes, they will be wonderful, caring, thoughtful and considerate parents with a warmth that will help heal the world. The journey of healing from trauma can also entail finding ourselves, that this is truly who we are and that should engulf us with power and happiness. Courage, beautiful days ahead!

How to React to Trauma Being Revealed

A lot of the time, it is very difficult for a person to talk about their trauma. Some might be ashamed of it, but a lot of us are aware that it is not something the average person either understands easily or feels comfortable talking about. Therefore, the most important thing the conversation partner can do is show that they are open to listening without judgement. It is not about immediate action to remedy as if to quickly discard and shove the issue under the rug, but of acknowledgement of what the sufferer has been through, believing them and showing understanding, love and concern. The victim wants to know that they will not be shunned for their past. They will also want to unload, some in a cathartic way, so practise empathic listening[104]. To be able to remain supportive, the listener should try to keep their body language and reactions in check. The victim has enough to deal with without having to worry about upsetting the listener too much. They are sharing their innermost feelings and thoughts, parts of themselves they've tried to hide from the world, sometimes for decades, so it is important to let them know that the listener appreciates the huge token of trust put in them with something similar to 'Thank you for telling me. I am very sorry for what happened to you. You know where I am if you need me. I can support you with this. What can I do to help?'

The victim's shame should be alleviated with something akin to 'It wasn't your fault. It was the only way you could get through it' or 'You didn't deserve that treatment.'

It is also important to acknowledge, however, that the listener might not be enough or sufficiently competent to fully undertake this mission. Therefore, they should suggest the sufferer should reach out for professional help as well, while putting emphasis on how they deserve to get help. They should be told they don't have to do it all alone. Words like 'you need help' can be misleading to a trauma victim as it can be misconstrued in their minds and further damage their low self-esteem as they are usually ready to take blame, thinking that everything is their fault. So it is crucial to think about any connotations specific words said can induce.

In any case, being non-judgemental is key, else the healing process might be stunted and the sufferer will not reach out any more. The one disclosing their secrets is looking for validation first and foremost. They need to know they will still be loved and not regarded in less esteem.

Things not to do are also worth knowing, such as not asking the person for details they are not prepared to share. They should be given space while the listener tries to create a safe space that might eventually allow the victim to share more of their experiences.

Giving advice can be very controversial. This is because with all the listener's good intentions, they will rarely be able to fully grasp the situation, even if they have been through similar experiences themselves. So one person's advice might not fit all. It might even offend the sufferer by appearing judgemental or as if their suffering was being minimised.

The most harmful reactions to disclosed trauma are the clueless or ignorant statements that appear to question the validity of what the individual went through, such as something along the lines of 'I know your alleged abuser, they wouldn't do that to you, they probably didn't mean it' or 'It's just how they are, you have to accept it'. This usually coming from another family member or a close friend's perspective, and appears to justify the abuser's actions. Some responses even attribute the blame to the sufferer or they negate the strength needed to deal with the abuse such as, 'You'll get over it.' Some people don't even realise that PTSD happens to someone other than a soldier. These reactions can obviously make the sufferer's illness or disorders worse and exacerbate suicidal thoughts.

How to Explain Trauma to People Who Won't Get It

There will always be people who will refuse to believe us or, due to ignorance or no experience in the matter, cannot imagine what impact it has to have been abused all the way through childhood. Unfortunately, there will also be situations where we might have to explain to someone why we are the way we are, a potential boyfriend for example, a medical professional, a colleague. It isn't an easy obstacle to overcome either because unless we educate them on what forms trauma can take and what effects it has, they are unlikely to appreciate our point of view. This is not to say that there aren't kind and empathetic people who will accept versions of events presented at face value and try their best to help despite not experiencing anything similar themselves. There are people who could do with reading this book, but the problem with that is that they are unlikely to be interested in it. Educating has to happen gradually, and be backed up with scientific evidence. It's crucial that the individual is prepared for what they're about to hear, that trauma isn't simply dumped upon them without them having a clue in advance. If the reveal is really necessary, the written word works better as it gives the reader time to ruminate. It should be made clear to them that the other person's experiences and resulting personality is very different and that there is an expectation for them not to understand. This drives home how dissimilar the circumstances are and makes them, in fact, more likely to understand.

Even therapists make mistakes with their patients, such as being too wary of re-traumatising them by going back to the point of origin of their suffering, or not showing them more than one or two approaches to treatment to be able to choose one from that works for them. Help is out there though, even if it means a change of therapist or source.

Inspirational and Factual Quotes

'Remember who you were when you pulled through the darkest night of the soul. Remember how you rallied, how you remained functional, even if barely. Remember how you changed, defied your genetics and kept on going. Remember how you held it all together as everything fell apart. Remember all the times you were stronger than you felt and wiser than you thought. Remember how you had a galaxy within you when you thought there was nothing left. So that the next time you know you're going to need a wildfire instead of a match to get through the darkness, remember the survivor within.' – Tanya Markul

'Don't let someone who did you wrong make you think there's something wrong with you. Don't devalue yourself because they didn't value you. Know your worth even if they don't.' – Trent Shelton

'Don't worry about what people think of you or about the way they try to make you feel. If people want to see you as a good person, they will. If they want to see you as a bad person absolutely nothing you do will stop them. Ironically, the more you try to show them your good intentions, the more reason you give them to knock you down if they are committed to misunderstanding you. Keep your head up high and be confident in what you do. Be confident in your intentions and keep your eyes ahead instead of wasting your time on those who want to drag you back. Because you can't change people's views, you have to believe that true change for yourself comes from within you, not from anyone else.' – Najwa Zebian

'One day, in retrospect, the years of struggle will strike you as the most beautiful.' – Sigmund Freud

'The crying is the healing, not the hurting. When we stop children from crying, they have to stuff the hurt inside instead of releasing it.' – Pam Leo

'Is there anything she can't handle? She has been broken. She has been knocked down. She has been defeated. She has felt the pain that most couldn't handle. She looks fear in the face. Year after year. Day after day. But yet, she never runs. She never hides. And she always finds a way to get back up. She is unbreakable. She's a warrior. She's you. Spread light, truth, love.' – unknown

'The strength of a person's spirit would then be measured by how much 'truth' he could tolerate, or more precisely, to what extent he needs to have it diluted, disguised, sweetened, muted, falsified.' – Nietzsche

'When we recover loudly, we contribute to keeping others from dying quietly.' – Melissa Anderson, MD

> 'I lied and said I was busy.
> I was busy; but not in a way most people understand.
> I was busy taking deeper breaths.
> I was busy silencing irrational thoughts.
> I was busy calming a racing heart.
> I was busy telling myself I am okay.

Sometimes, this is my busy – and I will not apologise for it.'– Brittin Oakman

'Effective Parenting 101: Teaching our children to control themselves is far more effective than trying to control our children. Model, don't manipulate. Lead, don't intimidate. Support, don't shame. Encourage, don't threaten. Guide, don't punish.' – L. R. Knost

'If you invite someone into your home and they start breaking things and insulting the decor, you don't have to hate them, but you wouldn't invite them into your home anymore. Boundaries are doing the same thing. Except your home is your mind. Your home is your heart. Your home is your time and your life. Uninvite the guests who don't know how to treat your home with respect.' – Doe Zantamata

'Vulnerability is not winning or losing; it's having the courage to show up and be seen when we have no control over the outcome. Vulnerability is not weakness; it's our greatest measure of courage. People who wade into discomfort and vulnerability and tell the truth about their stories are the real badasses.' – Brene Brown

'Our brains are wired for connection, but trauma rewires them for protection. That's why healthy relationships are difficult for wounded people.' – Ryan North, founder of One Big Happy Home

'Childhood trauma is associated with a 70% to 80% increased risk of adult hospitalisation with an autoimmune disease. Childhood trauma can dysregulate cortisol levels, the vagus nerve and the autonomic nervous system. The cumulative burden of childhood trauma has been shown to cause negative effects on physiological, cognitive, behavioural and psychological functions.' – Dr Jaban Moore

Appendices summarising the above

The 4F Responses

FIGHT:	FLIGHT:
Being Impulsive	Panic and anxiety
Assertive	Addictions
Critical	Staying busy
Demanding	Workaholic
Aggressive	Overachiever
Anger outbursts	Over-analyses everything
Rage	OCD
	Perfectionist
FREEZE:	**FAWN:**
Depression	People-pleasing
Isolation	No boundaries
Avoidance	Impressionable
Detachment	Avoids conflict
Escape to a fantasy world	Conformist
Manic creative episodes	Codependence
	Can't stand up for themselves
	Looks to others for guidance

Overview of Key Effects of Childhood Trauma by Type

Effects of Neglect:	Effects of Abandonment:
Low self-worth	Codependency
Anger	Fear of being left (out) – seeing it as a threat
Repressing issues	
Fear of showing vulnerability	Inability to form healthy relationships
Trouble making eye contact	Low self-esteem
Struggle to let go	Loud thoughts
Trouble saying no	Not liking being alone
Attracting people who don't appreciate them – as a mirror of how they feel about themselves	
Effects of Blame Shifting:	Effects of Betrayal:
No boundaries	No trust in anyone, sometimes including oneself
Not asking for help/needs to be fulfilled	Need of external validation
	Problems recognising, managing and expressing emotion
	Fear of being hurt
	Being insecure
	Feeling unsafe

Effects of Rejection:	Effects of Injustice:
Making negative assumptions about what others are thinking	Helplessness and hopelessness
Reluctance to let others in	Loss of trust in humanity
Finding compromise difficult	No sense of safety or predictability
Constant need to be productive	Moodiness and irritability

Glossary

apotheosise – idolise, rank high

brain zap – a startling sensory disturbance where the suffer feels like their head was suddenly jolted or had a tremor

déjà-poo – experiencing deja-vu in a rather unpleasant manner

derealisation – thinking that our surroundings can't be real

endocrine – to do with creating, releasing and coordinating hormones

hypo - low

inflation – perceiving of one's qualities as more beneficial than they are

narc – narcissist (https://www.merriam-webster.com)

References

1. The Long-term Health Outcomes of Childhood Abuse, An Overview and a Call to Action Kristen W Springer, MPH, MA,1 Jennifer Sheridan, PhD,1,2 Daphne Kuo, PhD,1,4 and Molly Carnes, MD, MS

2. "Trauma." Merriam-Webster.com Dictionary, Merriam-Webster, https://www.merriam-webster.com/dictionary/trauma. Accessed 6 Jan. 2022.

3. Bessel van der Kolk, The Body Keeps the Score: Brain, Mind, and Body in the Healing of Trauma. New York: Viking/Penguin, 2014.

4. "Narcissist." Merriam-Webster.com Dictionary, Merriam-Webster, https://www.merriam-webster.com/dictionary/narcissist. Accessed 7 Jan. 2022.

5. https://www.instagram.com/quotes_shots_of_wisdom/ [Accessed: 20 March 2023]

6. Bigelsen J. & Kelley, T. (2015) *When Daydreaming Replaces Real Life: Should elaborate fantasies be considered a psychiatric disorder?* Available at: https://www.theatlantic.com/health/archive/2015/04/when-daydreaming-replaces-real-life/391319/

7. Glausiusz, J. (2014) *Living in an Imaginary World*. Available atL https://www.scientificamerican.com/article/living-in-an-imaginary-world/# January 1, 2014

8. Nirit Soffer-Dudek, and Eli Somer, "Trapped in a Daydream: Daily Elevations in Maladaptive Daydreaming Are

Associated With Daily Psychopathological Symptoms". Front Psychiatry. 2018; 9: 194. Published online 2018 May 15.

9. Lindberg, S. (2022) *What Is Emotional Numbness?* Available at: https://www.verywellmind.com/emotional-numbing-symptoms-2797372

10. Dvir Y, Ford JD, Hill M, Frazier JA. Childhood maltreatment, emotional dysregulation, and psychiatric comorbidities. Harv Rev Psychiatry. 2014; 22(3): 149-161.

11. Weilenmann S, Schnyder U, Parkinson B, Corda C, von Känel R, Pfaltz MC. Emotion transfer, emotion regulation, and empathy-related processes in physician-patient interactions and their association with physician well-being: A theoretical model. Front Psychiatry. 2018; 9:389.

12. Luna, A. (2022) *Signs You're Struggling With Emotional Numbness (the Secret Illness)* Available at: https://lonerwolf.com/emotional-numbness/

13. Jackson MacKenzie, "Whole Again: Healing Your Heart and Rediscovering Your True Self After Toxic Relationships and Emotional Abuse", Paperback – January 8, 2019.

14. Barrett, D. L. The hypnotic dream: Its content in comparison to nocturnal dreams and waking fantasy. Journal of Abnormal Psychology, 1979, Vol. 88, p. 584 591; Barrett, D. L. Fantasizers and dissociaters: Two types of high hypnotizables, two imagery styles. In R. G. Kunzendorf, N. Spanos, & B. Wallace (Eds.) Hypnosis and Imagination, NY: Baywood, 1996; Barrett, D. L. Dissociaters, fantasizers, and their relation to hypnotizability. In Barrett, D. L. (Ed.) Hypnosis and Hypnotherapy: Vol. 1: History, theory and general research, Vol. 2: Psychotherapy research and applications, NY: Praeger/Greenwood, 2010.

15. Wilson, S. C. & Barber, T. X. (1983). "The fantasy-prone personality: Implications for understanding imagery, hypnosis, and parapsychological phenomena." In, A. A. Sheikh (editor), Imagery: Current theory, research and application (pp. 340–390). New York: Wiley. Republished (edited): Psi Research 1(3), 94 – 116. http://psycnet.apa.org/psycinfo/1983-22322-001.

16. Sherrie Hurd, A. (2018) *7 Subtle Ways Childhood Trauma Affects You When You Are an Adult.* Available at: https://www.learning-mind.com/childhood-trauma-effects/

17. Tavris, C. y Aronson, E. (2007). Mistakes Were Made (But Not by Me): Why We Justify Foolish Beliefs, Bad Decisions, and Hurtful Acts. Harcourt Books.

18. Louis de Canonville, C. (2023) *Understanding Cognitive Dissonance, Trauma Bonding and Infantile Regression.* Available at: https://narcissisticbehavior.net/understand-cognitive-dissonance-trauma-bonding-infantile-regression/

19. 'Dovetail Learning', (2023) Available at: https://dovetaillearning.org/

20. Dearman, B. (2019) *How psychological trauma physically affects you.* Available at: https://www.hypnotherapy-directory.org.uk/memberarticles/how-psychological-trauma-physically-affects-you#accept-cookies

21. Levine, B.. (2012) *Why Anti-Authoritarians Are Diagnosed as Mentally Ill.* Available at: https://www.madinamerica.com/2012/02/why-anti-authoritarians-are-diagnosed-as-mentally-ill/

22. Psychoneuroendocrinology, 51, 58-67. doi: 10.1016/j.psyneuen.2014.09.008

23. Ohio State University. "Childhood abuse, adversity may shorten life, weaken immune response among the elderly."

ScienceDaily. ScienceDaily, 16 August 2010. <www.sciencedaily.com/releases/2010/08/100815111450.htm>

24. 'The Wellness Coalition' (2015) *Health Effects of Physical and Emotional Abuse.* Available at: https://www.thewellnesscoalition.org/wp-content/uploads/2015/02/Health-Effects-of-Domestic-Abuse-M.-Beasley.pdf (Accessed: 11 May 2022)

25. 'Health Jockey' (2008) *Asthma in children linked to physical and sexual abuse.* Available at: https://www.healthjockey.com/2008/09/02/asthma-in-children-linked-to-physical-and-sexual-abuse/ (Accessed: 11 May 2022)

26. Stress, catecholaminergic system and cancer. Krizanova O., Babula P., Pacak K. Stress. 2016 Jul; 19(4):419-28

27. Chronic stress promotes tumour growth and angiogenesis in a mouse model of ovarian carcinoma. Thaker PH, Han LY, Kamat AA, Arevalo JM, Takahashi R, Lu C, Jennings NB, Armaiz-Pena G, Bankson JA, Ravoori M, Merritt WM, Lin YG, Mangala LS, Kim TJ, Coleman RL, Landen CN, Li Y, Felix E, Sanguino AM, Newman RA, Lloyd M, Gershenson DM, Kundra V, Lopez-Berestein G, Lutgendorf SK, Cole SW, Sood AK. Nat Med. 2006 Aug; 12(8):939-44

28. 'Northwestern Medicine' (2022) Available at: https://www.nm.org/healthbeat/medical-advances/how-the-brain-hides-traumatic-memories (Accessed: 11 May 2022)

29. 'Psychology Answers' (2023) *Why Do I Hate Being Touched?* Available at: https://psichologyanswers.com/library/lecture/read/167810-why-do-i-hate-being-touched (Accessed: 20 March 2023)

30. 'Fact of the Day' (2023) *did you know?* Available at: https://didyouknowfacts.com/facts/kids-have-a-strong-sense-of-self-esteem-by-the/#:~:text=New%20research%20shows%

20children%20as%20young%20as%205,years%20are%20
an%20extremely%20important%20foundation%20for%20
life (Accessed: 20 March 2023)

31. Buckner JD, Bernert RA, Cromer KR, Joiner TE, Schmidt
NB. Social anxiety and insomnia: the mediating role of
depressive symptoms. Depress Anxiety. 2008;25(2):124-
30. doi: 10.1002/da.20282. PMID: 17340615.

32. Anwar, Y. (2018) *Poor sleep triggers viral loneliness and
social rejection.* Available at: https://news.berkeley.
edu/2018/08/14/sleep-viral-loneliness/ (Accessed: 20
March 2023)

33. Anwar, Y. (2013) *Tired and edgy? Sleep deprivation boosts
anticipatory anxiety.* Available at: https://news.berkeley.
edu/2013/06/25/anticipate-the-worst/ (Accessed: 20
March 2023)

34. LeWine, H. (2019) *Does exercising at night affect sleep?*
Available at: https://www.health.harvard.edu/staying-
healthy/does-exercising-at-night-affect-sleep

35. 'Harvard Health Publishing' (2020) *Blue light has a dark
side.* Available at: https://www.health.harvard.edu/
staying-healthy/blue-light-has-a-dark-side

36. Knott, E. *Emily Victoria Knott's Profile Page [LinkedIn]*
[Accessed: 20 March 2023] Available at: https://www.
linkedin.com/in/emily-victoria-knott/

37. Pappas, S. (2018) *Weighted Blankets: How They Work*
Available at: https://www.livescience.com/59315-
weighted-blankets-faq.html (Accessed: 20 March 2023)

38. 'Psychology Today' (2023) *Stress.* Available at: https://
www.psychologytoday.com/us/basics/stress (Accessed:
20 March 2023)

39. 'Psychology Today' (2023) *Grief.* Available at:https://www.psychologytoday.com/us/basics/grief (Accessed: 20 March 2023)

40. 'Psychology Today' (2023) *Menopause.* Available at: https://www.psychologytoday.com/us/basics/menopause (Accessed: 20 March 2023)

41. Van Edwards, V. (2023) *7 Types of Toxic People and How to Spot Them.* Available at: https://www.scienceofpeople.com/toxic-people/ (Accessed: 20 March 2023)

42. 'Habit Stacker' (2023) *10 Types of Toxic People & How to Stop Them From Dragging You Down.* Available at: https://thehabitstacker.com/toxic-people/ (Accessed: 20 March 2023)

43. 'Cafe Whiz' (2033) Available from: https://www.cafewhiz.com/toxic-parenting-style/#:~:text=%20What%20is%20the%20Toxic%20style%20of%20parenting%3F,ignoring%20the%20child%E2%80%99s%20needs%20and%20feelings.%20More%20 (Accessed: 20 March 2022)

44. Foster, D. (2020) *Nine Types of Toxic Parents.* Available at: https://goodmenproject.com/featured-content/nine-types-of-toxic-parents/ (Accessed: 20 March 2023)

45. Wilkinson, N. (2022) *Wellbeing Workshop: Be Kind – To You and Others.* Available at: https://www.quest.nhs.uk/events/be-kind-to-you-and-others-2-2-3/#:~:text=The%20absence%20of%20empathy%20and%20understanding%20are%20sufficient.%E2%80%9D,There%20is%20one%20session%20with%2025%20places%20available. (Accessed: 20 March 2023)

46. 'OSHOtimes' (2022) *Emotions.* Available at: https://www.oshotimes.com/insights/health/emotions/ (Accessed: 20 March 2023)

47. Chopra. D. (2014) *Deepak Chopra Twitter Status. [Twitter]* Available at: https://twitter.com/DeepakChopra/status/501907947413180416 (Accessed: 20 March 2023)

48. Corelli, C. (2022) *Flying Monkeys – the narcissist's army of goons.* Available at: https://www.carlacorelli.com/narcissism-glossary/flying-monkeys/ (Accessed: 20 March 2022)

49. Bradberry, T. (2022) *The Art Of Saying No.* Available at: https://www.talentsmarteq.com/articles/The-Art-of-Saying-No-1545891057-p-1.html/ (Accessed: 20 March 2023)

50. Newman, S. (2017) *The Book of No: 365 Ways to Say it and Mean it—and Stop People-Pleasing Forever (Updated Edition).* Available at: https://www.amazon.com/gp/product/1683366905/ref=as_li_qf_sp_asin_il_tl?ie=UTF8&tag=rewme-20&camp=1789&creative=9325&linkCode=as2&creativeASIN=1683366905&linkId=3a85f7383dce574a6f886cbe349452ff (Accessed: 20 March 2023)

51. Borresen, K. *(2018) Am I Codependent? 10 Signs You Might Be, According To Experts.* Available at: https://www.huffingtonpost.co.uk/entry/signs-of-codependent-relationship_n_5a725f26e4b05253b27572ba (Accessed: 20 March 2023)

52. Granneman, J. (2020) *Why Is Writing Easier Than Speaking for Introverts?* Available at: https://introvertdear.com/news/introverts-words-hard-science/ (Accessed: 20 March 2023)

53. Sabater, V. (2021) *Your Daemon, According to Carl Jung.* Available at: https://exploringyourmind.com/your-daemon-according-to-carl-jung/ (Accessed: 20 March 2023)

54. Bubb EJ, Metzler-Baddeley C, Aggleton JP. The cingulum bundle: Anatomy, function, and dysfunction. Neurosci Biobehav Rev. 2018 Sep;92:104-127. doi: 10.1016/j.

neubiorev.2018.05.008. Epub 2018 May 16. PMID: 29753752; PMCID: PMC6090091.

55. Tuarez, J. (2021) *What Part Of The Brain Controls Emotions?* Available at: https://neurotray.com/what-part-of-the-brain-controls-emotions/ (Accessed: 20 March 2023)

56. Courtney, Elizabeth & Kushwaha, Monika & Johnson, Jeffrey. (2008). Childhood Emotional Abuse and Risk for Hopelessness and Depressive Symptoms During Adolescence. Journal of Emotional Abuse. 8. 281-298. 10.1080/10926790802262572.

57. De Bellis MD, Zisk A. The biological effects of childhood trauma. Child Adolesc Psychiatr Clin N Am. 2014 Apr;23(2):185-222, vii. doi: 10.1016/j.chc.2014.01.002. Epub 2014 Feb 16. PMID: 24656576; PMCID: PMC3968319.

58. 'Choice House' (2020) *Defining Types of Trauma and Appropriate Treatment.* Available at: https://www.choicehousecolorado.com/defining-types-of-trauma-and-appropriate-treatment/ (Accessed: 20 March 2023)

59. 'PsychCentral' (2021) *Not Aware of Your Symptoms? It May Be a Sign of Anosognosia.* Available at: https://psychcentral.com/health/anosognosia#definition (Accessed: 20 March 2023)

60. Porges, S. (2022) *polyvagal theory.* Available at: https://www.stephenporges.com/ (Accessed: 20 March 2023)

61. Mandeville, R. (2020) *Recognizing the C-PTSD-Based Fawn Response.* Available at: https://www.pacesconnection.com/blog/the-trauma-response-of-fawning-aka-people-pleasing-part-one (Accessed: 20 March 2023)

62. 'GoodTherapy' (2019) *Sexual Assault / Abuse.* Available at: https://www.goodtherapy.org/learn-about-therapy/issues/sexual-abuse (Accessed: 20 March 2023)

63. 'GoodTherapy' (2019) *Anger.* Available at: https://www.goodtherapy.org/learn-about-therapy/issues/anger (Accessed: 20 March 2023)

64. 'GoodTherapy' (2019) *Posttraumatic Stress.* Available at: https://www.goodtherapy.org/learn-about-therapy/issues/ptsd (Accessed: 20 March 2023)

65. 'GoodTherapy' (2019) *Compulsion.* Available at: https://www.goodtherapy.org/blog/psychpedia/compulsion (Accessed: 20 March 2023)

66. 'GoodTherapy' (2019) *Drug and Alcohol Addiction.* Available at: https://www.goodtherapy.org/learn-about-therapy/issues/drug-and-substance-abuse (Accessed: 20 March 2023)

67. Schmidt, B. (2015) *3 Simple Ideas to Build Mindfulness in Your Day.* Available at: https://www.nextavenue.org/3-simple-ways-to-build-mindfulness-in-your-day/ (Accessed: 20 March 2023)

68. Buffum Taylor, R. (2022) *Dialectical Behavioral Therapy.* Available at: https://www.webmd.com/mental-health/dialectical-behavioral-therapy (Accessed: 20 March 2023)

69. Fishwick, C. (2016) *I, narcissist – vanity, social media, and the human condition.* Available at: https://www.theguardian.com/world/2016/mar/17/i-narcissist-vanity-social-media-and-the-human-condition (Accessed: 20 March 2023)

70. Vater A, Moritz S, Roepke S. Does a narcissism epidemic exist in modern western societies? Comparing narcissism and self-esteem in East and West Germany [published correction appears in PLoS One. 2018 May 29;13(5):e0198386]. PLoS One. 2018;13(1):e0188287. Published 2018 Jan 24. doi:10.1371/journal.pone.0188287

71. Folk, J. (2023) *Anxiety Symptoms, Causes, Treatment.* Available at: https://www.anxietycentre.com/anxiety-disorders/symptoms/ (Accessed: 20 March 2023)

72. Folk, J. (2021) *Stress Response Hyperstimulation.* Available at: https://www.anxietycentre.com/anxiety-disorders/symptoms/hyperstimulation/ (Accessed: 20 March 2023)

73. Folk, J. (2021) *Heart Palpitations Anxiety Symptoms.* Available at: https://www.anxietycentre.com/anxiety-disorders/symptoms/heart-palpitations/ (Accessed: 20 March 2023)

74. Folk, J. (2022) *Chest Pain Anxiety Symptoms.* Available at: https://www.anxietycentre.com/anxiety-disorders/symptoms/chest-pain-anxiety/ (Accessed: 20 March 2023)

75. Folk, J. (2023) *Dizziness Anxiety Symptoms.* Available at: Https://www.anxietycentre.com/anxiety-disorders/symptoms/dizziness/ (Accessed: 20 March 2023)

76. Folk, J. (2021) *Muscle Weakness Anxiety Symptoms.* Available at: https://www.anxietycentre.com/anxiety-disorders/symptoms/muscle-weakness-anxiety/ (Accessed: 20 March 2023)

77. Folk, J. (2022) *Numbness Tingling Anxiety Symptoms.* Available at: https://www.anxietycentre.com/anxiety-disorders/symptoms/numbness-tingling/ (Accessed: 20 March 2023)

78. Folk, J. (2021) *Weak legs, jelly legs, rubber legs, shaky legs, leg weakness anxiety symptom.* Available at: https://www.anxietycentre.com/anxiety-disorders/symptoms/weak-legs/ (Accessed: 20 March 2023)

79. Folk, J. (2021) *Asthma Symptoms and Anxiety.* Available at: https://www.anxietycentre.com/anxiety-disorders/symptoms/asthma-symptoms-anxiety/ (Accessed: 20 March 2023)

80. Folk, J. (2021) *Excessive Yawning Anxiety Symptoms.* Available at: https://www.anxietycentre.com/anxiety-disorders/symptoms/excessive-yawning-anxiety/ (Accessed: 20 March 2023)

81. Folk, J. (2021) *Depersonalization Anxiety Symptoms.* Available at: https://www.anxietycentre.com/anxiety-disorders/symptoms/depersonalization/ (Accessed: 20 March 2023)

82. Folk, J. (2021) *Brain Zaps Anxiety Symptoms.* Available at: https://www.anxietycentre.com/anxiety-disorders/symptoms/brain-zaps/ (Accessed: 20 March 2023)

83. Folk, J. (2021) *Chronic Pain Anxiety Symptoms.* Available at: https://www.anxietycentre.com/anxiety-disorders/symptoms/chronic-pain/ (Accessed: 20 March 2023)

84. Folk, J. (2021) *Chronic Fatigue, Syndrome, Anxiety.* Available at: https://www.anxietycentre.com/anxiety-disorders/symptoms/chronic-fatigue-anxiety/ (Accessed: 20 March 2023)

85. Folk, J. (2021) *Body Jolt, Jolts, Shocks, Zaps, Tremors, Shakes – anxiety symptoms.* Available at: https://www.anxietycentre.com/anxiety-disorders/symptoms/body-jolt/ (Accessed: 20 March 2023)

86. Folk, J. (2021) *Muscle Tension, Aches, Pains – Anxiety Symptoms.* Available at: https://www.anxietycentre.com/anxiety-disorders/symptoms/muscle-tension/ (Accessed: 20 March 2023)

87. Folk, J. (2021) *Anxiety Lump In The Throat, Causes, Treatment.* Available at: https://www.anxietycentre.com/anxiety-disorders/symptoms/lump-in-throat/ (Accessed: 20 March 2023)

88. Joseph RM, Ehrman K, McNally R, Keehn B. Affective response to eye contact and face recognition ability in children with ASD. J Int Neuropsychol Soc. 2008 Nov;14(6):947-55. doi: 10.1017/S1355617708081344. PMID: 18954475.

89. Berub, A., Turgeon, J., Blais, C. and Fiset, D. (2023) *Emotion Recognition in Adults With a History of Childhood Maltreatment: A Systematic Review* in Trauma, Violence, & ABUSE 2023, Vol. 24(1) 278–294. Available at: https://journals.sagepub.com/doi/pdf/10.1177/15248380211029403 (Accessed: 20 March 2023)

90. LeDoux JE. Emotion circuits in the brain. Annu Rev Neurosci. 2000;23:155-84. doi: 10.1146/annurev.neuro.23.1.155. PMID: 10845062.

91. Grant MM, Cannistraci C, Hollon SD, Gore J, Shelton R. Childhood trauma history differentiates amygdala response to sad faces within MDD. J Psychiatr Res. 2011 Jul;45(7):886-95. doi: 10.1016/j.jpsychires.2010.12.004. Epub 2011 Jan 26. PMID: 21276593; PMCID: PMC3090525.

92. Dannlowski U, Kugel H, Huber F, Stuhrmann A, Redlich R, Grotegerd D, Dohm K, Sehlmeyer C, Konrad C, Baune BT, Arolt V, Heindel W, Zwitserlood P, Suslow T. Childhood maltreatment is associated with an automatic negative emotion processing bias in the amygdala. Hum Brain Mapp. 2013 Nov;34(11):2899-909. doi: 10.1002/hbm.22112. Epub 2012 Jun 13. PMID: 22696400; PMCID: PMC6870128.

93. Haxby JV, Hoffman EA, Gobbini MI. Human neural systems for face recognition and social communication. Biol Psychiatry. 2002 Jan 1;51(1):59-67. doi: 10.1016/s0006-3223(01)01330-0. PMID: 11801231.

94. Van Dam NT, Rando K, Potenza MN, Tuit K, Sinha R. Childhood maltreatment, altered limbic neurobiology, and substance use relapse severity via trauma-specific reductions in limbic grey matter volume. JAMA Psychiatry. 2014 Aug;71(8):917-25. doi: 10.1001/jamapsychiatry.2014.680. PMID: 24920451; PMCID: PMC4437819.

95. Trautmann, S. Rehm, J. & Wittchen, H. (2016) *The economic costs of mental disorders* in EMBO reports Vol 17 | No 9. Available at: https://www.embopress.org/doi/pdf/10.15252/embr.201642951 (Accessed: 20 March 2023)

96. Pollock, A. (2015) *The Brain in Defense Mode: How Dissociation Helps Us Survive.* Available at: https://www.goodtherapy.org/blog/the-brain-in-defense-mode-how-dissociation-helps-us-survive-0429155 (Accessed: 20 March 2023)

97. Harvey, S. (2019) *Screw Perfection: I'm Becoming Wilder, more Tender, more Myself.* Available at: https://www.elephantjournal.com/2019/06/screw-perfection-im-becoming-wilder-more-tender-more-myself-sarah-harvey/ (Accessed: 20 March 2023)

98. Molnar DS, Flett GL, Hewitt PL. Perfectionism and Perceived Control in Posttraumatic Stress Disorder Symptoms. Int J Ment Health Addict. 2020 May 26:1-15. doi: 10.1007/s11469-020-00315-y. Epub ahead of print. PMID: 32837419; PMCID: PMC7250265.

99. Beach, H. (2021) Em*otional Safety: Why kids need a safe space to feel, learn, and grow.* Available at: https://hannahbeach.ca/emotional-safety/#:~:text=Emotional%20safety%20is%20foundational%20to,feels%20like%20in%20practical%20terms. (Accessed: 20 March 2023)

100. 'NCTSN' (2023) *Trauma Types.* Available at: https://www.nctsn.org/what-is-child-trauma/trauma-types (Accessed: 20 March 2023)

101. Hobbs, A & Natale, N. (2019) *Why Do I Cry So Easily? Experts Break Down the Reasons Behind Your Tears.* Available at: https://drkatecummins.com/news/why-do-i-cry-so-easily-experts-break-down-the-reasons-behind-your-tears (Accessed: 20 March 2023)

102. From Firm Muscles to Firm Willpower: Understanding the Role of Embodied Cognition in Self-Regulation. Iris W. Hung and Aparna A. Labroo, Journal of Consumer Research Vol. 37, No. 6 (April 2011), pp. 1046-1064, Oxford University Press

103. Bahadur, N. (2018) *How to Stop Yourself From Crying.* Available at: https://www.nytimes.com/2018/10/14/well/mind/how-to-stop-yourself-from-crying.html?smid=url-share (Accessed: 20 March 2023)

104. Salem, R. (2003) *Empathic Listening.* Available at: https://www.beyondintractability.org/essay/empathic_listening (Accessed: 20 March 2023)

List of organisations that can provide support with abuse

The National Association for People Abused in Childhood (NAPAC)

NAPAC provides a national Freephone support line for adults who have experienced any type of abuse in childhood.

Helpline: 0808 801 0331. Monday–Thursday 10:00 am–9.00 pm and Friday 10.00 am–6.00 pm

Website: https://napac.org.uk/

Hub of Hope

Hubofhope.co.uk - UK-wide mental health service database for local, national, peer, community, charity, private and NHS mental health support.

Help for Adult Victims of Child Abuse (HAVOCA)

Havoca.org - Information and support for adults who have experienced any type of childhood abuse, provided by other survivors.

Support for Survivors - 0115 962 2722

hello@supportforsurvivors.org
supportforsurvivors.org
Help for adult survivors of child abuse.

Childline - 0800 1111

Childline.org.uk - Support for children and young people in the UK, including a free helpline and online chats with counsellors.

Kidscape - 0207 823 5430

kidscape.org.uk
Information and advice for parents, carers and young people with concerns about school bullying and abuse.

National Society for the Prevention of Cruelty to Children (NSPCC) - 0800 800 5000 (for adults concerned about a child)

nspcc.org.uk
Support and information for children or anybody with concerns about a child.

YoungMinds - 0808 802 5544 (Parents Helpline)
85258 (Crisis Messenger for young people – text the letters YM)

youngminds.org.uk
Committed to improving the mental health of children
and young people

Respond- 0207 383 0700

respond.org.uk
Services for people with learning disabilities or autism
who have experienced abuse or trauma.

One in Four - 0800 121 7114

oneinfour.org.uk
Providing advocacy, counselling and resources for adults
who have experienced trauma, domestic or sexual abuse
in childhood.

Southall Black Sisters - 0208 571 9595

southallblacksisters.org.uk
Information, guidance, support, practical assistance,
counselling and aid for BAME women and children who
have experienced domestic and sexual abuse, with phone
service in multiple languages.

Respect Not Fear

respectnotfear.co.uk
Advice for young people about domestic violence and
abusive relationships.

About the Author

Fantasy worlds can bring a lot of joy.

Rita Zbojan Ballantyne was born in the communist Romania of the '70s. Encouraged by her father to experience the world beyond the confines of the Iron Curtain, she explored many countries and cultures after the dictatorship's fall. A political activist, animal lover and trained Psychologist, she currently lives in Scotland with her husband and her youngest son, with the older children having recently flown the nest.